The Centrality of the Doctrine of Human Free Will in the Theology of Balthasar Hubmaier

Michael W. McDill

Volume 4

THE CENTRALITY OF THE DOCTRINE OF HUMAN FREE WILL IN THE THEOLOGY OF BALTHASAR HUBMAIER

MICHAEL W. MCDILL

ACADEMIC THEOLOGICAL STUDIES

The Centrality of the Doctrine of Free Will in the Theology of Balthasar Hubmaier
Copyright © 2024 by Michael W. McDill

Published by Northeastern Baptist Press
    Post Office Box 4600
    Bennington, VT 05201

All rights reserved. No part of this book may be reproduced in any form without prior permission from Northeastern Baptist Press, except as provided for by USA copyright law.

All Scripture translations are the author's unless otherwise noted.

Cover design by Leason Stiles & Jared August

Hardcover ISBN: 978-1-953331-34-2

To Becky

Contents

Series Introduction	i
Abstract	iii
Introduction	1
Free Will and the Reformation	3
Hubmaier a Catholic?	11
Overview	25
Chapter One	
Historical-Theological Context for Free Will	27
Pre-Augustinian Church Fathers	28
Augustine	38
Pelagianism	44
Donatism	45
Luther and Calvin	52
Luther and Erasmus	60
The Anabaptists and Free Will	65
Chapter Two	
Hubmaier's Doctrine of Free Will	71
Hubmaier's Historical Milieu	72
The Baptist View of Hubmaier	80
Hubmaier's Commitment to Scripture	83
Hubmaier's Doctrine of Free Will	103

Chapter Three
Analysis of the Doctrine of Free Will in
Respect to Hubmaier's Broader Theology   137

    Hubmaier, Luther, and Justification   138

    Hubmaier, Luther, and Faith versus Works   146

    Election, Freedom of Choice, and the Knowledge of Good and Evil   178

    Hubmaier's Ecclesiology: Believer's Baptism   190

    Religious Freedom   209

    Summary   219

Conclusion   223

    The Logic of Symmetry: Divine Grace and Human Free Will   226

    The Logic of the Personal: Relational Freedom in Divine Grace and Human Trust   232

Bibliography   249

Series Introduction

Northeastern Baptist Press publishes Christian books that inform, inspire, and encourage people to follow Jesus Christ. Realizing the need for an academic series that is tethered to the Baptist Faith and Message 2000, NEBP has developed the Academic Theological Studies (ATS) series.

The ATS series is comprised of doctoral dissertations as well as academic monographs that are carefully selected based on solid recommendations and rigorous peer review. Each study makes a unique and distinct contribution to the broader field of theology. Although all books in this series are specialized, they are not written for specialists. The ATS series provides the church at large with quality resources that have significant implications for practical issues. Toward this end, we publish within the fields of biblical studies, systematic and historical theology, Christian counseling, education, and pastoral ministry.

We foresee the ATS series growing into a significant collection of academic studies that provide the church with an accessible, yet academically rigorous avenue for theological inquiry.

Jared M. August
Ralph H. Slater
Series Editors

Abstract

Balthasar Hubmaier was a leading Anabaptist reformer in the early period of the development of that movement. His writings provided a framework from which later Anabaptists worked, especially his explication of the doctrine of believer's baptism. The Anabaptist view of salvation and discipleship was dependent on an affirmation of free will. Hubmaier was one of the strongest and most able proponents of human free will. He wrote two treatises dealing with free will, *On the Freedom of the Will*, and *The Second Book On the Freedom of the Will Of the Human Being*. He also featured this doctrine in many of his other writings, especially his Christian Catechism.

To show how central the doctrine of free will was to Hubmaier's theology, three chapters treat: the free will issue up to the time of the Reformation, Hubmaier's concept of free will, and free will as found in his theology in general. The first chapter gives an account of free will in the early Fathers of the church, and in Augustine as he attempted to battle opponents, especially Pelagius and the Donatists. It also reviews Luther and Erasmus' debate over free will during the Reformation, as well as the basic Anabaptist view of free will. An analysis of Luther and Calvin, as affirming an unfree will, and the effect of this on their ideas of assurance of faith is also included.

The second chapter attempts to explicate Hubmaier's view of free will by first dealing with possible sources for Hubmaier's thought and then with a discussion of Hubmaier's commitment to scriptural authority. A discussion of the Baptist view of Hubmaier is included in this chapter along with some analysis of the influence of mysticism and nominalism on Hubmaier's thought. Hubmaier's doctrine of free will is then described, featuring his use of the concept of the two wills of God, hidden and revealed, and his tripartite anthropology in which Hubmaier features each part, body, soul, and spirit, as possessing a will.

The third chapter lays out the various key components of Hubmaier's theology as a whole, considering for each how free will is central. In comparison and contrast with Luther, Hubmaier's theology of free will is analyzed concerning, first, justification, then, faith and works. Next the doctrines of election and ecclesiology are examined in light of the impact of free will on Hubmaier's theology in these areas. Finally, Hubmaier's stance on religious freedom is analyzed as it pertains to his view on free will. In this way human free will is shown to be central to Hubmaier's theology in that it plays a crucial role in his soteriology, anthropology, concept of faith, view of election, ecclesiology, view of baptism, and his advocation of religious freedom.

Free will is central in Hubmaier's soteriology because he insists on the element of human choice in faith. Hubmaier's tripartite anthropology allows for the spirit in man, however darkened by sin, to accept God's grace, and so does not eliminate free will after the Fall. For Hubmaier, free will is rooted in the image of God in man which cannot be obliterated, and thus still functions in fallen man's spirit, however weakly. This allows for a human response to God's grace in salvation. Hubmaier believes that man is able to respond to God's Word which is man's restored opportunity, in the gospel, to choose God through the sacrifice of Christ, while also leaving the option to reject Him.

Thus, free will becomes key to Hubmaier's concept of initial and ongoing faith in Christ. Free will is necessary in the initial human response of surrender to God in Christ in conversion. This results in an ongoing commitment to surrender the will to God in discipleship, demonstrated by works of brotherly love. Therefore, free will is central to Hubmaier's concept of faith as a decision for salvation as well as in a commitment to persistent and trusting Christian obedience. Free will, completely restored in God's power through Christ, continues to play a crucial role in the Christian's commitment to trust God daily, manifested in an obedient life of faithful discipleship.

Out of this soteriological foundation flows Hubmaier's requirement that baptism come after faith. Only one who has decided for Christ in his innermost being can publicly confess this and commit to following Christ with other believers through public baptism. As a result, free will was also essential to Hubmaier's ecclesiology. This is seen in his Anabaptist doctrine of the voluntary church, made up of those who have openly identified with fellow believers through their own choice by submitting to believer's baptism. To ensure the unity and integrity of this gathered church of faithful believers, church discipline, involving brotherly admonition and the ban, must be exercised. This points to an emphasis being laid on human free will as essential in the ongoing life of the church. The believer who chooses to live in public or grievous sin is admonished and then banned, but the one who chooses to return is joyously restored.

Finally, in Hubmaier's position on religious freedom it is clear that freedom of dissent derives from the belief that Christ is the supreme Judge, who refuses to compel to salvation, but draws men to Him in patience and mercy. Thus, no human being has the authority to condemn anyone in this world for his beliefs. This prevents premature human judgment and punishment. For Hubmaier, since God has given free will even in eternal matters, certainly no human authority should venture to take it away from his fellow man by use of physical restraint, torture, or execution simply because of differences in belief.

Introduction

The purpose of this monograph will be to explore the theology of Balthasar Hubmaier as it pertains to his doctrine of anthropology, specifically in the area of human free will. The influences upon Hubmaier from medieval theology and especially from the Reformation era, as well as his interaction with these, will give the context for Hubmaier's unique and significant strain of Anabaptist theology which, the monograph will endeavor to show, is heavily dependent on his doctrine of human free will.[1]

---

1 For the purposes of the monograph a basic definition of human free will can be used. Essentially it will be identified as self-determinism. However, this must be qualified in that the idea of self-determination acknowledges that factors such as heredity and environment do influence human behavior, but they are not ultimately the determining factors for that behavior. A human being's acts are caused by himself, even when God himself is taken into account as a causal agent. Norm Geisler elaborates: "Many object to self-determinism on the grounds that if everything needs a cause, then so do the acts of the will. Thus it is often asked, What caused the will to act? The self-determinist can respond to this question by pointing out that it is not the will of a person that makes a decision but the person acting by means of his will. And since the person is the first cause of his acts, it is meaningless to ask what the cause of the first cause is." Elwell, Walter A., ed., *Evangelical Dictionary of Theology* (Grand Rapids: Baker Book House, 1984), s.v. "Freedom, Free Will, and Determinism," by Norman Geisler. This short summary of the free will issue by Norm Geisler

in the *Evangelical Dictionary of Theology* explains that causal antecedents are to be taken into account but cannot adequately explain human actions: "There are three basic positions concerning man's choices: determinism, indeterminism, and self-determinism. Determinism is the belief that all of man's actions are the result of antecedent factors or causes. Naturalistic determinists, such as Thomas Hobbes and B. F. Skinner, argue that man's behavior can be fully explained in terms of natural causes. Theistic determinists, such as Martin Luther and Jonathan Edwards, trace man's actions back to God's controlling hand. The opposite position to determinism is indeterminism. On this view there are no causes for man's actions, antecedent or otherwise. The final position is self-determinism, or free will. This is the belief that man determines his own behavior freely, and that no causal antecedents can sufficiently account for his actions." More specific to the free will debate during the Reformation, and especially relevant to the Luther-Erasmus debate with which Hubmaier was conversant, is the basic definition given by Erasmus: "By free choice . . . we mean a power of the human will by which a man can apply himself to the things which lead to eternal salvation, or turn away from them." E. Gordon Rupp and Philip S. Watson, eds., *Luther and Erasmus: Free Will and Salvation* (Philadelphia: Westminster Press, 1969), 47. Luther disparages this definition as obscure, overambitious, and contradictory. See Rupp and Watson, *Luther and Erasmus*, 169–177. Harry McSorley writes, "Luther correctly points out the inadequacy of Erasmus' definition in light of the earlier statement . . . that apart from the mercy of God, neither the will nor the effort of man is effective." However, Luther is also "unfair to Erasmus in that he does not give sufficient recognition to Erasmus' statements on the need for grace." McSorley, *Luther: Right or Wrong?: An Ecumenical-Theological Study of Luther's Major Work, The Bondage of the Will* (New York: Newman Press, 1969), 286. Luther frames his argument in such a way as to make it appear that he allows for no freedom of will or choice in fallen humanity, and thus, has been charged with being a determinist (see Geisler above). He accuses Erasmus, on the other hand, of Pelagianism. Rupp and Watson, *Luther and Erasmus*, 173. In light of this, the full title of Hubmaier's first treatise on free will is instructive and serves comparatively as a definition: *On the Freedom of the Will which God through his sent Word offers to all people and thereby gives them the power to become His Children and also the choice to will and to do good. or else to let them remain Children of Wrath which they are by nature*. Balthasar Hubmaier, *Freedom of the Will, I*, in *Balthasar Hubmaier: Theologian of Anabaptism*, ed. Wayne Pipkin and John H. Yoder, Classics of the Radical Reformation (Scottdale: Herald Press, 1989), 427. The function, if any, of human free will in the operation of salvation is the crux of the debate.

Introduction

FREE WILL AND THE REFORMATION

One of the important debates during the period of the Reformation concerned human free will. The Reformation doctrine, *sola fide*, rested upon a conception of the grace and sovereignty of God which allowed for no trace of effort or work on man's part to obtain salvation. This swing away from the Roman system of works was adamantly defended by Martin Luther in his treatise, *The Bondage of the Will*. The debate between Luther and Desiderius Erasmus concerning free will continued the entrenchment of both sides in an age-old debate about human freedom.[2]

Early in this period, an eloquent and intelligent leader arose among the Anabaptists named Balthasar Hubmaier. He was known to Luther,[3] and was also mentioned by the Roman Church in the papal *Index* of prohibited books alongside the names of Luther and Ulrich Zwingli.[4] He has been acclaimed by some scholars as the "leading theologian" of Anabaptism.[5] One of the key el-

---

2 Erasmus defended human free will in his work, *On the Freedom of the Will*. This work and Luther's *The Bondage of the Will* are found in E. Gordon Rupp and Philip S. Watson, eds., *Luther and Erasmus: Free Will and Salvation* (Philadelphia: Westminster Press, 1969).

3 Luther writes, "Unfortunately, I know full well, dear sirs, that Balthasar Hubmaier has included my name among others in his blasphemous booklet on rebaptism, as if I shared his perverted views." Martin Luther, *Concerning Rebaptism* in *Martin Luther's Basic Theological Writings*, ed. Timothy Lull (Minneapolis: Fortress Press, 1989), 341.

4 See Meic Pearse, *The Great Restoration: The Religious Radicals of the 16th and 17th Centuries* (Carlisle: Paternoster Press, 1998), 72.

5 See Eddie Louis Mabry, *Balthasar Hubmaier's Doctrine of the Church* (Lanham: University Press of America, 1994), xvi. Another example is Gunnar Westin, *The Free Church Through the Ages*, trans. Virgil A. Olson (Nashville: Broadman, 1958), 94, where he writes: "Hubmaier was the foremost theologian and apologist for the Anabaptists." Also Torsten Bergsten, *Balthasar Hubmaier: Anabaptist Theologian and Martyr*, ed. W. R. Estep (Valley Forge: Judson Press, 1978), 45. R. J. Smithson writes, in *The Anabaptists: Their Contribution to Our Protestant Heritage* (London: James Clarke & Co., 1935), 143, that "Balthasar Hubmaier was without doubt one of the ablest advocates of the Anabaptist cause in the sixteenth century." William R. Estep calls Hubmaier "the leading Ana-

ements in Hubmaier's theology was a defense of human free will. Amidst the tumult over works, grace, and free will during the Reformation, a distinctive voice could be heard interpreting these matters from its radical wing. Hubmaier wrote two major theses on free will. Torsten Bergsten, in his definitive biography, *Balthasar Hubmaier: Anabaptist Theologian and Martyr*, claims that in these treatises "Hubmaier's teachings regarding free will do not coincide exactly with either those of Erasmus or of Luther.... Rather, he adopts a third point of view. As an Anabaptist theologian and leader he emphasized the ethical responsibility of man as well as a Reformed doctrine of sin."[6]

The prevailing outlook concerning free will among the Magisterial Reformers was a rejection of human free will due to a disdain for any hint of works-oriented justification. Among the Anabaptists, Hubmaier is one

---

baptist preacher" in *The Anabaptist Story: An Introduction to Sixteenth-Century Anabaptism*, 3d ed (Grand Rapids: Eerdmans, 1975), 103. Estep also mentions Hubmaier as one of three leading theologians among Anabaptists in *Renaissance and Reformation* (Grand Rapids: Eerdmans, 1986), 204, and as "the most vigorous and impassioned thinker of the Anabaptist movement," 216. Donald F. Durnbaugh says, in *The Believer's Church: The History and Character of Radical Protestantism* (Scottdale: Herald Press, 1968), 72, that Hubmaier "became the most prolific literary protagonist of the Anabaptist cause. His name and writings were later to lie cheek by jowl with Luther, Calvin, and Zwingli as the main heresiarchs in the Catholic Index of prohibited books." Cornelius Dyck notes in *Spiritual Life in Anabaptism* (Scottdale: Herald Press, 1995), 65; 96, that Hubmaier was "the best trained theologian among the Anabaptists," and that he "must be considered one of the top Anabaptist theologians, a very able and energetic pastor and a gifted preacher." The *Martyr's Mirror* introduces Hubmaier in this way: "At the time of Zwinglius there was also one Balthasar Hubmor of Friedberg, whom the papists called a doctor of the Holy Scriptures, a learned and eloquent man." Thielemann Van Braght, *The Bloody Theatre or Martyr's Mirror*, 2d English ed. (Scottdale: Herald Press, 1999), 465. Carl Leth writes, "Balthasar Hubmaier was the most prominent theologian of the first generation of Anabaptists," in "Balthasar Hubmaier's 'Catholic' Exegesis: Matthew 16:18-19 and the Power of the Keys," in *Biblical Interpretation in the Era of the Reformation*, ed. John Thompson and Richard A. Muller, 103-117 (Grand Rapids: Eerdmans, 1996).

6 Torsten Bergsten, *Balthasar Hubmaier: Anabaptist Theologian and Martyr*, ed. W. R. Estep (Valley Forge: Judson Press, 1978), 354.

Introduction

of the few to offer a substantial defense of this key doctrine. Hubmaier was more than willing to make his views known, although always in an honest and respectful manner.[7] In the context of the Protestant reaction against the established natural and rational scholastic theology of Catholicism, with the Reformers' emphasis on the dichotomy between God in His sovereignty and man in his helplessness, Hubmaier posited a claim for free will in man. Hubmaier was seeking to strike a balance between the tendency toward determinism in the Magisterial Reformers and the works-righteousness approach of the Roman Church.

The Reformation was invested in one dominant theological theme: justification by faith alone.[8] As a corollary doctrine, the bondage of the will became a foundation upon which the Reformation doctrinal program was generally built, most notably by Martin Luther and most systematically by John Calvin with his *Institutes of The Christian Religion*. The Reformers, turning to Augustine as a favored interpreter of the Scriptures, conceived a view of God and man that, because of sin, seemed to cancel man's status as God's image bearer. Man, who possessed a limited freedom, having been created in the likeness of God, lost his freedom after the Fall and became completely corrupted and worthless. Only God's giving of the gift of faith alters this status,

---

7 William Estep writes: "Hubmaier always demonstrated a willingness to accept new insights of truth even from those who would burn him. A lover of the academic debate and frequently caught up in the heat of a controversial issue, he never became bitterly caustic. He steadfastly refused to engage in personal innuendoes." Even in the face of imprisonment and torture in Zurich at the bidding of Ulrich Zwingli, Hubmaier refrained from vitriolic, bitter invective. Estep explains: "He did not refer to Zwingli by name in any of his tracts written against his position until after he had been imprisoned and tortured as his hands. Even then, in the polemical pamphlet on infant baptism, Hubmaier did little more than mention the methods [imprisonment, torture, starvation, being locked in the prison tower with the bodies of those who had died there under the same conditions] used by Zwingli against him and other Anabaptists." Insertion added. *The Anabaptist Story*, 97.

8 The principle of *sola scriptura* functioned as a key complement of *sola fide* since it involved the priesthood of all believers and the authority of the individual conscience in the interpretation of Scripture.

and only for the elect. Being predestined, they are rescued from the general pool of mankind who are doomed to remain in sin and thus to eternal death.

The concern of the Reformers to downplay human free will was not stressed primarily in the context of a doctrine of anthropology, but especially for their soteriology, in order to secure the doctrine of grace and to show clearly that man does not merit salvation in any way.[9] Thus, Calvin remarked:

> In order for us to come to a sure knowledge of ourselves, we must first grasp the fact that Adam, parent of us all, was created in the image and likeness of God. That is, he was endowed with wisdom, righteousness, holiness, and was so clinging by these gifts of grace to God that he could have lived forever in Him, if he had stood fast in the uprightness God had given him. But when Adam slipped into sin, this image and likeness of God was cancelled and effaced, that is, he lost all the benefits of divine grace, by which he could have been led back into the way of life. Moreover, he was far removed from God and became a com-

---

[9] Alvin Beachy writes: "Standing as they did within the context of the Pauline-Augustinian anthropology with its emphasis upon the bondage of the will and man's utter helplessness in sin, it is not difficult to see why the Magisterial Reformers often felt that the Radicals were guilty of the Pelagian heresy." Alvin J. Beachy, *The Concept of Grace in the Radical Reformation* (Nieuwkoop: B. De Graaf: 1977), 15. And again Beachy explains: "The Magisterial Reformers arrived at their concept of grace through an anthropology that centered in the bondage of the will and the doctrine of predestination. In Lutheranism, as well as within Calvinism, predestination was the solution to the problem posed by the bondage of the will. . . to both systems the bondage of the will was the necessary safeguard to the sovereignty of God in grace. . . . The Radical Reformers, on the other hand, felt that the bondage of the will, predestination, and invincible grace had to be rejected both to safeguard God's eternal goodness and man's moral responsibility." Beachy, *The Concept of Grace in the Radical Reformation*, 33. It is worth noting that while Beachy's analysis is generally on the mark, as far as predestination for the Anabaptists goes, Hubmaier does say: "God knows whom he has chosen from all eternity." Hubmaier, *Dialogue with Zwingli's Baptism Book*, Pipkin and Yoder, 203. This statement functions as a frank affirmation of predestination, especially marked by its emphasis on God's foreknowledge. But, for Hubmaier, it is not a view which cancels human free will.

plete stranger. From this it follows that man was stripped and deprived of all wisdom, righteousness, power, life, which . . . could be held only in God. As a consequence, nothing was left to him save ignorance, iniquity, impotence, death, and judgment.[10]

In the attempt to be sure of portraying man as being incapable of saving himself, Calvin ostensibly expunges the image of God in fallen man. Anthony Hoekema examines Calvin's view of the image of God in man after the fall by asking this key question: "*Is there a sense in which fallen man is still in the image of God?* Sometimes it seems as if Calvin's answer to this question would be a resounding No. For at times he speaks of the image of God as having been *destroyed* by sin, *obliterated* by the Fall, *wiped out* or *lost* by sin, *cancelled* by sin, 'as it were *blotted out* . . . by Adam's sin,' or *utterly defaced* by sin."[11]

This emphasis of Calvin suggests that man is "totally depraved," not just in every part, but entirely and completely in every measure possible. Yet Hoekema points out that Calvin seems also to indicate that man still has some vestiges of the image of God even after the fall into sin. He calls these the remnants or traces of the *imago dei* in man which include will and reason. Calvin expects Christians to be patient and show love to human beings based on this remaining image. Calvin's idea here of the image of God after the fall is of a grotesquely distorted likeness, and yet, he grants that there is an image.[12] This clashes with the other language Calvin uses which seems to point to *no* allowance for a remaining image of God in man.

These views appear to be in conflict, and Calvin apparently does not make clear which idea must prevail. Does man indeed retain the image of

---

10 John Calvin, *Institutes of the Christian Religion, 1536 Edition*, trans. Ford Lewis Battles (Grand Rapids: Eerdmans, 1986), 15–16.

11 Anthony Hoekema, *Created in God's Image* (Grand Rapids: Eerdmans, 1986), 43. Hoekema elaborates further: "Calvin held that what happened in the Fall was . . . that whatever gifts or abilities man retained, such as reason and will, were perverted and distorted by the Fall. 'Now, all man's faculties are, on account of the depravity of nature, so vitiated and corrupted that in all his actions persistent disorder and intemperance threaten.'" Hoekema, *Created in God's Image*, 45.

12 See Hoekema, *Created in God's Image*, 43–45.

THE CENTRALITY OF THE DOCTRINE OF HUMAN FREE WILL IN THE THEOLOGY OF BALTHASAR HUBMAIER

God after the Fall, however small the traces, or does he not? Hoekema is forced to make this criticism: "Calvin is inconsistent when he speaks about the image of God in fallen man: sometimes he says that the image has been destroyed, obliterated, or blotted out by sin, whereas at other times he states that the image has not been totally destroyed but that we must still see the image of God in all people, conducting ourselves toward them in the light of this understanding."[13] This kind of ambivalence, which has occasioned misconceptions and theological conflict, is what Hubmaier desired to clear away with his own unique doctrine of free will.

This monograph will endeavor to show that Hubmaier grasped the appropriate biblical tension in the matter of grace and sovereignty versus free will and human responsibility. If in theology one must ultimately appeal to mystery, two things must be done: make sure it is as late in the process as is logically possible (in other words to appeal to mystery too early may be to hedge), and make sure that the appeal to mystery echoes the Bible's sense of proportion. It is clear that the Bible allows certain crucial concepts, such as divine providence and human responsibility, to stand as apparent contradictions. Eddie Mabry has stated that Hubmaier is contradictory in his theology of free will and grace.[14] Perhaps he is simply biblical, embracing the proper tension which can be found in Scripture between God's sovereign grace and man's free responsibility as creature. In fact, a personal rather than a mechanistic model may alleviate the conundrum.

If Hubmaier can be characterized as having been more in line with the Bible's own balance between God's sovereignty and human free will, then it may also be demonstrable that Luther and other determinist theologians are perhaps essentially biblical in most areas but inconsistent when it comes to human freedom. Wilhelm Pauck describes this tension in Luther's theology in this area:

> In what terrific tension Luther held his faith! On the one hand he viewed it with radical seriousness as the work and gift of God who acts upon man from without. On the other hand, he experienced it as a concrete

---

13 Hoekema, *Created in God's Image*, 48–49.

14 See Eddie Louis Mabry, *Balthasar Hubmaier's Doctrine of the Church* (Lanham: University Press of America, 1994), 116–120.

personal decision and commitment. In contemplating this tension, one understands why religion was a perpetual crisis and an unceasing battle for Luther. . . . He felt that, in the light of the human need for security, the ambiguity of divine grace was unbearable. . . . Indeed, he held these agonies of faith to be unavoidable because he was aware that, from the viewpoint of ordinary human experience, faith was an impossibility.[15]

According to the logic of free will and its function in the concept of faith as a *genuine choice* to trust God, such agonies might possibly be ameliorated. In emphasizing free will, Hubmaier's theology avoids the disconnect between empirical faith and theological determinism arising from positing an unfree will in man, which seems to hamper Lutheran theology.

Alister McGrath recognizes this disconnect between justification by faith and the enslaved will in Lutheranism. He writes, "Luther appears to adopt a form of necessitarianism, either as the main substance of his defence of the *servum arbitrium*, or at least as an important supporting argument. His assertions that Wycliffe was correct to maintain that all things happen by absolute necessity, and that God is the author of all man's evil deeds, have proved serious obstacles to those who wish to suggest that Luther was merely restating an Augustinian or scriptural position."[16] McGrath disagrees with certain scholars who have seen Luther's bondage of the will and justification by faith concepts as two sides of the same coin, so that a declaration of one amounts to an utterance of the other. Instead, he writes that it must be pointed out "that Luther's doctrine of justification is not exhausted or adequately characterised by a statement of the doctrine of the *servum arbitrium*."[17] McGrath reasons that just because the will is enslaved, God is not required then to justify man *according* to that deficiency with an alien righteousness.[18]

---

15 Wilhelm Pauck, *The Heritage of the Reformation* (Glencoe: Free Press, 1961), 25.

16 Alister McGrath, *Iustitia Dei: A History of the Christian Doctrine of Justification*, 2^d ed. (Cambridge: Cambridge University Press, 1998), 202.

17 Ibid., 203.

18 Ibid., 203. McGrath explains this idea concerning Luther's theology: "Essential to his understanding of justification is the concept of *iustitia Christi aliena*, which is not necessarily implied by the doctrine of the unfree

Luther's theology, then, instead of being in harmony regarding the enslaved will and righteousness by faith, is actually at odds. McGrath writes that "the history of Lutheran theology indicates that a wedge was driven between the concepts of an alien justifying righteousness and an enslaved will at a comparatively early stage, the former being consistently maintained as *de fide*, the latter being abandoned or reduced to the mere assertion that man cannot justify himself–a far cry from its original meaning. This implicit criticism of Luther by Lutheranism may be taken as demonstrating that there is no fundamental theological connection between the two concepts."[19] McGrath asserts that righteousness by faith and the bondage of the will in Luther's theology "are two essentially independent statements about justification, related only by the personality of Luther."[20] Thus, he seems to be saying that justification by faith in an alien righteousness from God is not dependent on the doctrine of the bondage of the will. Perhaps it could be said, then, that, conceivably, human free will is compatible with justification by faith.

The centrality of free will in Hubmaier's theology is observable through contrasting his claims for free will with the Reformation theologies which surrounded him, especially that of Luther. When considering Hubmaier's theology, juxtaposed with Luther's *Bondage of the Will*, one finds free will to be pronouncedly pivotal. A compelling argument for seeing free will as central to Hubmaier is that the debate over free will was central to the Reformation itself, especially in connection with the hammering out of the crucial issue of righteousness through grace by faith. Luther certainly saw the free will issue as fundamental, as can be attested in one key overture he made toward Erasmus in their debate: "I praise and commend you highly for this also, that unlike all the rest you alone have attacked the real issue, the essence of the matter in dispute, and have not wearied me with irrelevancies about the

---

will. If man's free will is enslaved, it is certainly true that he cannot justify himself–but this does not place God under any obligation to justify him by means of an extrinsic righteousness, provided the source of justifying righteousness is conceded to be none other than God himself. That man's will is enslaved is one matter; that God should choose to justify him in one specific manner as a result is quite another."

19 McGrath, *Iustitia Dei*, 203.
20 Ibid.

papacy, purgatory, indulgences, and such like trifles (for trifles they are rather than basic issues), with which almost everyone hitherto has gone hunting for me without success. You and you alone have seen the question on which everything hinges, and have aimed at the vital spot."[21] Hubmaier also fastened on this key issue, responding to the Reformation affirmation of the enslaved will with his own understanding of free will. As Alvin Beachy asserts: "At no other point did the Radical Reformers differ so strongly with the Magisterial Reformers as on the question of the bondage of the will."[22] In this context the indispensable nature of the doctrine of human free will in Hubmaier's theology begins to emerge.

HUBMAIER A CATHOLIC?

In placing the Anabaptists and their views in historical perspective in the Reformation period, and for placing Hubmaier and his theology in context, an important development is the fairly recent trend in Anabaptist studies, beginning in the late 1960's, toward a pluralistic view of the derivation of the Anabaptists. Harold Bender's view that the Anabaptists grew out of the Reformation, in particular in Zurich under Zwingli, had for a good while been dominant.[23] J. Denny Weaver describes the state of Anabaptist scholarship as of the late twentieth century: "Bender described what he considered true

---

21 Martin Luther, *On the Bondage of the Will*, in E. Gordon Rupp and Philip S. Watson, eds., *Luther and Erasmus: Free Will and Salvation* (Philadelphia: Westminster Press, 1969), 333.

22 Alvin Beachy, *The Concept of Grace in the Radical Reformation* (Nieuwkoop: B. De Graaf: 1977), 46. Beachy goes on to write: "Not all of the representative leaders of the Radical Reformation . . . developed in a systematic way their doctrines of the freedom of the will. Those who did were Hans Denck, Balthasar Hubmaier, and Melchior Hoffmann . . . . All three of the men who did develop at least a well reasoned argument against the bondage of the will . . . did so in reaction to this doctrine as set forth in Luther's *De Servo Arbitrio*." 46–47.

23 See Harold S. Bender, *The Anabaptist Vision* (Goshen: Mennonite Historical Society, 1945).

Anabaptism as a rather homogeneous movement originating in Zurich and motivated by purely religious concerns. In contrast, the more recent writers depict several points of origin and describe influential roles for persons not considered representative Anabaptists by Bender and his colleagues."[24] More importantly, this heterogeneous view also claims a variety of reforming motivations for the Anabaptist movement.[25] Increasingly the Anabaptists are being viewed not so much as a radical or left "wing" of the Reformation but as what Timothy George calls a "movement which gave birth to a new form of Christian faith and life."[26] J. A. Oosterbaan has designated the Anabaptist movement a "reformation of the Reformation" or "a correction of the correction of Catholicism."[27] Hubmaier's life and writings are well described by this current, more independent and heterogeneous, picture of Anabaptism.

Despite the uniquely Anabaptist mold of Hubmaier's doctrine of free will, some scholars have identified Hubmaier's position, based on certain elements within it, as inclining toward Roman Catholicism. They tie him to Johann Eck, Hubmaier's mentor before his conversion as an evangelical, and to Eck's nominalist background. Hubmaier probably was influenced in his theology by nominalism, and by Eck, but there seems to be no direct way to gauge the degree of this influence. A salient observation on the difficulty of consigning Hubmaier, or for that matter anyone else in this time, to a nominalist predilection is made by Paul Peachey. He observes that in the attempt to label an individual Reformer's intellectual heritage during the Reformation "the difficulties are perhaps insuperable."[28] Intellectual background and training was not necessarily indicative of each thinker's final views. Peachey ob-

---

24 J. Denny Weaver, *Becoming Anabaptist: The Origin and Significance of Sixteenth-Century Anabaptism* (Scottdale: Herald Press, 1987), 14.

25 See Walter A. Elwell, ed. *Evangelical Dictionary of Theology* (Grand Rapids: Baker Book House, 1984), s.v. "Radical Reformation" by J. D. Weaver.

26 Timothy George, *Theology of The Reformers* (Nashville: Broadman Press, 1988), 255.

27 J. A. Oosterbaan, "The Reformation of the Reformation: Fundamentals of Anabaptist Theology," *Mennonite Quarterly Review* 51 (1977): 176.

28 Paul Peachey, "The Radical Reformation," in *The Origins and Characteristics of Anabaptism / Les debuts et les caracteristiques de l'anabaptisme*, ed. Marc Lienhard (The Hague, Netherlands: Martinus Nijhoff, 1977), 13.

Introduction

serves that, "one might expect nominalists to espouse the radical reformation, and realists to remain Catholic or at most join the magisterial reformation. But one has only to recall that the magisterial reformer Luther, his Catholic opponent Eck, and the radical reformer Hubmaier . . . all stood under nominalist influence, to sense the difficulty."[29]

Hubmaier did utilize certain nominalist categories, especially the hidden and revealed will of God, in his theology. However, these concepts do not seem to be employed by Hubmaier as strict dogma so much as useful formulas which were consistent with his own theology. Torsten Bergsten explains Hubmaier's attitude:

> Hubmaier, after his conversion to the evangelical faith, repeatedly criticized the theological training which he had received and taught during his years as a loyal son of the church. He testified that he had attained his doctorate without knowing the way to eternal life and without having read either the Gospels or the Pauline epistles in their entirety. Thomas Aquinas, Duns Scotus, Gabriel Biel, William Occam, The Decretals, legends of the saints . . . and other scholastic authorities had been until then his "hellish scriptures." The new Hubmaier now condemned all teachings and teachers without a sure foundation in the Word of God, such as Aristotle, Aquinas, Duns Scotus, Bonaventura, and Occam. . . . Notwithstanding, the Anabaptist theologian was quite happy to appeal to Roman Catholic authorities whenever he found in their writings some support for his own new convictions.[30]

For Hubmaier, there was evidently no great reason to dismiss any essentially useful and logical theological construct simply because of the persons or

---

29 Peachey, "The Radical Reformation," 13. Peachey continues with this scholarly caution: "No concept which one chooses, therefore, can avoid the difficulty that in real life most theories are mixed. The polar concepts here employed as ideal types simply identify contrasting sets of tendencies which are criss-crossed by other tendencies in the flux of events. At particular moments one or another tendency may emerge as decisive, but one may not absolutize."

30 Bergsten, *Balthasar Hubmaier*, 51–52.

systems from which it was generally perceived to have been derived. Steinmetz remarks concerning this: "Hubmaier understood himself . . . to be following a middle way between the Pelagianism of the late scholastics and what he regarded as the Stoicism of Luther. He saw no reason to reject a theme from late medieval nominalism simply because it had been put to bad use in Catholic theology."[31] Hubmaier desired to subject every idea to the test of Scripture.

There appears to be a tendency by some scholars to label Hubmaier's particular brand of Anabaptism, his soteriology and defense of free will, as "Catholic" through the use of guilt by association with Eck. This approach evidently brushes aside the equal significance of the fact that the major Protestant Reformers, who are never labeled as "Catholic," had been Roman Catholic themselves, and retained certain Catholic ideas of their own. One such idea held by Luther, Calvin, and Zwingli, which the Anabaptists were quick to reject on the basis of their reading of Scripture, was infant baptism. For Luther and Calvin, infant baptism was related to their deterministic soteriology and so gave their doctrine of salvation, especially in the context of the Magisterial Reformers' territorial 'Christendom' oriented ecclesiology, a decidedly "Catholic" tone.

In other words, because these Reformers held on to the idea of a Christian society into which each infant was baptized as a Christian citizen, a theological question arose. How does one tell who are the "real" Christians, destined for heaven, when it is so obvious that many do not live according to the moral strictures of the Bible indicating a new life? The answer was a heavy emphasis on predestination to explain why some are obviously not Christian by virtue of their lifestyle, although baptized into the church as babies. These are the goats; those predestined for hell. This syllogistic reasoning likely followed from the holdover of the notably Roman Catholic idea of a regional church, which necessitated infant baptism, and almost certainly influenced the theology of the Magisterial Reformers.

In fact, this was one of the basic mistakes of the Protestant Reformers from the viewpoint of the Anabaptists.[32] As Leonard Verduin asserts, "In its

---

31 Steinmetz, "Luther and Hubmaier on the Freedom of the Human Will," in *Luther in Context* (Grand Rapids: Baker Books, 1962), 70.

32 Kenneth Davis notes that "Hubmaier also condemns the system

final version, Reformation theology attempted a combination of the formula of salvation by sacramental manipulation with the formula of salvation by believing response to the preached Word. This swing to the right [i.e., Roman Catholicism] precipitated the exodus of those adherents [Anabaptists] who had been too much under the influence of the ancient anti-Sacramentalism to go along with the retrenchment."[33] Ironically, according to Christof Windhorst, Luther had deeply influenced Hubmaier by his writings on the matter of the sacraments: "Above all, Luther's criticism of the sacraments made a deep impression on him. Here he learned that what mattered was preaching God's Word, which was heard in faith and realized in love."[34] However, Hubmaier went on to embrace the logical and biblical conclusion of this truth learned from Luther and adopted the doctrines of believer's baptism and a believers' church, radical ideas in the Reformation period. In the meantime, Luther backtracked toward infant baptism (he never rejected his own baptism in the Catholic Church), claiming that the faith of the parents was the faith by which the infant was baptized in Lutheran territory.

---

which combined ecclesiastical and temporal powers because it produced an unholy, worldly clergy." Kenneth R. Davis, *Anabaptism and Asceticism* (Scottsdale: Herald Press, 1974; reprint, Eugene, OR: Wipf and Stock, 1998), 122.

33 Insertions added. Leonard Verduin, *The Reformers and their Stepchildren*, with a foreword by Franklin H. Littell (Grand Rapids: Eerdmans, 1964), 154–155. Another writer summarizes the basic difference between Protestants and Anabaptists: "Most reformers sought territorial reformation, to transform their churches *en masse*. In Anabaptism the Reformation produced a radical strain which questioned the validity of regional or national churches. If men were saved by faith alone, then it might be argued that only adults capable of faith could be numbered among the elect. . . . At Zurich a group under Conrad Grebel followed the logic of this, rejected infant baptism and separated themselves from the town's worship. Zwingli's rationalist theology was in fact very vulnerable to their arguments, but he justified a vicious suppression of the group, many of whom were executed, with grim humor, by drowning." Henry Chadwick and G. R. Evans, eds, *Atlas of the Christian Church* (New York: Facts On File, 1987), 102.

34 Christof Windhorst, "Balthasar Hubmaier: Professor, Preacher, Politician," in *Profiles of Radical Reformers: Biographical Sketches from Thomas Müntzer to Paracelsus*, ed. Hans-Jürgen Goertz (Kitchener: Herald Press, 1982), 147.

Nevertheless, David Steinmetz makes the case that Luther was actually *more* radical than Hubmaier in his soteriology because of Hubmaier's "Catholic" (read works-oriented) stance on soteriology as opposed to Luther's "justification by faith" position.[35] But the case for Hubmaier's Roman Catholicity in soteriology must be made clearer in order for this statement to stand. To see Hubmaier's soteriology as Catholic works righteousness is to ignore the many clear affirmations of salvation by grace and faith alone in Hubmaier's writings. For example, Hubmaier's definition of faith from his *Catechism*: "Faith is the realization of the unspeakable mercy of God, his gracious favor and goodwill, which he bears to us through his most beloved Son Jesus Christ, whom he did not spare and delivered him to death for our sakes that sin might be paid for, and we might be reconciled to him and with the assurance of our hearts cry to him: Abba, Father, our Father who are in heaven."[36] In addition, Hubmaier proposed to draw his arguments from Scripture when defending human free will and decidedly rejected any Roman Catholic authority. Estep writes, "It is clear . . . that the Bible, not Augustine, councils, nor 'schoolmen' of the church is the 'plumb line' of Christian doctrine for Hubmaier."[37]

Hubmaier found an overabundance of evidence for human free will in Scripture, which was clearly his principal authority and source. In affirming free will as biblical, his primary target was theological determinism like that of Luther, which he believed permitted God to be perceived as the author of sin. Alister McGrath agrees with this assessment of Lutheran determinism, stating that "For Luther, it is God who is the author of sin."[38] Hubmaier judged this idea to be unbiblical. Note the frequent appeal to Scripture and its authority in the preface to Hubmaier's *Freedom of the Will, II*, in which Hubmaier discusses this sort of necessitarian conception of God:

---

[35] See David C. Steinmetz, "Balthasar Hubmaier (1485?–1528): Free Will and Covenant," in *Reformers in the Wings* (Philadelphia: Fortress, 1971), 207–208.

[36] Balthasar Hubmaier, *A Christian Catechism*, in *Balthasar Hubmaier: Theologian of Anabaptism*, ed. Wayne Pipkin and John H. Yoder, Classics of the Radical Reformation (Scottdale: Herald Press, 1989), 349.

[37] William R. Estep, *The Anabaptist Story: An Introduction to Sixteenth-Century Anabaptism*, 3d ed (Grand Rapids: Eerdmans, 1975), 96.

[38] McGrath, *Iustitia Dei*, 202.

> For if all things happened from necessity . . . and God effected good and evil in us, he would no longer have the right to condemn people because of sin. He would have to condemn himself. Adam and Eve could have so easily excused themselves before God with the words, "Lord, that we have transgressed your commandment happened out of your providence and necessity. You made and ordered us to be so. Therefore, it had to happen." Such is far from God. He was, is, and remains righteous in all his works, Isa. 1, 5; Ps. 51:1–8; John 8:51; Matt. 19:17. Therefore he wants us to judge and decide ourselves and asks us to do that. . . . Accordingly, Gracious Prince and Lord, in order to *maintain with the Holy Scripture such freedom of the will in the human being, to whom God has sent his Word*, I now dedicate the second book to Your Princely Grace in which first of all *I introduce Scriptures to testify to the truth*.[39]

As here, Hubmaier's priority on Scripture over human wisdom is evident in all of his writings. In this he is planted firmly in the evangelical Anabaptist camp. To say he leans toward the Catholic position in these matters perhaps betrays a predisposition.

Another scholar who takes the "Catholic" view of Hubmaier is the Baptist theologian James McClendon. He makes the case for this in his essay, "Balthasar Hubmaier, Catholic Anabaptist." His argument seems to amount to finding similarities with Catholic theology in a few theological viewpoints of Hubmaier (which can be done with any Reformation theologian) while at the same time pointing to Hubmaier's background as a Catholic theology student under Eck. Most of these similarities Hubmaier only affirmed when in prison, before his death, when he agreed in several non-essentials with the Catholic authorities in a final attempt to save his own life. McClendon's argument may indicate an agenda, perhaps ecumenism. Hubmaier's theology is patently so much more Anabaptist than Catholic, that to add this label seems to be an anachronistic attempt to remake Hubmaier according to modern aspirations

---

39 Emphasis added. Balthasar Hubmaier, *Freedom of the Will, II*, in *Balthasar Hubmaier: Theologian of Anabaptism*, ed. Wayne Pipkin and John H. Yoder, (Scottdale: Herald Press, 1989), 451–452.

for Christian unity. Hubmaier clearly rejected the Catholic system, with all its jurisdiction, in favor of scriptural authority. McClendon even admits this in his article, stating that "by his life's end Balthasar Hubmaier's deepest convictions were radically biblical."[40] Hubmaier's own words make clear that he considered his Catholic training and ministry to have held him "captive to many errors, hypocrisies, and evil abominations."[41] Hubmaier continues:

> We have planted them and industriously (although ignorantly; we did not know any better at that time) built them up. Indeed, we ran all around the sea until, with teaching, persuading, cowls, tonsures, and with oil and chrism, we had made a priest or a fellow monk. But the almighty and merciful God in his divine mercy opened our eyes . . . [to] see, acknowledge, and confess ourselves, in the strength of our Lord Jesus Christ, henceforth to direct our lives according to his rule.[42]

In addition, one may consult the works of Hubmaier regarding his general conception of salvation to see that the tenor of his conviction concerning justification is much closer to Luther and the Reform than to the Roman Church. For instance, Hubmaier writes describing a new Christian, ready for baptism:

> *Even though admittedly guilty yet he believes firmly that Christ, through his own death, has forgiven those sins, and through his resurrection made him holy in the sight of God, our Heavenly Father. Therefore, he then consents from now on to confess publicly before men the faith and the name of Christ, having also himself previously promised to live according to the word and command of Christ. But not in human strength*, lest that befall him which befell Peter. "For without me ye can

---

40 James McClendon."Balthasar Hubmaier, Catholic Anabaptist." in *Essays in Anabaptist Theology*, ed. H. Wayne Pipkin, (Elkhart: Institute of Mennonite Studies, 1994), 77.

41 Balthasar Hubmaier, *A Christian Catechism*, in *Balthasar Hubmaier: Theologian of Anabaptism*, ed. Wayne Pipkin and John H. Yoder, Classics of the Radical Reformation (Scottdale: Herald Press, 1989), 342.

42 Ibid. This is but one sampling, among many, of this sentiment in Hubmaier's writings.

do nothing," says Christ except in the power of God the Father, and of the Son, and of the Holy Ghost.[43]

This assertion regarding salvation appears in Hubmaier's work on believer's baptism and was in that way very distinct in respect to Protestant theology. The statement's key elements, however, centering on Christ's efficacy and human weakness, were clearly nearer to Luther than to the Roman Catholic structure of sacraments and sacerdotal rituals and works which furnished salvation for communicants.

The stress on discipleship among Anabaptists, as seen in the statement above with the commitment to "to live according to the word and command of Christ," was another strong reason for Hubmaier to take up the argument in favor of human free will. Because of a pastoral concern for holiness within the church, Hubmaier criticized the Lutheran reform as too lackadaisical when it came to personal holiness. This was an effective challenge to the Magisterial Reformation advanced by the leaders of the Radical Reformation throughout the sixteenth century. Harold O. J. Brown is of the opinion that, "Constant pressure on the Lutherans from the Anabaptists . . . to emphasize works kept the Lutherans from making the logical distinction between 'works-righteousness' and the 'works of the righteous.' In the heat of the controversy, confessional Lutheranism sometimes became ensconced in a commitment to 'faith alone' that amounted to hostility to good works and a godly life and seemed to turn Christianity into theory only, with no discernable practical implications."[44]

This appears to be a discrepancy in Luther's theology, and one reason that he spurned the book of James as a 'right strawy epistle.'[45] Hubmaier believed that the determinism which bolstered Luther's strong claims to *sola gratia* and *sola fide* left those great truths at times without the scriptural balance of Christian works. Verduin elaborates:

---

43 Emphasis added. Balthasar Hubmaier, *On the Christian Baptism of Believers* in *Anabaptist Beginnings (1523–1533): A Source Book*, comp. and ed. William R. Estep, Jr. (Nieuwkoop: B. De Graaf, 1976), 69–70.

44 Harold O. J. Brown, *Heresies: Heresy and Orthodoxy in the History of the Church* (Peabody, Mass.: Hendrickson, 1988), 367–368.

45 Luther, *Preface to the New Testament*, 1522.

THE CENTRALITY OF THE DOCTRINE OF HUMAN FREE WILL
IN THE THEOLOGY OF BALTHASAR HUBMAIER

Balthasar Hubmaier complained that in the camp of the Reformers men had learned only the first two of three pivotal doctrines of the Christian faith . . . The first doctrine was . . . We are saved by faith. . . The second was "of ourselves we cannot do any good" . . . Both of these are true enough, says this teacher at the Second Front. But then, he goes on to say that "Under cover of these two half-truths all evil, unfaithfulness and unrighteousness have gained the upperhand completely." . . . "Everybody wishes to pass for a Christian and a good evangelical as far as taking a wife is concerned, eating flesh [in Lent], making no further sacrifice, fasting not, saying no prayers any more;" but otherwise one sees nothing but drinking, gourmandizing, blaspheming, practicing usury, lying, cheating, abusing, forcing, stealing, robbing, playing, dancing, flirting, loafing, committing adultery, tyrannizing, slaying, etc., etc. The third lesson, which men in the Protestant camp had not mastered, said this Hubmaier, is that faith without works is dead.[46]

Yet Alister McGrath points out that Luther has often been misunderstood regarding faith and works since "Luther's theological breakthrough was intimately linked with the realisation that man was not justified upon the basis of any human work, but through the work of God within man."[47] McGrath notes further that, "Luther does not, as he is frequently represented, reject the necessity of good works in justification . . . He frequently appeals to the biblical image of the good tree which bears good fruit, thus testifying to, rather than causing, its good nature."[48]

Although, as McGrath indicates, Luther did stress Christian works of love in other writings, the necessitarian statements he made, especially in *The Bondage of the Will*, implied that all things, including Christian obedience, were already determined. This led, in some instances of the evangelical Reform, to a de-emphasis on a holy lifestyle as Verduin noted above. This issue is associated with the residual Romanist idea of a regional church, the concept of 'Christendom,' which the magisterial reformers retained, along with its attendant sacra-

---

46 Verduin, *The Reformers and Their Stepchildren*, 105, n. j.
47 McGrath, *Iustitia Dei*, 203.
48 Ibid.

ment, infant baptism. These ideas often drove the layman back toward the old Romish trust in the state-church institution and its rites, a medieval appendage to faith in Christ alone. In rejecting infant baptism Anabaptists confirmed that it is Christ alone who gives new life, along with its fruit, a changed life demonstrated in discipleship. In contrast to the Magisterial Reformers' idea of the national church, Hubmaier wrote: "For baptismal Scriptures do not apply to them [infants] but to those who now believe and confess their faith orally. On this confession Christ built his church, Matt. 16:18. And this is the order: (1) Christ, (2) word, (3) faith, (4) confession, (5) water baptism, (6) church."[49] A voluntary church as opposed to a territorial church, then, was at the heart of the Anabaptist concern for true biblical discipleship.

Therefore, Hubmaier and the Anabaptists stressed a holy life and accountability. This was a major element in Hubmaier's doctrine of baptism. Baptism was the making of a *voluntary* covenant with other believers, to be accountable to live in accordance with righteousness as a sign of the new life that the ceremony represented. According to William R. Estep this type of commitment and its corresponding ecclesiology of gathered believers was unique to the Anabaptists: "*A most important fact often overlooked is that the very concept of the gathered church . . . was evidently Anabaptist in origin and not a conscious product of the Magisterial Reform.* None of the Reformers developed an ecclesiology of churches composed of committed disciples only."[50] Accordingly, part of the motivation for keeping free will in a central position for his Anabaptist theology was Hubmaier's concern for a *disciples' church*: a group of Christians who, because of a choice to trust Christ and follow him, are baptized on the basis of faith and gather freely to worship and fellowship.

Thus, the Anabaptist insistence on believer's baptism and a believers' church was connected with their emphasis on free will. Hubmaier encouraged this connection in Anabaptism and was probably the strongest defender of a distinctive doctrine of human free will among the Anabaptists. Furthermore,

---

49 Hubmaier, *On Infant Baptism Against Oecolampad*, in *Balthasar Hubmaier: Theologian of Anabaptism*, ed. Wayne Pipkin and John H. Yoder, Classics of the Radical Reformation (Scottdale: Herald Press, 1989), 286.

50 William R. Estep, ed., *Anabaptist Beginnings (1523–1533): A Source Book* (Nieuwkoop: B. De Graaf, 1976), 5.

his view of faith and of the order of salvation are two additional concerns keeping free will at the center of Hubmaier's Anabaptist theology. Hubmaier's *ordo salutis*, as seen in his definition of church, above, featured a strong emphasis on the Word of God and the gospel, to which the believer must respond in faith. This response was to be a decisive and total surrender to Christ, in concurrence with the work of the Holy Spirit in the believer's life. This is reflective of the Anabaptist stress on conversion and the 'new birth,' with its resultant amended life. As Abraham Friesen writes, "This emphasis . . . can be seen throughout Anabaptism."[51] Friesen notes that for the Anabaptists "conversion is spoken of in terms of dying to sin and being raised to 'newness of life.'"[52] "It was not enough to know and give intellectual assent to a creedal statement;" says Friesen, "one had to be raised up to 'newness of life.' Hence the *Schleitheim Confession* observed: 'we have no fellowship with [the evil ones in the world] and do not run with them in the confusion of their abominations.'"[53]

As distinct from the idea that faith is exclusively a 'gift,' emphasized heavily in Lutheran and Reformed theology so that (especially for Calvin) faith only comes after regeneration, to Hubmaier faith was essentially a decision of trust and surrender to the Word revealed in the Christ of the gospel. As Rollin Armour asserts, "Hubmaier was not 'Protestant' in the classical and normative sense . . . for he understood faith to be a human action of belief which brought divine grace rather than, as in Luther and Zwingli, a more passive trust created within man's heart *sola gratia*."[54] For Hubmaier faith cannot be seen as passive. It is the believer's submission of his will to the will of God in Christ. To Hubmaier human freedom is divinely ordained, so that man may *authentically* yield to God through the opportunity given in Christ's death and resurrection.

Though Armour helpfully describes Hubmaier's view of free will as it relates to faith and baptism, he also claims to find Hubmaier leaning toward

---

51 Abraham Friesen, *Erasmus, the Anabaptists, and the Great Commission* (Grand Rapids: Eerdmans, 1998), 104.

52 Ibid.

53 Ibid., 105.

54 Rollin Stely Armour, *Anabaptist Baptism: A Representative Study*, Studies in Anabaptist and Mennonite History (Scottdale: Herald Press, 1966), 34.

Introduction

a Catholic view just as Steinmetz and McClendon do. One of the evidences Armour offers is that "Hubmaier believed that the Christian could attain a relative perfection."[55] He goes on to write that Hubmaier's idea "is also very near the Catholic conception of grace as the gift of God which makes man acceptable in His sight and capable of living above sin."[56] Armour's critique is incisively refuted by Hubmaier's own words: "But to the charge that we boast that we can sin no more after baptism, and the like, is a monstrous injustice and untrue. For we know that both before and after baptism, we are poor and miserable sinners, and if we say we sin not, we are liars, and the truth is not in us."[57] Leonard Verduin defends the Anabaptists against this very old claim of perfectionism[58] when he maintains:

> It was easy, very easy, to slide from the "heretic's" censure of conductual-averagism to the charge that he was given to Perfectionism. But this would be quite unfair. The Reformers made themselves guilty of this unfairness, time without number. No one knew better than did the Restitutionists that a Church of wholly sinless people is unattainable; and it is historically not defensible to imply, much less to assert, that they visualized a Church of unambiguous saints.[h]

---

[h] Balthasar Hübmaier, an influential leader among the Stepchildren, was well aware that the Reformers were twisting the "heretics'" clamor for the changed life so as to make it add up to Perfectionism. He rejected this.[59]

---

55 Armour, *Anabaptist Baptism*, 34.

56 Ibid.

57 Hubmaier, *Concerning the Christian Baptism of Believers*, in *Anabaptist Beginnings*, ed. Estep, 67.

58 This aspersion was first used polemically by the Magisterial Reformers; Armour, reviving a similar slur against the Anabaptists, claims Hubmaier is "a step closer to Pelagianism" because he believed that "the human will is inherently capable of electing to believe the gospel." Armour, *Anabaptist Baptism*, 34.

59 Verduin, *The Reformers and their Stepchildren*, 102–103.

There appears, then, to be clear evidence that the Catholic label for Hubmaier's theology, especially referring to Perfectionism and Pelagianism, is imbalanced. In fact Armour goes on to balance his own assessment of Hubmaier by qualifying it as follows: "At the same time, it must be admitted that it is to a degree illegitimate to call Hubmaier's thought 'Catholic,' for he wholly repudiated the Catholic sacramental theology which was interwoven with all other aspects of Catholic thought, anthropology included."[60] Thus, Armour comes to the conclusion other scholars have about Anabaptism generally,[61] and Hubmaier specifically, "that he and those who agreed with him might best be classified as belonging to a third party, neither Protestant nor Catholic."[62]

William Estep characterizes Hubmaier as one who was not enamored of tradition, especially the teachings of his own Catholic training, but considered Scripture to be the authority for his theological views. Estep sees Hubmaier as a reformer who did "honestly attempt to discover what the Scriptures taught and to exegete them faithfully. It is also evident that the New Testament became for him the sole authority for the Christian life and the life of the church."[63] The theological debates during the Reformation were not casual colloquiums of cautious intellectuals, but intense battles among deeply religious men who were often prepared to die for truth. Hubmaier believed truth was derived from God's own Word. In a book which takes as its title Hubmaier's motto, *Truth Is Immortal*, Irwin Barnes calls Hubmaier "a fearless warrior for the truth, who drew his inspiration and authority . . . from the Scriptures," recalling that "Hubmaier paid for his beliefs with his life."[64] An intensely powerful testimonial demonstrating that Hubmaier was not "Catholic" in his thought is that he was executed for this very reason: a refusal to deny his Anabaptist faith and return to Catholic dogma.

---

60 Armour, *Anabaptist Baptism*, 34.

61 As evidenced by the title of one of Walter Klaassen's books: *Anabaptism: Neither Catholic or Protestant* (Waterloo, Ont.: Conrad, 1973).

62 Armour, *Anabaptist Baptism*, 34.

63 Estep, *The Anabaptist Story*, 97.

64 Irwin Barnes, *Truth Is Immortal: The Story of the Baptists in Europe* (London: Carey Kingsgate Press, 1955), 12.

Introduction

Overview

Chapter One will begin with a survey of the argument over human free will in the history of the church up to and including the Reformation, which will assist in placing Hubmaier within the larger theological-historical setting. Next, Hubmaier's free will doctrine shall be examined within the framework of Anabaptist and Reformation theology showing that the Magisterial Reformers were heavily influenced by Augustinianism, whereas the Anabaptists universally affirmed human free will. After the historical and theological context has been described, Chapter Two will concern itself with the idea of human free will in Hubmaier's own thought. An examination of the biblical, theological, and philosophical sources for Hubmaier's position will precede an explanation of the trichotomous features of Hubmaier's anthropology which allowed for his view of human free will.[65] This will include an analysis of Hubmaier's approach in his two treatises, *Freedom of the Will, I* and *Freedom of the Will, II*,[66] concerning: 1) three kinds of will (flesh, soul, and spirit) in trichotomous man; 2) two kinds of will in God in which Hubmaier distinguishes a hidden will (God's complete freedom) and revealed will (God's call for man to choose Christ), in order to account for God's sovereignty.

Finally, a treatment of the relation and impact of Hubmaier's doctrine of free will on Hubmaier's full theology will undertake to show the centrality of free will in his thought. The concept of volitional freedom in mankind will be presented as essential to Hubmaier's whole theology in Chapter Three.

---

65 See Mabry, *Balthasar Hubmaier's Doctrine of the Church*, 13.

66 In Wayne Pipkin and John H. Yoder, eds, *Balthasar Hubmaier: Theologian of Anabaptism,* Classics of the Radical Reformation (Scottdale: Herald Press, 1989). This is the latest English edition of Hubmaier's collected works. The German critical edition is *Balthasar Hubmaier Schriften*, Quellen zur Geschichte der Täufer IX, ed. by Torsten Bergsten and Gunnar Westin (Guetersloh: Gerd Mohn, 1962). An earlier English edition of Hubmaier's works is *The Writings of Balthasar Hubmaier*, ed. by W. O Lewis and George Dagged Davidson (Liberty: William Jewell College, 1939). The interview between Hubmaier and Faber while he was in prison in Vienna can be found in William R. Estep, *Anabaptist Beginnings*.

THE CENTRALITY OF THE DOCTRINE OF HUMAN FREE WILL IN THE THEOLOGY OF BALTHASAR HUBMAIER

John D. Rempel speaks of free will as a "preoccupation" for Hubmaier.[67] He notes that some key areas of intersection with free will in Hubmaier are the image of God in man, God's Word, original sin, Christian good works, soteriology, and ecclesiology (including baptism and the Lord's Supper).[68] Torsten Bergsten writes, "In Hubmaier's teaching on free will, his anthropological, soteriological, and ethical views are brought together."[69] The pivotal position of free will in Hubmaier's theology calls for a study of its development and nature, and its impact on his whole theology.[70]

The significance of the debate over human free will today, and the crucial role of the doctrine of free will in Hubmaier's theology, point to the potential importance of investigating the centrality of human free will in the theology of Balthasar Hubmaier. An analysis of the basic issues in the doctrine of the human free will, as well as some of the confusions and theological motivations in the historical background, presents the possibility for some additional enlightenment with regard to Anabaptist theology, Reformation theology, and the doctrine of human free will. This is especially true when the task is to see these things from the unique Anabaptist perspective taken by Hubmaier. The monograph's objective is to demonstrate the centrality of the doctrine of human free will in Hubmaier's Anabaptist theology, and thus provide a key to better understanding this unique and seminal Reformer.

---

67 John D. Rempel, *The Lord's Supper in Anabaptism: A Study in the Christology of Balthasar Hubmaier, Pilgram Marpeck, and Dirk Philips*, Studies in Anabaptist and Mennonite History 33 (Scottdale: Herald Press, 1993), 44.

68 Ibid., 44. Also see the discussion of Hubmaier's teaching on free will in Torsten Bergsten, *Balthasar Hubmaier*, 350–352.

69 Bergsten, *Balthasar Hubmaier*, 349.

70 As to Hubmaier's doctrine of anthropology, which is closely tied with his upholding of human free will, George Huntston Williams writes that "it imparted a distinctive character to the whole of his theology as we assemble it from his numerous works." G. H. Williams, *The Radical Reformation*, 3d ed. (Kirksville: Sixteenth Century Journal Publishers, 1962), 334.

Chapter One

Historical-Theological Context for Free Will

To understand the broader historical context for Hubmaier's theology of free will, a survey of the issue in church history is in order. Luther, Erasmus, and Hubmaier, were not the first to discuss and debate these matters. Beginning with the Fathers of the church and continuing to the Reformation it is evident that, as Norman Geisler asserts, "with the exception of the later writings of St. Augustine...virtually all the great thinkers up to the Reformation affirmed that human beings possess the power of contrary free choice, even in a fallen state."[71] According to this assessment the will-in-bondage anthropology has not been the dominant Christian view in most of Christian history.

During the patristic period of church history, free will was already a pivotal issue, especially in combating pagan deterministic worldviews prevalent during the early age of the church. Then, with Augustine and Pelagius the issue is thrust into its first great internecine battle in Christian history, which continued to erupt during the early Middle Ages, especially in the form of the semi-pelagian dispute.[72] During the Middle Ages prominent theologians like

---

71 Norman Geisler, *Chosen But Free* (Minneapolis: Bethany House, 1999), 145.

72 According to *The Oxford Dictionary of the Christian Church*, Semi-pelagianism is "the name given to doctrines on human nature upheld in the fifth century by a group of theologians who, while not denying the necessity of grace for salvation, maintained that the first steps toward the Christian life were ordinarily taken by the human will and that grace supervened later. Their position was roughly midway between the radically opposed doctrines

Abelard and Aquinas weighed in on the issue of free will, primarily favorably, while later medieval nominalists, such as Gabriel Biel, assigned excessive meritorious power to human free will regarding salvation. Finally, the famous debate between Luther and Erasmus marks the Reformation with the issue of free will and reopens in a slightly different form with the advent of the Dutch Reformed theologian Arminius. This latter is the form of the debate over which western Christians still struggle, separating into Calvinist and Arminian camps.

PRE-AUGUSTINIAN CHURCH FATHERS

In general, the early Fathers viewed man as free. "There can be no doubt whatever that the Greek and Latin Fathers of the church from the very beginning held to the natural freedom of man's will both before and after the fall of Adam."[73] So writes Harry McSorley in his study treating Luther's *The Bondage of the Will*. For the pre-Augustinian Fathers, at creation the soul is endowed with the ability to choose between good and evil. Some souls choose to turn from God and give themselves over to the sins of the flesh. But man is able, through the aid of God and living a Christian life, to return to God. **Archelaus** (fl. 278 AD) wrote: "For all the creatures that God made, He made very good; and He gave to every individual the sense of free will, in accordance

---

of Augustine and Pelagius. These teachings were first expressed *c.*425 by representatives of the monastic movement in southern Gaul, the most prominent of whom was John Cassian. Cassian was one of the first of the Semi-Pelagians, who rejected the view of Augustine that humankind generally is damned by the sin of Adam and that some souls are saved purely through the grace of God, which cannot be earned. Cassian's views were developed mainly in opposition to Augustine's later writings, which taught an extreme form of predestination, infallible perseverance, and a 'numerus clausus' [fixed number] of the elect." Insertion added. Livingstone, E. A., ed. *The Oxford Dictionary of the Christian Church*, 3rd ed., (Oxford, 2003), *s.v.* 'Semipelagianism'.

[73] Harry J. McSorley, *Luther: Right or Wrong?: An Ecumenical-Theological Study of Luther's Major Work, The Bondage of the Will* (New York: Newman Press, 1969), 57.

with which standard He also instituted the law of judgment. To sin is ours, and that we sin not is God's gift, as our will is constituted to choose either to sin or not to sin."[74]

Therefore, the freedom of man is real in that it empowers him to determine his estate forever. Jesus came to save man from sin. But sin implies guilt on the part of man and guilt is meaningless unless man is in some way responsible for his sin. Man cannot be held guilty for an immoral act unless he is able to act differently. Thus, only if man is free to choose can he be condemned for his sin. If man has sinned, he must be free. God, who is all good and perfect, cannot be responsible for evil and sin in the world. So, according to the early Fathers, man must shoulder this responsibility. The biblical fact of the imminent judgement of God requires this. McSorley elaborates:

> When the Fathers argued that free will was necessary for merit or demerit, they were not seeking to extol the power of man to merit his salvation. They were simply taking seriously the scriptural teaching that God judges all men according to their works, and from this theological standpoint—from the revealed truth of the coming judgment of God—they insisted against their pagan contemporaries . . . that the God who judges is the good God and that man had to have free will if a judgment of God is to be at all meaningful and just. One misunderstands the patristic teaching on free will, then, if one interprets it as mere moralism or as an assertion of autonomous humanism. It was much more an assertion of the justice and holiness of the one God, the recognition of the original goodness of his creation and a confession of the biblical faith in coming judgment of our works by God.[75]

This same misunderstanding (that an affirmation of free will necessarily means an affirmation of works salvation) was applied by Luther and others to the Anabaptist position on free will. Hubmaier's free will theology was similar to that of the Church Fathers as described above. Peder Liland describes

---

74 Archelaus, *The Acts of the Disputation with the Heresiarch Manes* 32 (*ANF* 6:378).

75 McSorley, *Luther: Right or Wrong?*, 61.

Hubmaier's position: "It is central to Hubmaier to state the integral place of an ethical obligation within the context of the religious commitment. This does not mean that the work of natural and re-generated will has any meritorious role in the question of salvation. The legalistic framework which Luther so vigorously rejected, is clearly rejected also by Hubmaier's less polemical affirmation of the Gospel."[76]

Justin Martyr (c. 100–165) likewise argued that man is not responsible for sin unless he has free will. Thus, God is just to punish and reward: "In the beginning He made the human race with the power of thought and of choosing the truth and doing right, so that all men are without excuse before God."[77] **Tatian**, a second century Christian apologist and a disciple of Justin, wrote: "Live to God, and by apprehending Him lay aside your old nature. We were not created to die, but we die by our own fault. Our free-will has destroyed us; we who were free have become slaves; we have been sold through sin. Nothing evil has been created by God; we ourselves have manifested wickedness; but we, who have manifested it, are able again to reject it."[78]

Justin and other early Christian apologists were concerned to defend Christianity against paganism by employing the doctrine of free will against the pagan idea of fate. They were determined to guard against the idea that God was in any way the author of sin. McSorley explains:

> In contrast to the Old and New Testament belief in God's providential care, the late Greek (Stoic and Pythagorean) concept of providence was a doctrine of destiny, fatalism or necessitarianism that left no place for the free will of man. The Christian Fathers, reacting against these originally Oriental ideas which found wide acceptance in the politically turbulent Graeco-Roman world, and which led to star worship and astrology, taught a doctrine of providence and predestination that respected man's natural freedom. A fatalism that took away man's responsibility

---

76 Peder Liland, "Anabaptist Separatism: A Historical and Theological Study of the Contribution of Balthasar Hubmaier" (Ph.D. diss., Boston College, 1983), appendix 9.

77 Justin Martyr, *The First Apology of Justin* 28 (ANF 1:311).

78 Tatian the Assyrian, *Address of Tatian to the Greeks* 11 (ANF 2:125).

for sin was abhorrent to them.... The early Church had to struggle against pagan dualism to uphold monotheism and the holiness of the one God. To the Fathers this meant that sin could not be attributed to any personal principle of evil co-existing with the good God, or to the material creation of a creator-God as opposed to the redeemer-God. It meant further that man could not have been created naturally evil by the good God and that the good God was in no way responsible for sin. Sin had to originate from some change in man for which man himself was responsible, a change that he freely willed.[79]

The preservation of the truth of God's essential goodness of character made free will integral to the apologetic of these early theologians. God must be the good Creator and just Judge of all things or the whole of the early Fathers' theology would not have made any sense. Hence, man must accept responsibility for evil, a responsibility acknowledged before a Holy God. As Thomas Oden states: "Such a sense of moral responsibility [in man] cannot be explained except by supposing the existence of a superior lawgiver, a Holy One who is present and impinging upon our responsibility with the claim that we do the good we know and avoid the evil we know.... In this way the will of the Creator is hypothesized as the necessary and sufficient reason for the existence of moral obligation."[80]

One of the leading proponents of free will in this early period was **Irenaeus of Lyon** (c.130–c.200). He appealed to the general tenor of Scripture[81]

---

79 McSorley, *Luther: Right or Wrong?*, 59–60.

80 Thomas C. Oden, *Systematic Theology*, vol. 1. *The Living God* (Peabody: Prince Press, 1987), 167.

81 Irenaeus finds man's free will implicit in the general tone of much of Scripture: "For this reason the Lord also said, 'Let your light so shine before men, that they may see your good deeds, and glorify your Father who is in heaven.' And, 'Take heed to yourselves, lest perchance your hearts be overcharged with surfeiting, and drunkenness, and worldly cares.' And, 'Let your loins be girded about, and your lamps burning, and ye like unto men that wait for their Lord, when He returns from the wedding, that when He cometh and knocketh, they may open to Him. Blessed is that servant whom his Lord, when He cometh, shall find so doing.' And again, 'The servant who knows his Lord's will, and does it not,

and specifically to the *imago dei* in man in his defense of human free will: "But because man is possessed of free will from the beginning, and God is possessed of free will, in whose likeness man was created, advice is always given to him to keep fast the good, which thing is done by means of obedience to God."[82] One of the logical arguments which made free will meaningful to Irenaeus was that God is free and thus freely created man and gave him freedom of choice. Being created in God's image meant, for Irenaeus, that man possessed free will and reason.[83] Justo González summarizes Irenaeus' thought: "As creatures of God with the purpose of growth, Adam and Eve were free. . . . Their freedom was in no way incompatible with the divine omnipotence, but was rather its result and expression."[84] So, for Irenaeus, man's moral responsibility is not an arbitrary assignment but arises from being made like his Creator, with reason and freedom.

Man's moral choice, then, is to seek out his Creator and do the good He commands, or to reject his Creator and turn to evil and his own devices. Irenaeus declared, "But man, being endowed with reason, and in this respect like to God, having been made free in his will, and with power over himself, is himself the cause to himself, that sometimes he becomes wheat, and sometimes chaff."[85] Irenaeus also relates free will to faith, which is especially vital for his soteriology:

---

shall be beaten with many stripes.' And, 'Why call ye me, Lord, Lord, and do not the things which I say?' And again, 'But if the servant says in his heart, The Lord delayeth, and begins to beat his fellow-servants, and to eat, and drink, and to be drunken, his Lord will come in a day on which he does not expect Him, and shall cut him in sunder, and appoint his portion with the hypocrites.' All such passages demonstrate the independent will of man, and at the same time the counsel which God conveys to him, by which He exhorts us to submit ourselves to Him, and seeks to turn us away from [the sin of] unbelief against Him, without, however, in any way coercing us." *Against Heresies* 4.37 (ANF 1:1032).

82 Irenaeus, *Against Heresies* 4.37 (ANF 1:1033).

83 See J. N. D. Kelly, *Early Christian Doctrines*, rev. ed. (New York: Harper Collins, 1978), 171.

84 Justo L. González, *A History of Christian Thought*, vol. 1, *From the Beginnings to the Council of Chalcedon* (Nashville: Abingdon, 1970), 163.

85 Irenaeus, *Against Heresies* 4.4 (ANF 1:926).

> And not merely in works, but also in faith, has God preserved the will of man free and under his own control, saying, "According to thy faith be it unto thee;" thus showing that there is a faith specially belonging to man, since he has an opinion specially his own. And again, "All things are possible to him that believeth;" and, "Go thy way; and as thou hast believed, so be it done unto thee." Now all such expressions demonstrate that man is in his own power with respect to faith. And for this reason, "he that believeth in Him has eternal life while he who believeth not the Son hath not eternal life, but the wrath of God shall remain upon him." In the same manner therefore the Lord, both showing His own goodness, and indicating that man is in his own free will and his own power, said to Jerusalem, "How often have I wished to gather thy children together, as a hen [gathereth] her chickens under her wings, and ye would not! Wherefore your house shall be left unto you desolate."[86]

Evidently, for Irenaeus, faith is not merely a passive gift as it seems to be with Luther. It involves a real choice: to trust God through His Son or to reject the Son, and hence the Father. Hubmaier indicated this same idea, contending that God "wills and draws all men unto salvation. Yet choice is still left to man, since God wants him without pressure, unconstrained, under no compulsion."[87]

Lactantius (c250–c325) was another church father and early apologist whose soteriology (and Christology) featured free choice prominently:

> When God had determined to send to men a teacher of righteousness, He commanded Him to be born . . . in the flesh, and to be made in the likeness of man himself, to whom he was about to be a guide, and companion, and teacher. But since God is kind and merciful to His people, He sent Him to those very persons whom He hated, that He might not close the way of salvation against them for ever, but might

---

86 Irenaeus, *Against Heresies* 4.37 (*ANF* 1:1033).

87 Balthasar Hubmaier, *On Free Will* in *Spiritual and Anabaptist Writers*, Library of Christian Classics, ed. George Huntston Williams and Angel M. Mergal (Philadelphia: Westminster Press, 1958), 135

give them a free opportunity of following God, that they might both gain the reward of life if they should follow Him (which many of them do, and have done), and that they might incur the penalty of death by their fault if they should reject their King.[88]

An ability to resist the grace of God was a common notion with the Church Fathers and also with the Radical Reformers. In fact, it is God's grace which *allows* for choice in this perspective. C. Arnold Snyder notes that the Radical Reformers "held that God's grace enabled sinners to choose freely either the path of salvation, or the path to perdition."[89] These ideas are embraced in Hubmaier's thought. "Thus, Hubmaier," writes Alvin Beachy, "in his development of a doctrine of the freedom of the will, shows concern not only for man's moral responsibility but also for the personal and voluntary character of Christian salvation with the implication that compulsion would be a violation of grace and for the protection of the moral character of God."[90]

The idea that God does not compel, since compulsion is contrary to grace, was championed by another early church father, **Clement of Alexandria** (c.150–c.215). He composed this declaration: "For choice depended on the man as being free; but the gift on God as the Lord. And He gives to those who are willing and are exceedingly earnest, and ask, that so their salvation may become their own. For God compels not (for compulsion is repugnant to God), but supplies to those who seek, and bestows on those who ask, and opens to those who knock."[91] One cannot help but notice how rich with supporting scriptures are the statements of the church fathers as they advocate for human free will.

It should also be noted that a significant aspect, indicating the quality of God's great grace and mercy, is the dignity which the call for faith affords to mankind. God does not force man to do his bidding. For the Church Fathers

---

88 Lactantius, *Divine Institutes* 4.11 (ANF 7:225).

89 C. Arnold Snyder, *Anabaptist History and Theology*, revised student ed. (Kitchener, Ontario: Pandora Press, 1997), 86.

90 Alvin Beachy, *The Concept of Grace in the Radical Reformation*, 53.

91 Clement of Alexandria, *On the Salvation of the Rich Man* 10 (ANF 2:1196).

the bestowal of free will to human beings appears to be part of the very definition of God's grace, a notion the Magisterial Reformers apparently neglected.

Hubmaier likewise emphasized this idea of God's grace in allowing for free will when he wrote, "No one may resist the will of God where God does not himself graciously offer freedom of will, Ps. 76:8; Rom. 9:19. However, where he offers the same to a person, his will once again takes place, either for good or for punishment which is also good to the one who recognizes its goodness. Heb. 12:6; Prov. 3:12."[92] Hubmaier is saying that God's will and man's free will are not incompatible; on the contrary God's will is done when man has free will to choose God's offered grace or reject it. For Hubmaier, it is a grace from God that man is given his own will, to accept or reject God's call. God's will takes place in both instances, as Hubmaier indicates, for good or punishment. Even temporary punishment is good if the one being punished for his sin repents and receives again the grace of God.

Thus, an element involved in the concept of punishment for sin, for Hubmaier, is that of the sinner being given over to further sin. He writes, "God wants the human being to do good. He also wants the one who does not want to do good to be the master of his own works, and to do evil, so that his separation from the good is thus punished, as sin with sin."[93] The point of this is for the man being punished in this fashion to come to his senses and repent. This then is also a grace of God.[94] By definition, then, the *God of*

---

92 Hubmaier, *Freedom of the Will, II*, Pipkin and Yoder, 467.

93 Ibid.

94 John Newport explains this idea that allowing further sin is punishment but is also a function of God's grace: "Through his judgment on sin, which often results in human suffering, God has made the way of the transgressor hard. But behind God's judgement is the ultimate purpose of mercy, not vengeance. God's wrath is motivated by his passionate love for his people. As the old preachers would say, God's painful judgments in this life are part of his 'blockade of the road to hell,' part of his 'trumpet call to the unconverted.' They are warnings lest men and women allow themselves to be destroyed in the Last Judgment. The apostle Paul gives a classic interpretation of God's judgment in Romans 1:18–32, which implies that the basic sin is idolatry—the rejection of God's self-revelation and rebellion against God's sovereignty. This idolatry creates a chain reaction: It provokes God's wrath; God's wrath causes immorality and injustice (Rom. 3:10–18); and immorality and injus-

grace will not compel men to be saved. Beachy describes Hubmaier's view in this way: Hubmaier affirms that God "wills that all men should be saved. . . . and draws men to salvation, yet choice is still left to man, since God wants him without pressure, unconstrained, under no compulsion. Only those who resist God's attracting will experience His repelling will as one of justice and punishment."[95]

The Latin Father, **Tertullian** (c.160–c.225) also emphasized human free will, especially with reference to man's innate morality, that is, his ability to respond to the claims of God his Creator. Tertullian remarked:

> I find, then, that man was by God constituted free, master of his own will and power; indicating the presence of God's image and likeness in him by nothing so well as by this constitution of his nature. For it was not by his face, and by the lineaments of his body . . . that he expressed his likeness to the form of God; but he showed his stamp in that essence which he derived from God Himself (that is, the spiritual, which answered to the form of God), and in the freedom and power of his will. This his state was confirmed even by the very law which God then imposed upon him. For a law would not be imposed upon one who had it not in his power to render that obedience which is due to law; nor again, would the penalty of death be threatened against sin, if a contempt of the law were impossible to man in the liberty of his will. So in the Creator's subsequent laws also you will find, when He sets before man good and evil, life and death, that the entire course of discipline is arranged in precepts by God's calling men from sin, and threatening and exhorting them; and this on no other ground than that man is free, with a will either for obedience or resistance.[96]

---

tice result in human suffering. In other words, God's wrath permits people to be what they desire to be in accordance with their idolatrous intent." *Life's Ultimate Questions* (Dallas: Word, 1989), 244.

95 Beachy, *The Concept of Grace in the Radical Reformation*, 53.

96 Tertullian, *Against Marcion* 2.5 (ANF 3:542–543).

Thus, Tertullian, like other church fathers, understood man's free will as a reflection of the image of God. He states further: "Therefore it was proper that (he who is) the image and likeness of God should be formed with a free will and a mastery of himself; so that this very thing—namely, freedom of will and self-command—might be reckoned as the image and likeness of God in him. For this purpose such an essence was adapted to man as suited this character, even the afflatus of the Deity, Himself free and uncontrolled."[97] J. N. D. Kelly writes of Tertullian: "Tertullian is a firm believer in free-will; he defends its existence against [Gnostics teachers] Marcion and Hermogenes, never ceasing to repeat that a man is responsible for his acts."[98]

Summary of Early Church Fathers' View of Free Will

To review, the pre-Augustinian fathers of the church were in support of free will in man for a variety of reasons. Some of the most important reasons were: Free will reflects the image of God in man, even after the Fall. Limited free will in man, the creature, reflects God the Creator's completely free nature. The moral nature of man and of God's claim on man, stressed prominently in Scripture, presupposes free will and responsibility for sin in human beings. Free will protects God's holy reputation and character as absolutely good, He cannot be the author of sin.

Further, God's merciful offer of salvation must be taken up via free choice by faith (there is also freedom to reject Him), affirming the fact that God desires all to be saved. This faith is never compelled, so that God's grace is a free gift, and is thus resistible. Even resistance is turned by God into mercy in allowing the sinner to damage himself further so that he will awaken to his woeful condition and repent. Free will explains the origin of evil and sin in the world and harmonizes with the Bible's consistent portrayal of God as the righteous Judge who will judge all in the end but is also a God of grace who pursues humankind.

---

97 Tertullian, *Against Marcion* 2.6 (*ANF* 3:543). 'Afflatus' refers to the act of blowing or breathing into from the Latin, thus in this context, the impartation of God's attribute of freedom to man made in His image.

98 Insertion added. Kelly, *Early Christian Doctrines*, 175.

AUGUSTINE

Augustine of Hippo (354–430) asserted that Adam had both the ability not to sin (*posse non peccare*) and the ability to sin (*posse peccare*) before his fall. He argued that man, in Adam, forfeited the former by employing the latter. Thus, the original freedom of man could only be recovered by the operation of divine grace. The crucial question, then, becomes whether man has the ability to accept or reject grace, and with that enquiry the problem of freedom is raised again. This was the question on which everything hinged in the Reformation. Luther, relying on Augustine, said no; others, like Erasmus and Hubmaier said yes. The matter comes down to whether the human will is active in faith or whether, as Augustine believed, the will is made willing by God, since the will is enslaved and in bondage.

In his *Enchiridion* Augustine summarizes his view of the role of man's will in salvation through faith:

> The whole work belongs to God, who both makes the will of man righteous, and thus prepares it for assistance, and assists it when it is prepared. For the man's righteousness of will precedes many of God's gifts, but not all; and it must itself be included among those which it does not precede. We read in Holy Scripture, both that God's mercy "shall meet me," and that His mercy "shall follow me." It goes before the unwilling to make him willing; it follows the willing to make his will effectual.[99]

---

[99] St. Augustine, *The Enchiridion on Faith, Hope and Love*, ed. Henry Paolucci (South Bend: Regnery/Gateway, 1961), 40. Hubmaier was not especially fond of Augustine and, specifically with the matter of infant baptism, did not hesitate to denounce him. In his work *On the Christian Baptism of Believers* he wrote, "I also know very well what Augustine wrote to Petrus Diaconus in his chapter *Firmissime*, [Most firmly] eleven hundred years ago. Would to God that he had said *Impiissime*, [Most impiously] for that, then he would have spoken the truth. But that is enough said about this. In this matter we do not need the testimony of men at all. Therefore we have only answered them very briefly with their own human junk." Pipkin and Yoder, 139. Hubmaier did quote Augustine in some instances to support believer's

With the Augustinian view, the matter of submitting to God in faith is rendered all but irrelevant since even the submission of the individual is completely a work of God's mercy; no 'synergism' is tolerated in this view. This idea appears to beg for the corresponding concept of double predestination in order to explain the overall plan of God, making of His mercy a force (monergism) which none can resist and which many are denied, apparently arbitrarily.

Alister McGrath observes that Augustine did not teach an explicit doctrine of double predestination even though it may be considered the logical outgrowth of his ideas about the enslaved will and divine grace. He writes, "Augustine was reluctant to acknowledge such a doctrine, no matter how logically appropriate it might appear."[100] But Augustine's insistence that the will is incapable of any role in salvation appears to rob the individual of genuinely surrendering his will, by faith, to trust in God's righteousness through Christ. This, then, amounts to a violation of grace and mercy, by many accounts, because grace becomes force, that is, irresistible and thus, by the Augustinian definition, loses its own essentially gracious nature.

Augustine, then, argued for irresistible and prevenient grace. Henry Chadwick describes Augustine's view: "If we are so corrupt that we no longer have free will to do good, grace must do all; and that this power is irresistible is a plain deduction from the divine decree of predestination which otherwise would be frustrated. . . . Accordingly, the empirical test of the operation of grace lies in a man's consistent goodness of character right through to the end of life, a 'final perseverance' which is a foreordained gift of God, independent of merit."[101] But this emphasis on irresistible grace was not always Augustine's view. The earlier Augustine had highlighted human free will when combating the dualistic religion of Manichaeism. At that time, Augustine wrote:

---

baptism, realizing his great influence down through the years and with Hubmaier's contemporaries, but on the whole was negative toward Augustine. See Bergsten, *Balthasar Hubmaier*, 281–283. Hubmaier even accused Augustine of lying. See Pipkin and Yoder, 254.

100 McGrath, *Iustitia Dei*, 203.

101 Henry Chadwick, *The Early Church*, rev. ed. (London: Penguin Books, 1993), 232.

> If man is good, and if he would not be able to act rightly except by willing to do so, he ought to have free will because without it he would not be able to act rightly. Because he also sins through having free will, we are not to believe that God gave it to him for that purpose. It is, therefore, a sufficient reason why he ought to have been given it, that without it man could not live aright. That it was given for this purpose can be understood from this fact. If anyone uses his free will in order to sin, God punishes him. That would be unjust unless the will was free not only to live aright but also to sin. How could he be justly punished who uses his will for the purpose for which it was given? Now when God punishes a sinner what else do you suppose he will say to him than "Why did you not use your free will for the purpose for which I gave it to you, that is, in order to do right?" Justice is praised as a good thing because it condemns sins and honors righteous actions. How could that be done if man had no free will? An action would be neither sinful nor righteous unless it were done voluntarily.[102]

Here Augustine sounds much like the earlier fathers of the church with a similar concern for the justice of God and the same stress upon free will as necessary for human responsibility.

Augustine also stated, "Nothing makes the mind a companion of cupidity, except its own will and free choice."[103] This is a statement from his early work on the subject of the meaning and origin of evil, *On Free Will*. Since evil's genesis is found in the free will of the rational human creature, the title reflects this emphasis. It was an attempt to counter Augustine's former philosophical home (Manichaeism), which had been satisfactory to him for a time, before his conversion to Christianity, since it purportedly explained evil. Similar to the Gnostic doctrine in this respect, it simplified the presence of evil by positing a dualism in the nature of things, seeing spirit as good and material as evil.

---

102 Augustine, *On Free Will*, in *Augustine: Earlier Writings*, ed. J. H. S. Burleigh, Library of Christian Classics (Philadelphia: Westminster Press, 1953), 135.

103 Ibid., 125.

Pelagianism

Augustine's affirmation of free will in his attack against the Manichees left him open to assault by Pelagius (c.360–c.420), a British monk who was known to quote from Augustine's *On Free Will* in their battles over the issue of salvation. Pelagius' view of free will as neutral led him to the conclusion that man had the ability to achieve perfection and thus, in Augustine's view, win his own salvation. In Pelagius' view, salvation was achieved by the help of the general grace of God, but Pelagius also reasoned that God would not have given moral commands that men were incapable of fulfilling. Divine commands are unconditionally binding upon Christians. According to Pelagius, the commands reflect the ability God has given humanity to obey, so that no defect in human nature bars fulfilling God's requirements. Augustine's response was to attack Pelagius' rejection of original sin, and to uphold a doctrine of grace without which man cannot hope to be right with God. McSorley writes that, essentially, Augustine believed that "fallen man indeed has free will (and can choose even ethically good acts), but that he is not free to do that which is truly good, that is, a good which has value for salvation, unless he is liberated by faith in Christ."[104]

Overall, Augustine wants to affirm both grace and free will. The question is how well he achieves this. McSorley believes he did: "The initiative in man's liberation from sin and his movements toward justification, faith and salvation is always taken by God. His grace prepares the will of man for faith and justification, but never excludes the operation of free will."[105] Whether or not Augustine was able to maintain this balance between grace and free will is a matter of dispute,[106] but he did render a service to Christianity in

---

104 McSorley, *Luther: Right or Wrong?*, 110.
105 Ibid.
106 McSorley gives his interpretation of the debate: "The question debated among Augustine scholars is not: Did the later Augustine deny his earlier teaching on the existence of natural freedom in fallen man? There is simply too much evidence that he did not. The controversy has centered much more around the question: Granted that Augustine had no intention of denying the natural freedom of man's will, does his doctrine of all-powerful, efficacious

combating the Pelagian form of works righteousness. Yet, in his struggle with Pelagianism, one could characterize Augustine's theology as having been too heavily weighted toward the irresistible grace side, allowing only a nod toward free will. Justo Gonzalez makes clear the crucial question, and direction, for Augustine's theology concerning the Pelagians: "If all that we can do is sinful, how are we to take the step that will lead us from our present state to that of the redeemed, especially if one takes into account the fact that such a step cannot be called sin? The answer is inescapable: by ourselves, we cannot take such a step. This was the focal point of Augustine's polemic against the Pelagians, as well as of his doctrine on grace and predestination."[107]

Free will has no role in the theology Gonzalez describes here. Augustine, then, has said two different things concerning free will and seemingly has contradicted himself. This has caused confusion and strife over the free will issue down through the centuries. There appear to be two major possibilities for interpreting Augustine in order to make sense of these apparent contradictions. Simply to force together the two, free will and irresistible grace, is one alternative. Justo L. González's attempt at integrating Augustine's disparate thought simply affirms both ideas without explanation:

> Grace is irresistible. It is inconceivable for the will to reject that grace which is given to it, for grace acts in the will, leading it to will the good.

---

grace and predestination in fact leave any room for natural, psychological or, as some call it, metaphysical freedom of the will? Do Augustine's statements affirming free will have 'only a purely formal significance?'" The view taken in this paper is that the answer to the last question is yes, and that in fact Augustine drifted toward irresistible grace and greatly diminished free will, while never absolutely denying it, in his later writings. McSorley takes the view that Augustine did retain a healthy balance between grace and free will: "Augustine faithfully upholds the dialectic between grace (and predestination) and free will which he finds in Scripture. To surrender either of these realities—the ever-present and supernatural divine action or the free, human activity—would be, in his eyes, heretical. It would be a surrender to either the Pelagians or the Manichaeans." *Luther: Right or Wrong?*, 108–109. McSorley goes on to make the point that Augustine was not trying to systematize any balance here, that this was a concern of later theology.

107 Justo L. González, *A History of Christian Thought*, vol. 1, 46.

This does not mean that Augustine has forgotten or forsaken his defense of free will, for grace does not oppose freedom. Grace does not force us to make a decision against our own will. It is rather that God, through grace, boosts the will, strengthens and stimulates it, so that the will itself, without any coercion, will desire the good. We do not save ourselves, nor are we saved against our will. "Neither the grace of God alone, nor he alone, but the grace of God with him." Grace moves the will, but only through a "soft-violence" that acts in such a way that the will agrees with it.[108]

Perhaps a better solution is offered by Norman Geisler when he differentiates between the early Augustine and the late Augustine. Augustine's earlier works tend to be moderate on the question of free will and grace and predestination. The later harden into a more extreme form of predestinarianism and grace which borders on being fatalistic and dismantling free will. This later Augustine, says Geisler, has triggered the complications and turmoil over these issues:

> As a result of his controversy with the Pelagians (who emphasized free will at the expense of grace), Augustine overreacted with an emphasis on grace at the expense of free will. Likewise, in response to the Donatists, a schismatic group that had broken away from the Catholic Church, he overreacted by affirming that heretics could be coerced to believe *against* their free choice to confess the Catholic faith. The logic seemed irresistible to him: If the Church can coerce heretics to believe against their will, then why can't God force sinners to believe against their will? This, of course, fit with his long-held belief that infants could be regenerated apart from any free choice on their part. Why, then, he reasoned, could not God force adults to be saved against their will? . . . The hardening of Augustine's theological arteries is manifested in several areas. In his early view, the same one held by all the Fathers throughout church history up to Luther, he embraced *unlimited* atonement; later he affirmed limited atonement. In the early period, he held that God

---

108 Justo L. González, *A History of Christian Thought*, vol. 2, *From Augustine to the Eve of the Reformation* (Nashville: Abingdon, 1971), 47.

never coerces a free act; this was discarded in favor of irresistible grace on the unwilling in his later years. This, of course, resulted in a hardened view of predestination where God was active in both the destiny of the elect and the non-elect, and in a denial that there are any conditions for receiving God's gift of unconditional salvation. In fact, for the later Augustine, in contrast to the earlier, mankind is so totally depraved that he has no free choice with regard to spiritual matters. In short, Augustine moved from moderate "Calvinism" to extreme "Calvinism."[109]

Another scholar who takes this approach to Augustine is historian Paul Johnson: "His earliest writings show an insistence on free will which was close to Pelagius's own. Later, as a militant bishop and persecutor, Augustine developed a grim determinism of his own. He took from Paul's epistle to the Romans a theory of grace and election which was not wholly unlike Calvin's."[110] Desiderius Erasmus was also of the opinion that Augustine changed his position on free will. He wrote of this shift in Augustine's thought in a comparison of Augustine and Luther in which he regards Luther, whom Erasmus sees as having made a similar adjustment over time, as the more extreme: "After his battle with Pelagius, Augustine became less just toward free choice than he had been before. Luther, on the other hand, who had previously allowed something to free choice, is now carried so far in the heat of his defense as to destroy it entirely."[111] A further example of this view is Augustine scholar John Burnaby. He writes in the preface to his edition of *Augustine: Later Works*, that at a certain period between A.D. 410 and 420 Augustine became "wholly absorbed by the Pelagian controversy, which forced him to imprison his doctrine of Grace in a system of rigid logic—the 'Augustinianism' whose authority has weighed so heavily and so unhappily upon Christian thought, though it has never been accepted by the *consensus fidelium*."[112]

---

109 Geisler, *Chosen But Free*, 162.

110 Paul Johnson, *A History of Christianity* (New York: Touchstone, 1995), 119.

111 Desiderius Erasmus, *On the Freedom of the Will*, in *Luther and Erasmus: Free Will and Salvation*, ed. E. Gordon Rupp and Philip S. Watson (Philadelphia: Westminster Press, 1969), 90.

112 John Burnaby, ed., *Augustine: Later Works*, Library of Christian

Historical-Theological Context for Free Will

DONATISM

In his dealings with Pelagius, Augustine's theology of grace had crystallized, inasmuch as it began to solidify during the earlier Donatist controversy. He saw Pelagius, as he had the Donatists, as undermining the authority of the institutional Catholic church. His emphasis on overpowering grace, at the expense of free will in man, can be linked to his coercionism in dealing with the Donatists.[113] Those who wanted to follow a voluntaristic approach to the

---

Classics (Philadelphia: Westminster Press, 1955), 13. A New Testament scholar, Bruce Corley, locates the decisive date of the change earlier, at 396: "We owe to the bishop of Hippo a recasting of the grace and free will debate in distinctly new terms.... A radical change of perspective, which we now call 'Augustinian,' can be traced, not to the *Confessions* (ca. AD 400) but to Augustine's *Retractions* on Romans 7 and 9, which were written in 396. No one had ever formulated an interpretation of divine grace and human responsibility like the one Augustine offered in 396—nor until 396, in fact, did Augustine. So, how did it come about? We need look no further than Augustine's account of Paul's conversion, where he develops a retrospective insight to God's power over the human will: 'The only possible conclusion is that it is wills that are elected. But the will itself can have no motive unless something presents itself to delight and stir the mind. That this should happen is not in any man's power. What did Saul will but to attack, seize, bind and slay Christians? What a fierce, savage, blind will was that! Yet he was thrown prostrate by one word from on high, and a vision came to him whereby his mind and will were turned from their fierceness and set on the right way towards faith, so that suddenly out of a marvellous persecutor of the Gospel he was made a still more marvellous preacher of the Gospel.' ... What Augustine found in common with Paul was not a burdened conscience but a vanquished will. Paul's conversion taught him the power of grace and the inability of human striving. The Augustinian theme of 'the violent capture of a rebel will' dominated all subsequent portrayals of Paul's conversion in the medieval period." Bruce Corley, "Interpreting Paul's Conversion—Then and Now," in *The Road from Damascus: The Impact of Paul's Conversion on His Life, Thought, and Ministry*, ed. Richard N. Longenecker (Grand Rapids: Eerdmans, 1997), 6-7.

113 This connection between the Pelagian and Donatist controversies in Augustine's theology may be summarized as follows: "Some scholars see in Augustine's condemnation a realization that Pelagian ideas undercut church

make-up of the church and desired to go their own way were justly forced, in Augustine's mind, to be brought back into sacral unity with the Catholic church, with its state sponsorship via Constantine. In this way the Church, with its institutional sacraments, became the means for salvation, by dispensing the grace of God to its members. Must she not force the sacral medicine on those who went astray for their own good? They must not be left to go their own way. A catholic Christian society could not countenance them.

Early on, Augustine believed sin originated with free will, which is created good. Free will implies the ability to do evil. It is a voluntary, noncompulsory, self-determined act. Augustine appears to have later contradicted this view when he concluded that the Donatists, who wanted to remain independent from a monolithic Constantinian Christianity, should be forced to believe against their will. As Dean Inge bluntly stated:

> Augustine was in favour of liberty of conscience while the Donatists held ascendancy in Africa, but when the Catholics got the upper hand, he frankly changed his mind.... Henceforward his view was precisely that surmmarised [sic] by Macaulay in his Essay on Mackintosh. "I am in the right, you are in the wrong. When you are the stronger, you ought to tolerate me, for it is your duty to tolerate truth; but when I am the stronger, I shall persecute you, for it is my duty to persecute error." This has always and everywhere been the attitude of the Roman Catholic Church, which has never listened to Cromwell's quaint remonstrance, "In the bowels of Christ think it possible that you may be mistaken."[114]

---

authority; the bishop's attack on Pelagius paralleled his earlier condemnation of the Donatists, another group that challenged the orthodox establishment. In Augustine's view, humanity could be saved only through an alliance between a unified, hierarchical church and the imperial government. Only through church-directed government, he believed, could peace and order be imposed on a sinful humanity—even on baptized Christians. His pessimistic views on humanity and nature triumphed over Pelagian freedom and moral choice and continued to dominate Christianity for centuries afterwards." Chas S. Clifton, *Encyclopedia of Heresies and Heretics* (New York: Barnes & Noble, 1998), 111.

114 William Ralph Inge, *Christian Ethics and Modern Problems* (New York: G. P. Putnam's Sons, 1930), 180.

Another scholar takes up the same line of thought concerning the connection between Augustine's dealings with the Donatists and the shift of his view of free will:

> He insisted that the use of force in the pursuit of Christian unity, and indeed total religious conformity, was necessary, efficacious, and wholly justified. He admitted he had changed his mind on this point. He wrote to a Donatist friend that he had seen his own town, originally Donatist, "brought over to the Catholic unity by fear of the imperial edicts." That had convinced him. In fact heretics in their hearts welcomed persecution: they would say "fear made us become earnest to examine the truth . . . the stimulus of fear startled us from our negligence." And then, this was Christ's own way. Had not he, "by great violence," "coerced" Paul into Christianity? Was not this the meaning of the text from Luke, 14:23: "Compel them to come in?" It was Augustine who first drew attention to this, and a number of other convenient texts, to be paraded through the centuries by the Christian apologists of force.[115]

In examining Augustine's application of the Apostle Paul's conversion on the Damascus road to justify force, Leonard Verduin writes, "The length to which Augustine went in his effort to find New Testament warrant for coercionism is almost unbelievable."[116]

Verduin understands the coercive tendency of the Catholic Church in the Reformation (and also of Luther and Calvin), to the great detriment of the "heretic" Anabaptists, as being derived from Augustine and his championing of coercion against the Donatists. Verduin sees in the very word "heretic," with which the Anabaptists were branded by nearly all in power during the Reformation, a connection to free choice: "The word 'heretic' is derived from the Greek verb *hairein* which means 'to exercise option in the presence of alternatives.' Those who saw the Christian life to be a matter of choice between alternatives were for that reason called 'heretics,' by those who thought

---

115 Johnson, *A History of Christianity*, 116.
116 Verduin, *The Reformers and Their Stepchildren*, 68.

in terms of a 'choiceless Christianity.' For this reason the word 'heretics' was used interchangeably with 'schismatics.'"[117] It is no coincidence that Balthasar Hubmaier, the so called "arch-heretic" and champion of free will, was one of the first to write an impassioned, thoughtful plea for religious tolerance in one of his most well-known works, *On Heretics and Those Who Burn Them*.

Coercionism and double predestination intersect with Augustine's promotion of infant baptism, which was also taken up by Luther, Calvin, and Zwingli. This was the chief signifying distinction in the Reformation for the Anabaptists, who struggled, even to the death, for their doctrine of *believer's* baptism. For the Anabaptists, faith must precede baptism because only then can it function, as intended, as an outward sign of an inward change wrought by faith in Christ. Jaroslav Pelikan elaborates on the Anabaptist view:

> "Inward baptism" by the Holy Spirit was to precede "outward baptism" with water. The parallel between circumcision and baptism, which was being used to support infant baptism, did not refer to "outward baptism" at all, but to "inward baptism." Because man was "by nature unclean in body and soul," outward baptism by itself was useless. Thus the age-old mutual dependence between the doctrine of original sin and the practice of infant baptism was broken: Hubmaier attacked Zwingli for underestimating the power of original sin [Zwingli's supporters had used the idea that infants are innocent and "unspotted" (don't have their "own" sin) to argue for pedobaptism; see Pipkin and Yoder, 284–285] and attacked Luther for underestimating the power of free will; but he attacked both of them, and the entire tradition with them, for teaching that a baptism administered involuntarily to infants was a cure for original sin. The biblical terminology about baptism "for remission of sins," which had, in conjunction with the practice of infant baptism, helped to establish original sin as a doctrine, did not mean that, in Luther's words, "baptism effects forgiveness of sins," but that baptism bore testimony to "the inward yes in the heart," which did effect it.[118]

---

117 Verduin, *The Reformers and Their Stepchildren*, 72.

118 Insertion added. Jaroslav Pelikan, *The Christian Tradition: A History of the Development of Doctrine*, vol. 4, *Reformation of Church and Dogma*

Evidently, Augustine's defense of infant baptism and his concept of the church as identified with society and with salvation spurred his turn to coercionism and ultimately his determinism. Historian Williston Walker analyzes these connections in Augustine:

> The effect of . . . saving grace is twofold. Faith is instilled, and sins, both original and personal, are forgiven at baptism. . . . As such it is immediate justification. But grace does much more. . . . It is a gradual transformation of nature, a sanctification. Through us, God does good works, which He rewards as if they were men's own and to which he ascribes merit. No man can be sure of his salvation in this life. He may have grace now, but, unless God adds the gift of perseverance, he will not maintain it to the end. It would seem that Augustine may have been led to this conclusion largely by the doctrine of baptismal regeneration. It is evident that if men receive grace at baptism, many do not keep it. This doctrine of grace was coupled in Augustine with a high valuation of the visible Catholic Church.[119]

Augustine's commitment to the idea of 'Christendom' likely prejudiced his theology against voluntaristic notions. The Donatists, on the other hand, appealed to Scripture in the face of the threat of force. Leonard Verduin writes, "The Donatists pointed out that this [coercion] would be to deviate from the policies of the Master, who had not raised a finger, much less a sword, to restrain people from going away. More than that, when a sizable group walked out He had confronted His disciples with the wistful question, 'Do you not also want to go?'"[120] This passage in John's gospel was also quoted by Hubmaier as an example of the concept of free will in Scripture: "Christ says to his disciples, 'Do you also want to go away?' It follows that going away or remaining with him must be in the power of the disciples."[121]

(1300–1700) (Chicago: University of Chicago Press, 1984), 317–318.
    119 Williston Walker, *A History of the Christian Church* (New York: Scribners, 1959), 165–166.
    120 Insertion added. Verduin, *The Reformers and Their Stepchildren*, 65.
    121 Hubmaier, *Freedom of the Will, II*, Pipkin and Yoder, 464.

But Augustine's answer to the Donatists' use of this Scripture betrays his conviction that the church was destined to be allied with the state. He wrote in a letter to a Donatist:

> I hear that you often quote and draw attention to the fact recorded in the Gospels that seventy disciples withdrew from the Lord and were left to their own choice in this wicked and undutiful desertion, and that to the other twelve who remained it was said, "Will ye also go away?" But you neglect to draw attention to the fact that then the Church was just beginning to sprout with the new shoots and that as yet that prophecy had not received fulfilment in her: "All kings shall fall down before him, yea, all nations shall serve him;" it is in proportion to the more complete fulfilment of that prophecy that the Church enjoys greater authority, so that she not only invites, but actually compels men to goodness.[122]

Augustine's use of the power of the state's authority to "compel" all to unify with the Catholic Church was based on what he perceived as the fulfillment of world domination by Christianity in the conversion of Constantine.[123]

Those, like the Donatists, who claimed liberty in the matters of faith, were only pressured even more. To Augustine, their claim for freedom represented a schism, an evil that must be forcefully eradicated. In the same letter Augustine told Donatus:

> You say that God has given man free-will and that therefore no one should be forced even to good. . . . Mark well then a point you refuse to take into consideration: the reason why a good will expends itself in

---

122 Augustine, *Selected Letters*, trans. James Houston Baxter, rev. ed., Loeb Classical Library (Cambridge: Harvard University Press, 1953; reprint 1993), 299–301.

123 Verduin writes, "The Constantinian change . . . caused the technique of coercion to be imported into the affairs of the Church. Because of it the cause of Christ lost the dimension of voluntaryism, which is native to true Christianity, and with it the cause of Christ picked up the dimension of coercionism, which is foreign to the true faith." *The Reformers and Their Stepchildren*, 63.

works of mercy is to provide guidance for man's evil will. For who does not know that man is not damned unless for his evil will, nor, on the other hand, granted deliverance, unless he has a good will? Still it does not follow that those we love are to be cruelly left to enjoy their evil will without correction, but where the power is granted, they are to be both prevented from evil and forced to good.[124]

Verduin gives another example of this appeal to coercionism in an assessment of a bit of Augustinian exegesis:

> Augustine managed to overpower still another Scripture passage that he could turn to suit his purpose, great allegorizer that he was. He found it in the family situation of Abraham, where there were two wives; one a free-woman and the other a bond-servant. The former lived her life in the climate of voluntaryism and the latter lived hers in that of coercionism. In this way Augustine justified the presence of two kinds of Christians in the Church, one there by choice and the other by coercion. Moreover, the allegory also justified it that the former afflicted the latter—had not Sarah pommelled Hagar? This bit of sophism also became a part of the panoply of the medieval exponent of "Christian sacralism." It was repeated in Reformation times.[125]

It is not surprising then to find that one of the appellations the Reformers affixed upon the Anabaptists was "Donatist."[126] Constantinianism was the plague of the Anabaptists during the Reformation. The Anabaptists were a threat, just as the Donatists had been, to the ideal of a monolithic Christian society. As one writer points out, "The Anabaptists . . . did not announce

---

124 Augustine, *Selected Letters*, 285–287. Letter written in 416 to Donatus, a priest in the movement, contemporary of Augustine, not the original namesake of the movement who died in 355.

125 Verduin, *The Reformers and Their Stepchildren*, 68.

126 Verduin writes, "One of the terms of reproach used by the Reformers as an incriminating label of the Second Front was 'Donatists'; the form 'neo-Donatist' also occurs in the sources. This reproachful name was used very freely and frequently." *The Reformers and Their Stepchildren*, 21.

a program for changing the social order, but their doctrine of a believers' church, their simple egalitarianism as well as their missionary zeal so threatened both church and state in central Europe that persecution and martyrdom swiftly descended upon them."[127]

LUTHER AND CALVIN

The brand of authoritarianism modeled by Augustine suggests a blinkered elitism, bequeathed as the proper way of thinking about society to the sixteenth century via the Middle Ages. For society to function properly, the masses must be kept in their place of subordination.[128] To grant free will as

---

127 *Concise Dictionary of Christianity in America* (Downers Grove: InterVarsity Press, 1995), 20. The matter of troubling the structures of society was a serious problem to the Magisterial Reformers, who charged the Anabaptists again and again with being schismatics. Henry Vedder describes an episode between Hubmaier and Zwingli which illustrates this tendency. Hubmaier had written *The Christian Baptism of Believers*, which was aimed, to a great extent, at Zwingli's teachings. Zwingli's reply was "entitled *A True, Thorough Reply to Dr. Balthasar's Little Book on Baptism* . . . . It contains little that is new, reiterating the arguments of his former treatise, with occasional attempts to meet the objections of his adversary. . . . *He presses again the objection that the Anabaptists are schismatics, and that their course will result in the division of the Church and the destruction of the standing order.*" Emphasis added. Vedder, *Balthasar Hübmaier: The Leader of the Anabaptists* (New York: Putnam, 1905; reprint, New York: AMS Press, 1971), 118.

128 C. S. Lewis explains the medieval perspective regarding 'Christian society' still dominant in the time of Reform: "No man claimed for himself or allowed to another the right of believing as he chose. All parties inherited from the Middle Ages the assumption that Christian man could live only in a theocratic polity which had both the right and the duty of enforcing true religion by persecution. Those who resisted its authority did so not because they thought it had no right to impose doctrines but because they thought it was imposing the wrong ones. . . . When Calvin led the attack on Servetus which ended in his being burnt at Geneva, he was acting on accepted medieval principles. A man's beliefs, like his actions were to be ruled by his Betters. . . . . And all Betters, whether secular or spiritual, had an authority of divine ori-

essential to humanity was to open the doors of society to freedom of conscience. Double predestination does not readily allow for that kind of view of human beings. Everyone is either a sheep or a goat, in addition the sheep are only chosen by the mystery of God's grace and are wholly undeserving, being stripped of any innate good. This theology of a nearly, if not completely, effaced *imago dei* led to a particularly negative view of humanity. Despite the personal warning inherent in this low view of human nature, a supreme confidence in their own movement's authority led the great Reformers, Luther and Calvin, to persecute and to recommend death for those who disagreed with their theology.[129]

---

gin: disobedience was sin as well as crime. What we should now call 'Church' and 'State' were (by our standards) deeply confused. . . . The common man might have—I think he had—a conscience and a religion; a conscience much burdened by his own unchastity, profanity, or deficiency in alms-giving, and a religion deeply concerned with the state and the possibility of making a good end when his time came. But the great controversies were too hard for him. And he was not directly faced either with pope or king; squire and parson, parents and neighbours, an itinerant preacher on one or the other side, were the immediate factors in his problem. We may well believe that such a man, though baptized in the Old Religion and dying in the New, did not feel that he had, in any clear sense, either committed apostasy or undergone conversion. He had only tried to do what he was told in a world where doing what he was told had been, according to all his Betters, the thing mainly demanded of him." C. S. Lewis, *English Literature in the Sixteenth Century*, New York: Oxford University Press, 1954.

129 Paul Johnson writes of the Reformers: "They were motivated by the . . . Augustinian concept of creating the city of God on earth. By the mid sixteenth century . . . there were three varieties of state religion in the West: papal Catholicism, state Christianity (Lutheranism), and Calvinist theocracy. Each, at any rate in theory, was universalist in its aims: it foresaw a future, and to some extent worked for it, when its doctrines and institutions would be imposed on the whole of Christendom. Each was organically linked to the state where it existed. Each was a compulsory religion, claiming a monopoly of the Christian ministry where it held power. Luther, as a heresiarch, had begun by pleading for tolerance, for (this was a new expression) 'freedom of conscience.' He did not want to 'triumph by fire but by writings.' Among his propositions condemned by Rome was: 'To burn heretics is against the will of the spirit.' The secular pow-

THE CENTRALITY OF THE DOCTRINE OF HUMAN FREE WILL IN THE THEOLOGY OF BALTHASAR HUBMAIER

Since one could never know for sure about each man's salvation, this view called for an iron hand to control the depraved masses of humanity, whether truly Christian or otherwise. Who would do this controlling except the leaders of the church in concert with the leaders of the city or state? It was their great burden and responsibility. This was in fact the actual state of affairs with Augustine, as well as Luther, Calvin, Zwingli, and in other Reformation cities. While Luther may have been somewhat less authoritarian than Calvin was in Geneva, the peasants' war, when he advocated the killing of the uprisers, was a black mark on his record as a Christian reformer. A. G. Dickens laments, "Luther's detestable advice to the princes that they should mercilessly slay the peasant rebels reflected the terror of 'responsible' leaders in the face of impending anarchy. However intelligible the fears of a religious leader who saw the impending ruin of his work, his historical reputation would have been better served had he silently left this bloody task to the princes, who could be trusted to discharge it with a full measure of harshness."[130]

---

er should 'busy itself with its own affairs, and let each one believe this or that as he can and as he chooses, and not use any force with anyone on this account.' He even, at first, urged the princes to be tolerant towards millenarians, anabaptists and others of the Munster type, 'because it is necessary that there be sects and the word of God must enter the lists and wage battle.' This early moderation did not survive Luther's increasing dependence on the princes. Once his teaching became established as a state religion, all other forms of Christianity had to be eliminated, at least in their open expression.... By 1527 he had passed to positive, rather than defensive intervention to ensure uniformity by organizing state ecclesiastical visitations, and in 1529 he went further still to deny 'freedom of conscience:' 'Even if people do not believe, they should be driven to the sermon, because of the ten commandments, in order to learn at least the outward works of obedience.' Two years later he agreed that anabaptists and other Protestant extremists 'should be done to death by the civil authority.' Calvin, by contrast, had never asserted that consciences should be free. How could the perfected society of the elect tolerate among it those who challenged its rules? The obvious answer to critics was to expel them from the city, following excommunication. If they attempted to remonstrate they were executed." *A History of Christianity*, 288–289.

130 A. G. Dickens, *Reformation and Society in Sixteenth-Century Europe* (London: Harcourt, Brace & World, 1966; reprint 1968), 80–81.

It is difficult to review these authoritarian realities in the Magisterial Reformation without recalling how much Luther and Calvin were opposed to any doctrine of free will in man. The theology that promoted God's irresistible grace at the expense of free choice, making faith a passive matter, dovetailed beautifully with the Augustinian doctrine of double predestination and with the maintenance of a highly sacral Christianity in which infant baptism and citizenship and Christianity were all blended to form a new Christendom. Thus, Luther and Calvin came to speak of individual faith in oxymoronic terms, since all the while the real destiny of men lay in the eternal decrees of predestination. Luther was so intent upon basing justification solely on the work of God that he spoke of faith primarily as a 'gift' while at the same time being convinced of the necessity to trust in God's work for his salvation rather than his own works. This trust, of course, is a choice of the human heart. Luther, however, associated free will not so much with choice as with human works. But in ridding his theology of free will, he seemed to leave no place for authentic human decision.

Assurance of Faith in Luther and Calvin

According to Randall Zachman, one of the points of similarity between Martin Luther (1483-1546) and John Calvin (1509-1564) is in their respective doctrines of assurance and the associated role of the conscience. Zachman's thesis is that both Luther and Calvin founded Christian assurance upon God's grace in Christ. But both also insisted on a good conscience as confirmation of true faith. Zachman asserts that the confirmation of faith by the good conscience leads to an inherent instability in the theologies of Calvin and Luther because of the potential for overemphasizing the good conscience as a proof of the Christian's faith in God's grace in Christ. He points to Theodore Beza (1519-1605) as an example of this theological instability: "The possibility is left open that the foundation and confirmation of faith might be reversed, as in fact happened in Beza and Westminster (that is, since the grace of Christ only benefits the elect, then one must first assure oneself of one's election through the testimony of a good conscience before one can confidently believe in Christ)."[131] Ironically, this is the very thing Luther and Calvin were trying to avoid: a bolstering of the conscience based on religious works as a confirmation of salvation, as in the old Roman Catholic system.

Zachman discusses several different issues that bear upon the role of the conscience and the assurance of faith. These can be shown in the basic difference in the theologies of Calvin and Luther. Luther held to a basic theological principle he called the *theologia crucis*, theology of the cross, which he contrasted with the *theologia gloriae*, theology of glory, of the Roman Church. The theology of the cross finds the truth hidden in the appearance of contradiction. Thus externals are of no consequence. In particular, this led Luther to subsume sanctification under justification in his theology, and to claim that images in the church are merely externals which should be left to crumble from the weight of their own insignificance.

Calvin on the other hand emphasized a trinitarian doctrine in which the twofold grace of God the Father (the Creator) in justification and sanctification are given in Jesus Christ (the Redeemer) through the Holy Spirit. Because Christ alone is the image of the invisible God, all images are to be done away with as idolatry. Sanctification is the goal of adoption and thus becomes externally significant as progressive evidence of faith. Luther grounded assurance in Christ's work of justification and the forgiveness of sins while Calvin grounded assurance in Christ Himself as the fountain of all good from the Father. While both agreed that the Law testifies to the conscience of the sinfulness of man, Calvin relied more on the Holy Spirit to make man aware while Luther emphasized the terrifying nature of the Law itself which drives the conscience toward Christ and God's mercy. This allows for Luther's emphasis on the abrogation of the law while Calvin sees greater unity between law and gospel.

In the theologies of both Luther and Calvin, Zachman finds a tension between a universal reconciliation in Christ and an individual reconciliation in election which he views as the source of the instability inherent in the mix-

---

[131] Randall C. Zachman, *The Assurance of Faith: Conscience in the Theology of Martin Luther and John Calvin* (Minneapolis: Fortress Press, 1993), 246.

up between assurance based on God's grace and an insistence on proof of a good conscience:

> In light of universal reconciliation in Christ, the assurance of faith is grounded in the fact that God is gracious to sinners in Jesus Christ alone; and the terrified conscience before the judgement seat of God makes it necessary to seek assurance of the mercy of God not in ourselves but in the testimony of Christ to us in the gospel. In light of individual reconciliation by faith in Christ, the assurance of faith is qualified by the fact that God is gracious only toward those sinners who sincerely believe in Christ, making it necessary for believers to find confirmation of their assurance within themselves; and the testimony of a good conscience before the judgment seat of God confirms that we are the godly to whom God has promised to be merciful in Christ.[132]

Zachman sees a solution to this instability in Calvin's concept that Christ is the image of the Father, but he does not develop the idea. He writes, "Calvin does point to a promising resolution of this problem in his understanding of Christ as the image of the Father, in whom the Father has laid up all of the good things to be offered to sinners in the wonderful exchange. However, the one good thing the Father does not set forth in the wonderful exchange in Christ is election."[133]

This exclusion of the source of election as 'in Christ' is highlighted in Zachman's appeal to Karl Barth's critique of Calvin in which he finds Calvin's anthropological conclusion (individual election) and his Christological starting place (universal reconciliation) to be discordant.[134] Is Zachman hinting that we should eject the notion of an individual reconciliation and place election in Christ as the Elect One so that we conclude simply that reconciliation is universal based on the wonderful exchange between Christ and humanity in which he took our impotence and sin and gave us righteousness and eternal life? While this is not at all clear, his dependence on Barth (who asserted that

---

132 Zachman, *The Assurance of Faith*, 246.
133 Ibid.
134 Ibid., 7.

man simply needs to be told he is saved) and his suggestion that the solution is Christ, as the image of the Father, so that election is also part of the grace from the Father in Christ for sinners, seems to imply a definite direction for Zachman's own thinking. This direction, while not explicitly expressed, could veer toward universalism.

If one locates election *in Christ,* and not apart from Christ as in decrees (a division that does appear to be a flaw in Calvin's theology), it may not necessarily infer universalism if a genuine choice of faith is allowed. But individual assurance of salvation and the role of a good conscience must necessarily be founded on God's grace alone, appropriated through faith. Since the nature of faith is to fasten on the object of faith, the question of assurance of faith can only send the individual back to Christ. The good conscience in sanctification, then, is a confirmation of Christ's work in the life of the believer, but it does not bear the weight of salvation itself or its assurance, it is the *product* of salvation. Thus, even sanctification is by faith. It is not a matter of proof, but of evidence, of faith, which is grounded in the reality of the power and gifts of Christ in the life of the believer.

Hubmaier regarded assurance as being grounded in Christ, through faith in Him. He writes of this in his treatise, *On the Christian Baptism of Believers*: "Water baptism does not wash away our sin, nor does it save us, but only the certain knowledge of a good conscience toward God *through the resurrection of Christ Jesus.* This knowledge is nothing but . . . faith, in which we are sure and certain that we have a gracious and favorable Father in heaven."[135] The intercessory work of the resurrected Christ becomes a source of security to the believer based on trust in the eternal mediation of Christ before the Father. Hubmaier describes this intercession: "He pleads for you before God his Father with faithful intercession, that he may abstain from his anger, and also be gracious and favorable to you through the grace and favor which he has toward Christ. Here then the Father neither wants nor can deny

---

[135] Emphasis added. Hubmaier, *On the Christian Baptism of Believers*, Pipkin and Yoder, 134. Note the good conscience here comes through the victory of the resurrection of Christ on our behalf not through spiritual or religious works which somehow 'prove' election.

anything to his most beloved Son but he grants him his request and thus forgives you your sin through Jesus Christ, our Lord."[136]

Hubmaier wrote movingly of faith in Christ and His finished work, as if Jesus, pictured here in terms of the parable of the good Samaritan, were appealing to us in his own words:

> "Believe the gospel. It truly shows you that I have laid you on the beast of my humanity, that I have suffered death and martyrdom for you, and that through my sufferings I have registered you in the inn of the Christian church. I have commended you to the servant of the house, that is, to those who preach to you my gospel and proclaim to you the *certain forgiveness of your sins*, namely, that I am your physician who has come into this world to make the sinner just and righteous, that I am also your reconciler, intercessor, mediator, and peacemaker unto God, my Father, so that whoever believes in me will not be damned but have eternal life." Through such words of comfort the sinner is enlivened again, comes to himself, becomes joyful and henceforth surrenders himself entirely to this physician Christ.[137]

This image of submitting to the Great Physician is a powerful one not only for the initial trust the Christian places in Christ but for an ongoing surrender to Him in sanctification as the essence of the Christian life. Thus, we see the foundation here of the Anabaptist emphasis on being a *Nachfolger*, a disciple, as elemental to Christianity.

Hence, it is at the point of assurance that the breakdown of Lutheran and Calvinistic theologies can best be seen. If the prerequisite for Salvation is *not* the Christian's own choice in belief, as we find with the denial of free will in matters of soteriology for Luther and Calvin, then he is either a sheep or a goat on condition of the inscrutable decree of election or reprobation. But if free will is in place, Christian works of sanctification, as an outflow of a salvation already received, have no salvific merit but are the trusting acts of obedience, love, and surrender in discipleship. This theological interpretation of the Christian life

---

136 Hubmaier, *On the Christian Baptism of Believers*, Pipkin and Yoder, 145.
137 Emphasis added. Ibid., 144.

appears to be in accord with Scripture and with the *imago dei*. On the other hand, the temptation, for the Lutheran or Calvinist, is to see Christian works as proof of election. But this can easily be turned on its head, making the Christian life a pursuit of works which secure assurance of salvation.

This emphasis on works for the Christian is not what Luther and Calvin intended, but it is what they get as the resultant psychology of emphasizing double predestination. Thus, the Reformed and Lutheran theological exclusion of free will would appear to cause a collapse at the point of assurance. For the Christian who sees his salvation as completely accomplished in Christ, accepted through a decision of trusting belief, the question of assurance of salvation is directed again and again back to the object, the promises and Person on which faith is fixed. The *quality* of belief is not the foundation of salvation, but the quality of the *object* of belief, who is faithful and has offered salvation to "whosoever" will trust in Him. Consequently, Christ Himself is the center of assurance just as he is of salvation. This is what Calvin and Luther desire, but what they unintentionally forfeit when they eject free will in favor of double predestination.

LUTHER AND ERASMUS

In his own time, Desiderius Erasmus (c. 1469–1536) was deemed, along with Luther, to be a shining star in the struggle against the darkening status quo of medieval Catholicism. He was even considered by some to be Lutheran, or to have functioned as a sort of mentor to Luther. Erasmus, being primarily a humanist academic and not a theologian, sought to achieve change by mocking the abuses and silliness of the Roman Church and by producing scholarly work, such as his translation of the Greek New Testament. He sought the role of mediator more than that of reformer and was never comfortable being called Lutheran. In *On Free Will*, he declared, "I have never accepted the doctrines of Luther."[138] John Olin writes, "Differences of scriptural interpretation . . . separated Erasmus and Luther from

---

138 Erasmus, *On Free Will*, in *The Portable Renaissance Reader*, ed. James Ross and Mary McLaughlin (New York: Penguin Books, 1981), 678

the beginning, though superficially at first it appeared that Luther was engaging in the same reform efforts as Erasmus and was contending with the same opposition."[139]

The great rift between Erasmus and Luther came over the issue of free will after Erasmus challenged Luther, composing his treatise, *On Free Will*. This was an issue about which Erasmus truly differed with Luther. Luther's response, in *The Bondage of the Will*, was acerbic and personally critical, and the whole episode drove Erasmus further away from the Protestant camp. Luther saw Erasmus' view as lacking a real understanding of the need for man to be saved by the power of God alone. Man had no capacity to save himself and could not even turn toward God. This must be done by God since man only has the capacity to be turned in the right direction, not to do the turning. For Luther, God must turn man's will to Himself, to unity with God, if he is to be saved.

Roland Bainton examines Luther's differences with Erasmus:

> Luther's fundamental break with the Catholic Church was over the nature and destiny of man, and much more over the destiny than the nature.... Erasmus was interested primarily in morals, whereas Luther's question was whether doing right, even if it is possible, can affect man's fate. Erasmus succeeded in diverting Luther from the course by asking whether the ethical precepts of the Gospels have any point if they cannot be fulfilled. Luther countered with characteristic controversial recklessness that man is like a donkey ridden now by God and now by the Devil, a statement which certainly seems to imply that man has no freedom whatever to decide for good or ill. This certainly was not Luther's habitual thought.... Man is capable of the integrity and valor displayed by the Romans of old or the Turks of today.... But in the eyes of God "there is none righteous, no, not one." Motives are never pure. The noblest acts are vitiated by arrogance, self-love, the desire of the eye and the lust of power. From the religious point of view man is a sinner.

---

139 John C. Olin, ed., *Christian Humanism and the Reformation: Selected Writings of Erasmus*, 3d ed. (New York: Fordham University Press, 1987), 25.

He has therefore no claim upon God. If man is not irretrievably lost it can only be because God designs to favor him beyond his desert.[140]

Erasmus countered with a key question: "Is it not unjust that God should create man incapable of fulfilling the conditions for salvation and then at whim save or damn for what cannot be helped?"[141] Luther simply replied that natural reason, although offended, "must admit the consequences of the omniscience and omnipotence of God."[142]

Erasmus detected the difficulty for human reason in the paradox between the power and goodness of God. He preferred to limit the power of God in allowing free will to man, rather than diminish the goodness and holiness of God. Luther, in effect, did the opposite. Within his deterministic theology, he viewed the great injustice attributed to God "when he damns those who do not deserve it,"[143] as an unfathomable mystery of His justice. And Luther's idea that man was only an instrument in the great struggle between God and the Devil conveyed the impression that man is a mere automaton.[144] It also seemed to depict God as arbitrarily unjust and cruel. Erasmus explains his position affirming free will in these words: "In order to have something to impute justly to the wicked who have voluntarily come short of the grace of God, in order that the calumny of cruelty and injustice may be excluded from God, that despair may be kept away from us, that complacency may be excluded also, and that we may be incited to endeavor. For these reasons, almost everyone admits free choice, but as inefficacious apart from the perpetual grace of God, lest we arrogate aught to ourselves."[145]

According to Bainton, "Erasmus agreed that man cannot be perfect. He agreed that salvation is by faith alone. At the same time he wished to do

---

140 Roland Bainton, *Here I Stand: A Life of Martin Luther* (Nashville: Abingdon, 1978), 196.

141 Bainton, *Here I Stand,* 196.

142 Luther, *The Bondage of the Will,* quoted in Bainton, *Here I Stand: A Life of Martin Luther,* 197.

143 Ibid.

144 See Roland Bainton, *Erasmus of Christendom* (New York: Crossroad, 1969), 187.

145 Erasmus, *On the Freedom of the Will,* Rupp and Watson, 96.

justice to the passages in Scripture which offer rewards for good deeds."[146] Erasmus believed in a synergism between human free will and divine grace, with grace being primary. He wrote:

> Two causes work together in the same individual act: namely, the grace of God and the will of man. Grace is the principal cause, and the will is the secondary cause, which can do nothing without the principal cause, while this cause suffices in itself alone. Thus fire burns by its natural virtue, although the principal cause of the burning of the fire is God, who acts through the fire and who would be sufficient alone, whereas the fire could do nothing without this cause, if it were withdrawn. By reason of this working together man owes all his salvation to the reception of divine grace, since the share which pertains directly to the free will is so small, and it even derives finally from the grace of God, who in the beginning created the free will, and then delivered it, and restored it to health. Thus those men would be reassured—if they can be reassured—for whom man can have no good which he does not owe to God. . . . On the other hand, those who deny absolutely the existence of free will, and claim that everything is done by pure necessity, assert that God produces in all men not only good works but also bad. It follows, then, that if man has no claim to be considered the author of his good works, he also cannot be regarded as the author of his bad works. This conclusion . . .seems manifestly to attribute injustice and cruelty to God.[147]

Both men made plausible arguments. Yet, Erasmus did, at times, give the impression that he was concerned merely about morals and not as much about salvation. Also, Luther did not give any answer to the charge that his ideas ended in making God responsible for sin and evil, except to repeat the axiom that He is sovereign. Luther proclaims, "This, therefore, is also essentially necessary and wholesome for Christians to know: that God foreknows and does all things according to His immutable, eternal, and infallible will. By

---

146 Erasmus, *On the Freedom of the Will*, 188.
147 Erasmus, *On Free Will*, in *The Portable Renaissance Reader*, 686–687.

this thunderbolt free will is thrown prostrate and utterly dashed to pieces."[148] Ernst Winter summarizes the impasse between the two thinkers:

> The two protagonists become symbolic for two camps, unable to meet.... Luther says that man is unable to do anything but continue to sin, except for God's grace. The whole work of man's salvation, first to last, is God's. Both proceed from different vantage points. Erasmus dismisses both the excessive confidence in man's moral strength, held by the Pelagians, and what he believed to be St. Augustine's view, the excessive hopelessness of a final condemnation passed on man. He identified Luther with the latter. Erasmus calls Scripture to help in outlining his reasonable and conciliatory middle way, really a philosophical and pragmatic statement of man's essential freedom. Luther interprets this to mean assigning free will to divine things, because his interest lies in practical implementation of a classical Christian paradox, which he thought solved. His solution is "faith alone sets us free."[149]

The problem with Luther's answer may be that his emphasis on God's grace not only "prostrates" free will but also distorts the essence of faith to some degree. If faith is only God turning the will toward God's grace, seeing it solely as part of the gift of elective grace, what room is there for an active trust and obedience, a purposeful surrender to God's grace, so to speak, in Luther's theology? Where is the receipt of the gift of grace in Christ on the part of the person? The very notion of a gift excludes the idea of something being forced on another person. On the other hand, Hubmaier describes the individual faith of the Christian in this way: "Accordingly, when he recognizes this grace and kindness [of remittance of sin through Christ], he surrenders himself to God and commits himself internally in his heart to live a new life according to

---

148 Luther, *The Bondage of the Will*, in *The Portable Renaissance Reader*, 697.

149 Ernst F. Winter, ed., *Erasmus-Luther: Discourse on Free Will* (New York: Continuum Publishing, 1989), x.

the Rule of Christ."[150] This relational and personal language corresponds with the tenor and plainness of the Bible.

THE ANABAPTISTS AND FREE WILL

As has been mentioned, among the Magisterial Reformers there was a strong aversion to the doctrine of human free will because of a dread of any hint of justification based on works, as in the Roman Catholic system. As Hendrikus Berkhof writes, "The freedom of the will as inherently a datum of creation leads Roman Catholic theology to attribute a cooperative factor to the actualized will in the work of redemption. Conversely, Reformation theology was and is inclined, for fear of the latter, to minimize freedom as a created structure."[151] Although Luther and Calvin both recognized free will as an element in human creation they believed that the Fall so corrupted man's whole being that he essentially has no choice but to sin.

This view of man appears to place fallen human beings in a situation in which they essentially do not have any genuine ability to choose, and thus cannot be responsible or accountable. This theology may effectively obscure the constant biblical injunctions for man to choose God and not evil. Anthony Hoekema writes:

> The understanding that human beings have this capacity for choice, and that they retain this capacity even after the Fall, is . . . an essential emphasis in the Christian doctrine of man. The Bible always addresses humans as persons who can make decisions and who are responsible for the decisions they make. God does not deal with the human being as if he or she were a "stick" or a "stone;" he deals with man as with a

---

150 Insertion added. Hubmaier, *On the Christian Baptism of Believers*, Pipkin and Yoder, 117.

151 Hendrikus Berkhof, *Christian Faith* (Grand Rapids: Eerdmans, 1979), 185.

person who must respond to him, and who is held accountable for the nature of her or his response.[152]

Hoekema observes that Luther and Calvin would rather not even have used the term "free will."[153] To them it was identified with the Catholic theology of works salvation.

However, from among the Anabaptists, who generally considered the doctrine of free will essential,[154] Hubmaier steps forth to vigorously defend the liberty of the human will, even to the point of challenging the redoubt-

---

[152] Anthony Hoekema, *Created in God's Image*, 228–229.

[153] "Both Luther and Calvin also preferred not even to use expressions like 'free will' or 'the freedom of the will' as descriptions of the state of fallen human beings today. Luther put it this way: 'I wish that the word "free will" had never been invented. It is not in the Scriptures, and it were better to call it "self-will," which profiteth not. Free-will is plainly a divine term, and can be applicable to none but the divine Majesty only: for He alone "doth, (as the Psalm sings) what He will in Heaven and earth." (Ps. cxxxv. 6.).... Wherefore, it becomes Theologians to refrain from the use of this term altogether, whenever they wish to speak of human ability, and leave it to be applied to God only.' Calvin expressed a similar sentiment: 'Then [according to Peter Lombard] man will be said to possess free will in this sense, not that he has an equally free election of good and evil, but because he does evil voluntarily, and not by constraint. That, indeed, is very true; but what end could it answer to decorate a thing so diminutive with a title so superb?'" Hoekema, *Created in God's Image*, 233–234. Leonard Verduin in, *Somewhat less than God: The Biblical View of Man* (Grand Rapids: Eerdmans, 1970), 91, also comments on this: "Well-intentioned theologians have shown a reluctance here, a reluctance to accept the idea of freedom to choose; they have tended to resist the idea that man in the modality of fallenness is still free, free to choose in an either-or sense. They were driven by the fear that if such freedom were granted, salvation would turn out to be, to an extent at least, a human achievement. This fear was commendable, especially in light of the fact that man's act of acceptance was sometimes delineated as a sort of good work, a human act of sufficient worth to merit salvation, in part at least. The question may be asked, however, whether the act of acceptance can be so construed, seeing that it is the acceptance of *grace*. Surely there is no pride-gendering implication in the idea that man in the modality of fallenness can opt to accept the hand of *grace*."

[154] See Torsten Bergsten, *Balthasar Hubmaier*, 13.

able German reformer, Luther himself.[155] In the context of the Reformation reaction against the scholastic Roman church dogma of natural and rational theology, toward an emphasis, as seen in Luther and Calvin, on the dichotomy between God in His sovereignty and man in his helplessness, Hubmaier posited a strong claim for free will in man. According to David Steinmetz, Hubmaier attempted "to steer a middle course between Luther and the older traditions of medieval theology."[156]

Reformation theology was committed to one overarching idea: justification by faith alone. As a reinforcement for *sola fide*, the concept of the bondage of the will became a commonplace, unquestioned foundation upon which the Reformation doctrinal structure was built. Torsten Bergsten observes that "According to Hubmaier, his opponents believed that everything happened by divine decree and that it was God who evoked good and evil in man. The Christian himself could do no good, since it is God who works in him both desire and its fulfillment."[157] Bergsten further notes that "These arguments and Hubmaier's rebuttal lead to the conclusion that the Lutheran doctrine of the enslaved will had found its way to Nikolsburg."[158] This was the city where Hubmaier spent the last and most productive years of his life as Anabaptist Reformer.

Contrary to the Lutheran doctrine, Anabaptists collectively held to the doctrine of free will in man even after the Fall. Robert Friedmann explains:

> As Hubmaier says... "The image of God is not altogether erased in us,"... Thus no total depravity is ever possible; in fact, the very core of man has remained uncorrupted and able to grasp God's grace and goodness. Of course, he admits that "we are poor and miserable sinners," but through divine grace the original freedom of man has been restored, even if imperfectly. If we surrender ourselves to God in childlike obedience, then

---

[155] Bergsten writes that Hubmaier's works on free will "represent an attack on Luther's views concerning the will, and also concerning man." *Balthasar Hubmaier*, 353.

[156] David C. Steinmetz, "Balthasar Hubmaier (1485?–1528)," 202–205.

[157] Bergsten, *Balthasar Hubmaier*, 349.

[158] Ibid.

we are truly free and able to do God's will, and thus we become disciples of Christ. This, in brief, is also general Anabaptist teaching concerning man as found nearly everywhere in Anabaptist writings, whether by Grebel or Marpeck, by Hutter or Menno Simons, and many others. Our inborn sinfulness is no unconquerable barrier to this task; for sin—that is, original sin—must never be understood as a kind of fate. Something in man has remained unspoiled and good, and "the fall of the soul is remediable through the Word of God."[159]

Thus, it is evident that Hubmaier's theology in general, and especially when it came to the doctrine of free will in man, was distinctly Anabaptist in nature. Bergsten confirms this: "Sebastian Franck writes concerning the Anabaptists: 'They are unanimous in holding the doctrine of free will, so far as I have discovered. Though, God comes to us, knocks at the door, woos us, and lays the first stone. After that it is up to us and to our free will, whether we accept this proffered grace or throw it to the wind.' This is an apt description of Hubmaier's viewpoint."[160]

Hubmaier appealed to Erasmus' works occasionally, as did other Anabaptists, and his second treatise on *Freedom of the Will* appears to have been modeled after Erasmus' *On the Freedom of the Will* in some ways. But the ideas in Hubmaier's theology, including his theses on free will, are decidedly

---

159 Robert Friedmann, *The Theology of Anabaptism: An Interpretation*, Studies in Anabaptist and Mennonite History (Scottdale: Herald Press, 1973), 59–60. Albert Henry Newman also wrote of the Anabaptists concerning free will: "They were almost without exception opposed to the Augustinian system of doctrine, especially in its Lutheran and Calvinistic forms, insisting upon the freedom of the will and necessity of good works as the fruit of faith, and regarding faith as a great transforming process whereby we are brought not simply to participate in Christ's merits, but to enter into the completest union with him in a life of utter self-abnegation. They were unanimous in regarding Luther's teachings regarding the will and good works as in the highest degree immoral and opposed to the spirit of the gospel." A. H. Newman, *A Manual of Church History*, vol. 2, *Modern Church History (A.D. 1517–1932)* (Philadelphia: American Baptist Publication Society, 1953), 154–155.

160 Bergsten, *Balthasar Hubmaier*, 350.

his own.¹⁶¹ Bergsten writes that "Hubmaier's teachings regarding free will do not coincide exactly with either those of Erasmus or of Luther in this respect. Rather, he adopts a third point of view. As an Anabaptist theologian and leader he emphasized the ethical responsibility of man as well as the Reformed doctrine of sin."¹⁶² While Erasmus' influence is clearly recognizable in the Anabaptists, especially with free will, it is not so much as a fountainhead but as a consultant for their beliefs, that he functions. Scripture was, first and last, the foundation upon which the Anabaptists sought to stand.¹⁶³ Estep writes, "The truth of the matter is that Hubmaier was no slavish disciple of either Luther or Erasmus—in fact, many of the ideas he espoused were markedly different from theirs."¹⁶⁴

One of the objections that Hubmaier almost certainly made regarding Luther's stance on free will was its rigid syllogistic reasoning. When Luther proceeds logically from the sovereignty of God to the impossibility of free will in the human being, he is effectively denying man part of his humanness. To Hubmaier, Luther's simplistic formula was contrary not only to human experience, but to the Scriptures. Harry McSorley names Luther's argument "necessitarian" because of its use of narrow philosophical reasoning, and because it results in a form of determinism. He describes the problematic theological implications of this logic: "A careful analysis of the necessitarian

---

161 See n. 8, Pipkin and Yoder, 453: "The clearest indication of the dependence of Hubmaier on Erasmus is that Hubmaier tends to use the same Scriptures as Erasmus in the order in which Erasmus used them. As a rule, however, the arguments are not those of Erasmus, but of Hubmaier, who develops his own exegesis and interpretations."

162 Bergsten, *Balthasar Hubmaier*, 354.

163 Timothy George describes the Radical Reformers' tie to Scripture: "Despite their many differences they all wanted to cut back through accretions of ecclesiastical tradition, through what Balthasar Hubmaier called 'the mud holes and cesspools of human dogma,' to the authentic rood (*radix*) of faith and order. Each branch of the Radical Reformation attached itself to a distinctive 'root.' For the Anabaptists it was the Bible, especially the New Testament. They desired not merely to reform the church, but to restore it to its pristine apostolic purity." *Theology of the Reformers*, 254–255.

164 William Estep, *Renaissance and Reformation* (Grand Rapids: Eerdmans, 1986), 214.

argument ... leads Luther into a theological predicament, since it makes it impossible for him to explain in a convincing way that man alone—and not God—is the cause of sin. It furthermore leaves no place in his theology for a personal decision of faith."[165] A personal faith decision was vital to Hubmaier's view, which he believed was in accord with Scripture.[166] William Estep characterizes Hubmaier's thought as "affirming the voluntary nature of the faith-response to God's gracious offer of salvation in Christ. In other words ... the proclamation of the gospel was predicated upon an uncoerced response, for Christ came to invite, not to compel, men and women to discipleship."[167]

---

165 McSorley, *Luther: Right or Wrong?*, 369.

166 The biblical call for decision is highlighted by Michael Green. He writes that in evangelizing, the apostles "*looked for a response. The apostles were not shy about asking men to decide for or against the God who had decided for them. They expected results. They challenged men to do something about the message they had heard. 'What shall we do?' was the response of the crowd on the day of Pentecost. The answer is clear enough in the pages of the New Testament. . . . They must first and foremost repent, change their attitude to their old way of life, be willing to let go their sins. It involved a radical break with the past. It could not be real in the absence of 'deeds which demonstrated repentance.'"* Green, *Evangelism in the Early Church* (Grand Rapids: Eerdmans, 1970), 151.

167 William Estep, "Church and State," in *The People of God: Essays on the Believers' Church*, ed. Paul A. Basden and David S. Dockery (Nashville: Broadman & Holman, 1991), 271.

Chapter Two

Hubmaier's Doctrine of Free Will

An understanding of Hubmaier's doctrine of the freedom of the will begins with contextual observations. The first task is to assess the likely influences on Hubmaier's thought, especially concerning his doctrine of free will. The approach taken here will be to establish an awareness of possible influences, but Hubmaier's work will not be evaluated through any specific ideological lens. Instead, his works will be analyzed, as much as is possible, as they come from his own pen. The background, motivations, and authorities staked out by Hubmaier himself will form the primary context for the content of his arguments and theology. Hubmaier was exposed to a number of ideologies from all sides of the Reformation spectrum, each of which he took into account as he sincerely and independently sought the truth, principally and definitively from the Bible, which he considered his final authority. Because of this, it might be said that Hubmaier was an original thinker. William Estep's assessment of Hubmaier's thought, from the very beginning of his work as a Reformer, is that "there are some independent and apparently new ideas which find public expression here for the first time in the Reformation era. From his earliest published work, Hubmaier demonstrated an independent and creative mind."[168]

This approach (Hubmaier as independent and original) is warranted since the focus will be on explaining Hubmaier's thought on free will in this

---

168 Estep, "Balthasar Hubmaier: Martyr Without Honor," *Baptist History and Heritage* 13, no.2 (April, 1978): 7–8.

chapter, but also because of the indeterminate nature of the scholarship relating to possible antecedents of Hubmaier's thought. A review of Hubmaier scholarship, in light of his Reformation context and his own unique Anabaptist theology, as Bergsten writes, "reveals that scholars have sharply contrasting views of the man and his work."[169] Thus, it is not the purpose here to sort out all the possible sources and interpretations of Hubmaier's thought, but to let Hubmaier's own words be reflected. However, to provide a description of the context in which Hubmaier worked to solidify his individual beliefs, a condensed inspection of several possible sources involved, and some of the views taken concerning his theology, will serve as the first steps toward assessing Hubmaier's doctrine of free will. One of the key factors in this investigation will be Hubmaier's commitment to Scripture.

HUBMAIER'S HISTORICAL MILIEU

The influences upon the Anabaptists, and thus upon Hubmaier, have been variously described as mysticism, nominalism, humanism (as in Erasmus), asceticism, scholasticism, etc. These have been named by assorted scholars as direct or indirect medieval or Renaissance endowments to Anabaptist thought. The impact of these ideologies upon Anabaptist theology has been depicted as substantial or negligible, depending on the writer. George Huntston Williams presents a general list of "late medieval and Renaissance impulses: humanism, the lay spirit (anticlericalism), sacramentarianism, mys-

---

169 Bergsten, *Balthasar Hubmaier*, 45. Bergsten explains the disparity in Hubmaier scholarship: "Hubmaier was one of the leading figures in the early days of the Anabaptist movement. At the same time he stood both theologically and practically in a close relationship to the Magisterial Reform. His particular significance for church history lies in his dual role as Reformer and Anabaptist leader. This fact also accounts for the widely divergent views of his life and work in the world of Reformation scholarship. In addition, the wide variety of ways in which the Anabaptists have been understood has also affected Hubmaier research. A fairly comprehensive body of scholarly literature on Hubmaier exists in which the ecclesiastical allegiance of the respective writers has played a decisive role." *Balthasar Hubmaier*, 25.

ticism, apocalypticism."[170] As for the effects of the assorted likely influences on Hubmaier, Estep writes: "While there is no doubt that Hubmaier was an independent thinker who refused to wear any man's collar, he was influenced by the various currents of Reformation that coursed through the sixteenth century. There is no consensus as to which became the most influential element in his own thought processes."[171]

As for the Reformation influence on Anabaptists generally, Williams notes further:

> Lutheranism as the generic initial term for revolt or renewal . . . brought about the mutation of still other Christian motifs in the consequent variations of still further radicalized theology and the proliferation of a congeries of interrelated churches, sects, and seekers for whom Luther for his own part had his own generic term of derision, *Schwärmer* (fanatics), and who constitute in their partial interrelatedness and interdependence a radical reformation different from the territorial, magisterial reformation.[172]

This Radical Reformation was the great heaving lump of "others" into which Hubmaier and the Anabaptists have been cast by scholars, who have tried, from assorted angles, to find the key source for this mass of "fanatics." Whether this can really be done in the case of the Anabaptists, and with Hubmaier in particular, remains to be seen. Thus, an analysis of the sources of Hubmaier's theology, specifically his free will doctrine, is in order.

As far as direct sources are concerned, John Rempel, a Mennonite scholar, does not see the progress of Hubmaier's theological development as primarily that of absorbing the ideas of others. Instead, Rempel characterizes Hubmaier's intellectual journey as a process of responding to what he saw as deficient notions in his time which served as antitheses for the working out of his own theological principles. Rempel characterizes "the impact of

---

170 George Huntston Williams, *The Radical Reformation*, 3d ed. (Kirksville: Sixteenth Century Journal Publishers, 1962), 27.

171 Estep, "Balthasar Hubmaier: Martyr Without Honor," 10.

172 Williams, *The Radical Reformation*, 27.

his contemporaries," on Hubmaier as being "foils for him, stepping stones toward convictions which transcended all of them."[173] Hans-Jürgen Goertz makes a similar observation in a study of some key Anabaptists, including Hubmaier: "Certainly the Anabaptists made use of medieval and humanist ideas, some of them more, others less, but they did not go into the Reformation with a ready-made concept of faith. They only discovered their concepts in the course of fierce struggles and bitter experience."[174]

This interpretation represents an insightful appraisal of Hubmaier's Anabaptist theology. Considering the difficulty of situating him as descendant of any individual movement or person, Rempel warns against "trying to identify Hubmaier completely with any one theology or trying to locate all his notions in the writings of known theologians."[175] He *made use* of certain theological ideas which he found expedient, but to classify him as a member of any one medieval or Reformation party (any of the '-isms' previously mentioned), except Anabaptism, overlooks the essentially radical nature of his reform. Carl Leth states it this way: "Hubmaier's theology reflects *his own synthesis* of catholic, nominalist, humanist, and Reformation influences."[176] It is evident, therefore, that Hubmaier's theology must be regarded as strongly

---

173 Rempel, *The Lord's Supper in Anabaptism*, 45.

174 Hans-Jürgen Goertz, *The Anabaptists*, trans. Trevor Johnson (London: Routledge, 1988), 66–67.

175 Rempel, *The Lord's Supper in Anabaptism*, 43. Emir Caner strikes the same note concerning influences, claiming that "Hubmaier was influenced by such giants as Erasmus, Zwingli, and Eck. Erasmus impressed upon Hubmaier the idea of free will, Zwingli affected Hubmaier's beliefs on the Mass and Images, and Eck swayed Hubmaier on mariology. Yet, this is not to say that Hubmaier incorporated all that he heard from his mentors; rather, Hubmaier used his literal hermeneutic of Scripture and applied it to the theologies of his day." Emir Fethi Caner, "Truth is Unkillable: The Life and Writings of Balthasar Hubmaier, Theologian of Anabaptism" (Ph.D. diss., University of Texas at Arlington, 1999), 164.

176 Emphasis added. Carl M. Leth, "Balthasar Hubmaier's 'Catholic' Exegesis: Matthew 16:18–19 and the Power of the Keys," in *Biblical Interpretation in the Era of the Reformation: Essays Presented to David C. Steinmetz in Honor of His Sixtieth Birthday*, ed. John Thompson and Richard A. Muller (Grand Rapids: Eerdmans, 1996), 103.

independent, and as Anabaptist, so that he holds a unique place within the Anabaptist movement.

Torsten Bergsten agrees with this assessment. He characterizes Hubmaier as an influential and seminal Anabaptist, defying any simple association with theological streams of the age. Bergsten applies this evaluation especially to Anabaptist writings on free will, Hubmaier being the foremost Anabaptist defender of that doctrine:

> In this literature one can detect a united front against the Lutheran doctrines of predestination and free will, and an emphasis on the Christian life of discipleship. The relevant documents arose from within the Anabaptist circles in South Germany.... which indicates that ... this ... Anabaptist movement cannot be equated either with the mysticism of the late Middle Ages or with the humanism of Erasmus and the spiritualism that belonged to the Reformation period. However, the Anabaptist movement did take over certain elements from all these religious currents, especially the concept of discipleship, and was stamped most clearly with the marks of the Lutheran and Zwinglian Reformation. Thus, the Anabaptists represent an independent movement within the religious milieu of the Reformation era. The Anabaptists more insistently than the other reformers stressed personal piety and the moral responsibility of Christians and differed from the mystics and the radical Spiritualists in attributing a greater significance to the outward Word and sacraments. Over against these latter, together with the humanists, the Anabaptists attempted to gather churches of regenerate believers according to the New Testament pattern. To a considerable extent Hubmaier was responsible for the shape of this movement in South Germany.[177]

In an analysis of medieval influences on the Anabaptists (including humanism, asceticism, mysticism, scholasticism, apocalypticism, and anarchism), Jarold Zeman affirms the difficulty in completely identifying Anabaptism with any of these ideological impulses. He declares that "an interpretation of Anabaptism which sees it exclusively, or primarily, as an expression of

---

177 Bergsten, *Balthasar Hubmaier*, 360.

medieval *Weltanschauung* is, in my opinion, untenable."[178] Zeman claims that the reverse is actually the case, asserting that "in their central aspirations of personalism, pluralism, and egalitarianism,[179] and in the actual realization of these in daily life, the Anabaptists looked forward to the modern era rather than back to the Middle Ages."[180] John Allen Moore, a Baptist scholar, applies the same type of evaluation to Hubmaier: "An honest and adventurous thinker for his day, practical minded and determined, eloquent and creative, he must surely rank among the most modern in spirit of the great church reformers of the sixteenth century."[181]

Hubmaier's theology is doubly difficult to place in context, not only because it is Anabaptist, but also, in some cases, because it has been deemed *not* so Anabaptist. Hubmaier is Anabaptist in emphasizing discipleship, believer's baptism and a believers' church. But he departs from typical Anabaptism by allowing for Christian magistrates and soldiers.[182] Also, as a fairly comprehensive theology with some systematic qualities, Hubmaier's thought is sometimes deemed less than Anabaptist, (or more than Anabaptist, depending on the viewpoint taken) since some scholars see in the essence of Anabaptism a predisposition toward ethics and discipleship and away from theology *per se*, as a cerebral undertaking.

---

178 Jarold Knox Zeman, "Anabaptism: A Replay of Medieval Themes or a Prelude to the Modern Age?," *Mennonite Quarterly Review* 70 (1976): 264.

179 As an explanation, these three "central aspirations" might better be named relational theology, religious liberty, and social equality. The Anabaptists, along with Hubmaier, were primarily concerned with discipleship not with general societal matters such as personalism, pluralism, and egalitarianism. What these words mean to a 20th century reader would not correspond exactly with Anabaptist beliefs and may be somewhat anachronistic. But the Anabaptists did stress following Christ personally, freedom of belief without state control, and equality within the fellowship of believers who are all forgiven and made free in Christ.

180 Zeman, "Anabaptism: A Replay of Medieval Themes or a Prelude to the Modern Age?," 269.

181 John Allen Moore, "Balthasar Hubmaier: Truth Is Immortal," in *Anabaptist Portraits* (Scottdale, PA: Herald Press, 1984), 165.

182 Many scholars (particularly Harold Bender) have described Anabaptism as being essentially pacifist. See Bender, *The Anabaptist Vision*.

For instance, Robert Friedmann believes the Anabaptists to have been decidedly *not* theological in their approach to Christianity since their focus was essentially discipleship:

> It is clear that besides Balthasar Hubmaier (d. 1528), who was a doctor of theology . . . there were no trained theologians in the broad array of Anabaptist writers and witnesses. Hubmaier was a special type, greatly esteemed by Christian radicals but not really emulated and followed after. Many of his theological ideas crept into Anabaptist thinking, such as, for instance, his doctrine of the freedom of the will . . . . But otherwise, theology of the Hubmaier kind was by and large bypassed by Anabaptists as something it would be better not to indulge in too deeply. They may have felt that it could easily lead the faithful astray from the narrow path of discipleship which is, in principle, nontheological.[183]

Here we see what seems to be a typical Mennonite treatment of Hubmaier: as essential for the theology of the Anabaptists in some of the most crucial areas, and yet as non-essential in that he never gained a following like that of Simons or Hutter, and did not conform to the pacifist mold of Anabaptism.[184] But Roger Olson sees Hubmaier's influence as foundational to the

---

183 Robert Friedmann, *The Theology of Anabaptism*, 19. Friedmann then proceeds to write the rest of the book on Anabaptist theology, as per the title, which in itself rather obscures his case for nontheological Anabaptism.

184 It should be observed here that Hubmaier is perhaps more Anabaptist even in these respects than some picture him to be. His initial and continuing influence on Anabaptists and others is perhaps greater than some more conventional Anabaptist leaders *because* of his strong and lucid Anabaptist theology. For instance, the *Hutterite Chronicle,* written by those who followed Jacob Hutter's pacifist doctrine, described Hubmaier's writings as having "powerfully . . . defended true baptism and opposed infant baptism with proofs from Holy Scripture. In the same thorough way he threw light on the Lord's Supper according to the truth and refuted the idolatrous mass and its great error and deception." *The Chronicle of the Hutterian Brethren*, ed. the Hutterian Brethren (Rifton, NY: Plough Publishing, 1987), 49. Also, although he saw no problem with supporting and serving in government,

Anabaptist movement, rather than, as Friedmann puts it, as one that somehow "crept" into Anabaptism: "Although Balthasar Hubmaier was not the founder of any particular church or group of Anabaptists, his legacy was profoundly influential among all Anabaptists. During his two to three years as a leader of the radical Protestant movement, he gave it a theological foundation upon which to build."[185]

Such an assessment seems to suggest that Hubmaier rendered a great service to the movement by providing Anabaptism with profound theological undergirding. Yet Hubmaier is seen by scholars such as Friedmann as

he was committed until the end to nonresistance. Estep writes: "Hubmaier was the first major theologian among the Anabaptists. His influence became pervasive: his teachings upon the role of faith and the necessity of the new birth that occurs with the hearing of the Word under the convicting power of the Holy Spirit became a major thrust of sixteenth-century Anabaptism. He undergirded with solid biblical exegesis the Anabaptist positions on the necessity of the new birth, believer's baptism, the nature of the church, and the limitations of the authority of the state. The churches he fostered at Waldshut and later at Nikolsburg, while true to the ecclesiological insights of Anabaptism, were more positively oriented toward the state than were Anabaptist churches elsewhere. However, his position on the sword never became widely accepted by sixteenth-century Anabaptists. Regardless of Hubmaier's view of the Christian's obligation to support the magistracy, his final position was one that advocated personal nonresistance. . . . Hubmaier was the most vigorous and impassioned thinker of the Anabaptist movement. In him can be seen the Anabaptist conception of the cross both as an event that happened once and for all in the history of redemption and also as a principle of life for the people of God. Through his martyr's death, Hubmaier showed that he adhered to the 'original Anabaptist' demand for individual nonresistance." Estep, *Renaissance and Reformation*, 216.

185 Roger E. Olson, *The Story of Christian Theology: Twenty Centuries of Tradition and Reform* (Downers Grove: InterVarsity Press, 1999), 422. Olson continues the discussion of Hubmaier's overall influence on Anabaptism: "For the most part Anabaptists like Menno Simons built on that foundation [Hubmaier's theology] so that they remained committed to basic Protestant principles in a radical perspective and with a strongly synergistic flavor. Their emphasis was on individual conversion and communal discipleship as well as separation from the world and freedom of conscience." Insertion added. 422–423.

perhaps too theological and systematic in his approach to make the Anabaptist movement, as it continued through the years, comfortable with him, especially since he differed concerning certain Anabaptist distinctives: the oath, government service, and pacifism. David Steinmetz disagrees with this estimate of Hubmaier. Rather, he places him solidly within the Anabaptist fold: "However, since Hubmaier did represent on the question of believers baptism, the voluntary Church, grace and free will, the views taught by other Anabaptist leaders, there is no reason to separate him from the Anabaptist movement as a whole."[186]

Some scholars have regarded Hubmaier as desirous of establishing a state-church in the cities where he ministered, and some see him as fomenting rebellion and anarchy in a connection with the peasants' war.[187] But William Estep refutes these descriptions of Hubmaier's reform effort in the article on Hubmaier in *The Mennonite Encyclopedia*: "Although he was not a thorough-going pacifist, neither was he the militant advocate of war he has at times been represented. . . . In all major doctrines he was in step with the majority of Anabaptism."[188] Hubmaier himself wrote a statement concerning his view of violence and rebellion, making clear his basic view that the Christian life was not in any measure radically political, but primarily characterized by faith in Christ:

> A Christian does not fight, strike, or kill unless he is a magistrate or commissioned to do it by a proper authority. Otherwise a Christian will surrender his cloak and his coat before he takes the sword. He

---

186 David C. Steinmetz, "Scholasticism and Radical Reform: Nominalist Motifs in the Theology of Balthasar Hubmaier," *Mennonite Quarterly Review* 45 (April 1971) : 124.

187 See the review of Hubmaier scholarship in the introduction of Bergsten. See also a concise summary of several scholars' views of Hubmaier's political position in Estep's introduction of Hubmaier's *On the Sword* in *Anabaptist Beginnings*, 107.

188 William Estep, "Hubmaier (Huebmör), Balthasar," in *Mennonite Encyclopedia: A Comprehensive Work on the Anabaptist-Mennonite Movement*, vol. 5, ed. Harold S. Bender, C. Henry Smith, and Cornelius Krahn (Scottdale: Mennonite Publishing House, 1955–59, 1990).

offers his cheek, indeed, life and limb. The Christian way is peaceful for that is the victory of the Christian, even faith which overcomes the world (1Jn. 5)."[189]

Torsten Bergsten comments on the attempts that some scholars have made to color Hubmaier largely in political shades: "Even on the basis of a very complete knowledge of the sources and the best of intentions, it is impossible to make a case for Hubmaier as a political leader at the expense of Hubmaier, the Anabaptist reformer."[190]

THE BAPTIST VIEW OF HUBMAIER

Baptist scholars like William Estep have seen Hubmaier as a sort of "proto-Baptist," a theologian modern Baptists identify with strongly. Torsten Bergsten writes: "Hubmaier can be regarded as a prototype of the Baptist movement."[191] Estep observes: "Hubmaier's appeal for Baptists is obviously not because he was a Baptist nor due to any direct influence he may have had upon the rise of the English Baptist movement. Rather, it is based upon a theological identity which Baptist scholars have often felt with the early Anabaptist theologian."[192] Bergsten describes the Baptist view of Hubmaier:

> For a long time, Hubmaier has been given a place of honor in Baptist scholarship and fellowship. He is generally regarded as the most important Anabaptist leader. There is also a readiness to recognize in him a spiritual brother who represented in all essentials the major principles of the English Baptist movement which emerged in the early seventeenth century. . . . Baptist church historians are in accord with

---

[189] Balthasar Hubmaier, "Justification," in *Anabaptism in Outline*, ed. Walter Klaassen (Scottdale, PA: Herald Press, 1981), 250. This is from the *Apologia* found also in Pipkin and Yoder, 560.
[190] Bergsten, *Balthasar Hubmaier*, 45
[191] Ibid., 46.
[192] Estep, "Balthasar Hubmaier: Martyr Without Honor," 10.

others, engaged in Anabaptist research, who see in the movement the beginning of the modern Free Church movement. . . . Since he also manifested a positive and constructive attitude toward the state and society, he was a prototype of modern Baptist leaders. . . . Hubmaier followed a middle course between two extremes among the Anabaptists: one was violent, meeting disaster in the Munster catastrophe; the other was pacific, adopting a negative attitude toward civil authority. . . . Hubmaier was a genuine free churchman, the first of a significantly larger group which was to come after him. The truly converted congregation in Waldshut was the largest and most active gathering in Europe at that time. . . . Hubmaier's beliefs [are] a remarkable synthesis of the radical concepts of the Anabaptists and the more conservative ideas of the Magisterial Reformers.[193]

As far as a direct link between Hubmaier and modern Baptists, there is little evidence. Some early English Baptists may have read Hubmaier and thus he had an influence in that way. Irvin Horst writes of Hubmaier that, "evidence exists that he and his writings were known in England during the early Reformation period."[194]

The Baptist scholar Gunnar Westin, editor of the critical German edition of Hubmaier's works along with Bergsten, describes Hubmaier's ministry in Waldshut as completely unparalleled in his time: "The altogether unusual took place in Waldshut, for the cause of the Reformation developed in an evangelical free church with the baptism of believers as the accepted practice."[195] In other words an entire city was under the influence of an Anabaptist ecclesiological establishment. Hubmaier had introduced believer's baptism as the practice of the reformed church in Waldshut. He had already resigned as priest and become pastor of the free church which replaced the established Catholic church. The city was not dominated by a Catholic or Protestant ter-

---

193 Bergsten, *Balthasar Hubmaier*, 39–41.

194 Irvin Buckwalter Horst, *The Radical Brethren: Anabaptism and the English Reformation to 1558* (Nieuwkoop: B. de Graaf, 1972), 131, n. 135.

195 Gunnar Westin, *The Free Church Through The Ages*, trans. Virgil A. Olson (Nashville: Broadman, 1958), 67.

ritorial church but formed a voluntary evangelical church. Other Anabaptists had important ministries, but they were mostly on the run.[196] Hubmaier was to be on the run also, as well as being imprisoned by Zwingli in Zurich, but later he was leader of another Anabaptist church which was remarkably successful in Nikolsburg in Moravia. Thousands were persuaded to embrace Hubmaier's Anabaptist theology and were baptized, even the local lords among them. After these achievements, Hubmaier was arrested by Catholic authorities, imprisoned in Austria and burned at the stake as an Anabaptist martyr in 1528.[197]

Robert Torbet's assessment of Hubmaier in his *A History of the Baptists* is a useful example of the Baptist sentiment regarding his place in history: "It was Balthasar Hubmaier, that stalwart Anabaptist, who dared to challenge Zwingli . . . He insisted . . . that 'in all disputes concerning faith and religion, the Scripture alone, proceeding from the mouth of God, ought to be our level and rule.' Baptists have maintained this consistent stand through all the centuries that have followed Hubmaier's day, even at the expense of their personal safety."[198] One of the great draws toward Hubmaier for Baptists through the centuries has been the recognition of his staunch advocacy and high regard for Scripture. This commitment to Scripture was the primary consideration, for Hubmaier, in the development and refinement of his theological works. As Rollin Armour writes, "Hubmaier's final views came only after considerable thought and his own investigation of Scripture."[199]

---

196 Westin writes: "Moreover, the Lutheran territories were becoming much like the Catholic and Reformed countries: the organization of a national church demanded strict uniformity. There was no religious freedom; all were forced to follow the rigid religious regulations. As for the Anabaptists, this meant a martyr's death, or in some cases, banishment." *The Free Church Through The Ages*, 79.

197 John Allen Moore, a European Baptist scholar, writes the following tribute to Hubmaier's tenacity in seeking the truth: "He worked hard, dared much, suffered greatly to find and follow the truth as best he was able to discover it—and he sealed that faith finally with his blood." Moore, "Balthasar Hubmaier: Truth Is Immortal," in *Anabaptist Portraits*, 165.

198 Robert G. Torbet, *A History of the Baptists*, 3d ed. (Valley Forge: Judson Press, 1963), 513.

199 Armour, *Anabaptist Baptism*, 24.

Hubmaier's Commitment to Scripture

The best way to understand Hubmaier's theology may be to get a sense of the historical and theological context in which he moved, along with an understanding that he was a man attempting to surrender his whole life and thought to the authority of Scripture. William Estep asserts, "Above all, Hubmaier desired to be a biblical theologian. In the final analysis, the New Testament itself, at least in his own mind, became the determinant of his theology. Consequently, his contribution took on the character of lasting significance."[200] To be fair, giving Hubmaier the benefit of the doubt regarding his own explicit goals and principles, his ideas should be understood in the context of his stated desire to appeal to the Bible as final authority. To label them according to the movements or personalities of the time, rather than as a sincere attempt to derive truth from Scripture, only works to obscure Hubmaier's thought.

One reason this is evident is that Hubmaier, because of his training and acumen, examined virtually every important idea in his time and attempted to evaluate each in light of the Bible. Eddie Mabry calls attention to Hubmaier's distinctiveness, even amidst the many ideas and personalities that may have affected him:

> While he seems to have been influenced by late medieval Augustinianism, late medieval nominalism, by some of the ideas of Luther, and some of the views of Erasmus and humanism, Hubmaier, again, does not seem to fit comfortably in any of these categories. Rather, his theology seems to be a blending of theological views and practices from all of the various theological influences to which he was exposed. At the same time, there seems to be something which keeps Hubmaier's theology essentially and distinctly his own. Hubmaier, of course, claims that this is due to his own study of the Scriptures. From this theological foundation, Hubmaier can interact with the various views, agree and disagree with them, without really becom-

---

200 Estep, "Balthasar Hubmaier: Martyr Without Honor," 10.

ing a member of any particular camp. He remains consistently somewhere in between them all.[201]

Hubmaier's originality and unique contribution, then, can be seen as deriving from this combination: the variety of Reformation influences and his theological training along with a deeply felt reliance upon Scripture, read in a simple, commonsense way. Emir Caner concurs: "In the end, what Hubmaier believed was uniquely his own. He combined what he saw as the best from all sides as it agreed with his interpretation of the Scripture."[202]

Once Hubmaier decided to make the Bible his ultimate authority, he never strayed from that commitment. This does not mean that his interpretations were free of any error or bias, but, as Hubmaier claimed, his words were "spoken in simplicity, and my speech can only be and will only be and may only be thus. For the Son of the carpenter who never went to a university has bidden me speak thus, and, in that I may write it, has himself fashioned my pen with his carpenter's hatchet."[203] Pipkin and Yoder note in their translation of *Freedom of the Will, II*, that Hubmaier's overwhelming citation of passages from the Bible makes it "graphically clear as to how deeply grounded in Scripture Hubmaier's approach was."[204] Thus, as is evident in all his writings, the Bible was Hubmaier's principal and direct source, what he called the "right, proper, and true arbiter."[205] Robert Macoskey insists that, regarding Hubmaier, "we must conclude that his beliefs were first and foremost the results of his New Testament study and the consequent re-thinking of the true nature of the church."[206]

---

201 Mabry, *Balthasar Hubmaier's Doctrine of the Church*, 201.

202 Caner, "Truth is Unkillable," 216.

203 Balthasar Hubmaier, "Von der Kindertaufe" (On Infant Baptism), in *Balthasar Hubmaier: Schriften*, ed. Gunnar Westin und Torsten Bergsten (Gütersloh, 1962), 269; trans. and quoted in Walter Klaassen, "Speaking in Simplicity: Balthasar Hubmaier," *Mennonite Quarterly Review* 40 (April 1966): 139.

204 Pipkin and Yoder, *Balthasar Hubmaier*, 450, n. 5.

205 Balthasar Hubmaier, *A Public Challenge to All Believers*, Pipkin and Yoder, 80.

206 Robert A. Macoskey, "The Contemporary Relevance of Balthasar Hubmaier's Concept of the Church," *Foundations* 6 (April 1963): 116.

Therefore, though some dependence on others like Eck, Erasmus, Luther, Zwingli, and fellow Anabaptist Hans Denck can be cited, Hubmaier's primary and conscious source was Scripture. This is apparent especially when one considers that Hubmaier's theology, as it developed and crystallized, was neither Catholic, humanist, or spiritualist. Despite the fact that he had been influenced by the humanists and their champion Erasmus, by his fellow Anabaptist, and spiritualist, Denck, and by his Catholic teacher Johann Eck before his conversion to evangelicalism, Hubmaier's distinctive theology reflects his intention to rely chiefly upon Scripture. William Estep views Hubmaier's thought as deriving principally from Scripture, though, of course, within the historical and theological milieu of the Reformation. Estep conveys this view as he explains the context for Hubmaier's soteriology (most clearly expressed in his writings on free will):

> The theological context within which Hubmaier hammered out his Anabaptist soteriology was first Roman Catholic, then Lutheran, and later Zwinglian. He was for most of his theological career a Roman Catholic theologian and according to scholastic categories a Nominalist. Lutheran and Zwinglian concepts became influential in his development as a Protestant thinker, but others such as Erasmus and Hans Denck had a hand in the final shape of his soteriology. Above all, Hubmaier aspired to be a biblical theologian. Everything he had ever been taught, every concept, traditional or reformed, was subjected to a critical analysis in the light of the New Testament.[207]

Another scholar who strongly affirms Hubmaier's theology as self-consciously scriptural is Wilhelm Wiswedel who states, "Hubmaier's high estimation of the Scripture is well known."[208] Wiswedel describes Hubmaier's out-

---

207 William Estep, "The Anabaptist View of Salvation," *Southwestern Journal of Theology* 20, no.2 (1978): 35.
208 Wilhelm Wiswedel, "The Inner and Outer Word: A Study in the Anabaptist Doctrine of Scripture," in *Essays in Anabaptist Theology*, ed. H. Wayne Pipkin (Elkhart: Institute of Mennonite Studies, 1994), 53.

look regarding Scripture, including a catalogue of Hubmaier's own statements of confidence in God's Word:

> The Holy Scripture is for him the straight edge by which all spiritual things are decided: it is the touchstone by which all doctrine should be tested. God's Word alone should be the judge. It is clear that Hubmaier means the entire written and printed Bible. "Nothing should be added to or subtracted from the word of Christ." "One must bring Scripture; that will sound the harp of David." "I consider the Scripture to be a Hercules." "I call upon heaven and earth to bear witness that I have faithfully said, cursed is he who dissolves the slightest word and does not say amen to it." "The Word of God stands firm as a stone wall." "The Scripture is the friend of God in which Jesus lives, dwells, and rests; there is no spot in it."[209]

In addition, Wiswedel alludes to the measure of Hubmaier's allegiance to scriptural authority, referring to a hymn attributed to Hubmaier, who apparently extolled the virtues of God's Word even in worship: "In his *Preislied des gottlichen Wortes* [*A Song in Praise of God's Word*] each of the eighteen stanzas contains the line, 'For God's Word will stand forever.'"[210] Hubmaier expressed his devotion to God's Word in his appeal, "that we humble ourselves under the powerful Word of God and not go forth any more according to our own brain."[211]

It seems clear, then, that the consistent, definitive measure for Hubmaier's theology was Scripture. Henry Vedder marks Hubmaier as having "taken his stand on the principle that for him the voice of Scripture is the only voice of authority, and consequently the only voice that he will obey."[212] Scripture

---

209 Wiswedel, "The Inner and Outer Word," 53.

210 Ibid. This hymn has been translated and printed in Estep, *Anabaptist Beginnings*; Vedder, *Balthasar Hübmaier*; Pipkin & Yoder, *Balthasar Hubmaier*.

211 Hubmaier, *Dialogue with Zwingli's Baptism Book*, Pipkin and Yoder, 232.

212 Vedder, *Balthasar Hübmaier: The Leader of the Anabaptists* (New York: Putnam, 1905; reprint, New York: AMS Press, 1971), 66.

must be, in Hubmaier's estimation, the ultimate and authoritative source for truth: "I want always to give God the glory and to allow his Word to be the sole judge; to him I herewith desire to submit and subject myself and all my teachings."[213] Emir Caner describes Hubmaier's devotion to Scripture as one of the "basic principles of his life: the sole authority of the Bible in faith and practice, on which all other doctrine is founded."[214] Walter Klaassen views Hubmaier as faithful *and* able in regard to this principle: "There seems to be no question about Hubmaier's gift for clear and persuasive biblical interpretation and the compelling force of his arguments."[215]

Contrasting Hubmaier with the Magisterial Reformers, Walter Klaassen comments on the key Reformation tenet, *sola scriptura*:

> He shared with all Reformers the Reformation principle of *sola scriptura*, the conviction that only the Bible could be regarded as authority in matters of faith. But as solid a principle as it appeared in the first flush of the Reformation, it soon turned out to be frustratingly elusive, to the very considerable satisfaction of the Catholics. For Luther it meant one thing, for Zwingli and his fellow Reformers another, and for the Anabaptists something else again. Hubmaier was more radical in his application of the principle than either Luther or Zwingli. The sole authority of Scripture is defended against all other claims to authority.[216]

Klaassen observes further that "For Hubmaier the Scriptures were clear and transparent and pure and luminous and simple."[217] According to Klaassen, Hubmaier's "approach was the unabashedly direct approach of the layman, whereas he viewed his educated opponents as using the tools of their scholarship to hide the truth and to confuse the simple."[218] Hubmaier denounced

---

213 Hubmaier, *A Public Challenge to All Believers*, Pipkin and Yoder, 80.
214 Caner, "Truth is Unkillable," 55.
215 Walter Klaassen, "Speaking in Simplicity: Balthasar Hubmaier," *Mennonite Quarterly Review* 40 (April 1966): 143.
216 Klaassen, "Speaking in Simplicity," 141.
217 Ibid., 140.
218 Ibid., 143.

his opponents' scholarly methods, in this case writing against Zwingli's work concerning infant baptism:

> One ought not to juggle so the treasure of the divine Word, for if one did so, out of holy theology there would be left only something resembling the philosophy of Anaxagoras [who said 'all things have a portion of everything'], and one would be forced to accept a new faith as often as the New Testament was printed. For every fickle minded person inserts into it a baptism to match his doctrine, without any basis in Scripture, and at last out of a pumpkin a new Christ create. It is not so with us dear friend; we wish to interpret the text in all simplicity."[219]

Due to his great confidence in Scripture, Hubmaier's view of tradition and of the Church Fathers was severely reductionistic. He would only give credence to views which, to him, accorded with Scripture. "I will trust Cyprian, councils,

---

[219] Insertion added. Hubmaier, *On the Christian Baptism of Believers*, in *Anabaptist Beginnings*, ed. Estep, 76–77. Walter Klaassen, in *Anabaptism: Neither Catholic nor Protestant*, 39, cites an instance of the kind of scholarship which motivated Hubmaier's denunciation of Zwingli: "A dramatic example of this is to be found in the minutes of the debate between Anabaptists and some Zwinglian (or reformed) clerics in 1538 in Bern, Switzerland. The argument about the legitimacy of infant baptism was finally won by the clerics to their satisfaction by the use of a logical device know as *syllogism*. It works like this: All who belong to God have the Holy Spirit; Children belong to God; Therefore children have the Holy Spirit. Since the Spirit is necessary to faith, the possession of the Spirit argues that infants have faith. When therefore the New Testament says that those who have faith are to be baptized it legitimizes the baptism also of infants. This bit of sophistry joined to the divine revelation in Scripture was for them an acceptable basis for the practice of infant baptism. . . . The Anabaptists were convinced that error is the only outcome of using such devices in interpreting Scripture, for it always made possible a softening, a neutralizing of the commands of Christ. By such means, stated Balthasar Hubmaier in one of the . . . humorous passages in Anabaptist writings, one could make a new Christ out of a pumpkin. Anabaptists insisted that such ideas were not necessarily related to the concrete facts of church life and personal discipleship and were therefore at best suspect and at worst deceptive. Thus was rejected an entire medieval legacy — a combination of the products of man's reason with biblical revelation."

and other teachings just as far as they use Holy Scripture, and not more," Hubmaier declared.[220] He lamented his own training in the Catholic tradition:

> In order to confess my own ignorance with my own blushes, I say without subterfuge, and God knows I am not lying, that I became a doctor in Holy Scriptures (as this sophistry is called), and still did not understand . . . . Yes, and at that time I had never read a Gospel, or an epistle by Paul, from beginning to end. What kind of a Holy Word could I then teach others or preach to them? Of course: Thomas, Scotus, Gabriel, Occam, decree, decretals, legends of the saints and other scholastics. These were previously our hellish scriptures.[221]

Klaassen conveys Hubmaier's resolve concerning the issue of Scripture: "His rejection of the Fathers and of tradition is based on his conviction that in many places they contradict the Bible. . . . No considerations of personal prestige, antiquity or social order may qualify the principle of *sola scriptura*. If we accept the word of men as authoritative, how can we have any certainty since their words do not agree?"[222]

Hence, as part of Hubmaier's commitment to Scripture, he rejected any mixture of human ecclesial rationalizations, no matter how authoritative, with the truths of the Bible. The Anabaptists were suspicious of any mitigating philosophy applied to Scripture in order to support traditional doctrines. Ac-

---

220 Hubmaier, *On Infant Baptism*, Pipkin and Yoder, 280.

221 Hubmaier, *A Christian Catechism*, Pipkin and Yoder, 343. In response to the defenders of the Catholic tradition Hubmaier, in *A Christian Catechism*, Pipkin and Yoder, 343–344, penned these words: "No matter that some . . . boast and shout: We have always and ever heard, learned, and even preached the gospel. Answer: Dear friends, I grant that this is your claim and cry, but not that it is the truth. For even if some bits and patches have been drawn forth from the gospel, so much chaff and grit of human comments and additions are mixed with them that we have not tasted the sweetness of the real wheat and kernel. We were led so far astray from the spring of living water that we have been drinking nothing but muddy, filthy and poisoned cistern water sullied by human feet. How then could health and salvation have been there?"

222 Klaassen, "Speaking in Simplicity," 141.

cording to Christof Windhorst in his study of Hubmaier, when a conviction concerning the precedence of Scripture over human tradition is embraced, "all human doctrines and customs of the old church become superfluous."[223] This was Hubmaier's uncompromising stand. R. J. Smithson observes, "He was emphatic in his rejection of all human authority in religion."[224] Hubmaier is heard to say: "One should ask the Scriptures and not the church."[225] And again in the same work: "The Holy Scripture is such a whole, consistent, genuine, infallible, eternal, immortal Word that cannot wear away nor can the smallest letter or the smallest point be changed, Luke 21:33. Heaven and earth

---

[223] Christof Windhorst, "Balthasar Hubmaier: Professor, Preacher, Politician," 148.

[224] R. J. Smithson, *The Anabaptists: Their Contribution to Our Protestant Heritage* (London: James Clarke & Co., 1935), 145. Smithson writes further, "Hubmaier emphatically repudiated the Romish contention that unless men accept the Church as the infallible interpreter the Scriptures will lead them astray. The humblest believer is able to understand the Scriptures, so much at any rate as is necessary to salvation." Smithson also points out that Hubmaier and the Anabaptists chose Scripture even over an appeal to love: "One of Œcolampadius' books against the Anabaptists has a chapter bearing the title, 'The Abandonment of Infant Baptism is Contrary to Christian Love.' Hubmaier undertook to answer the argument that believer's baptism is contrary to Christian love. He wrote: 'If the Scriptures teach that baptism has been instituted for the instructed and the believers, and not for infants, then this is the truth. Now Paul writes that love rejoiceth in the truth, I Cor. 13. What, is now the truth contrary to love? But perhaps you speak of the love of the world which may not endure divine truth, for its works are evil, therefore it hates the light, John 3.' The Anabaptists would not agree that love, instead of the Scripture, should be the final judge in the controversial points. They maintained that the love which causes men to ignore God's word is not Christian love, whatever it may be. With them the Scriptures were the only authority for faith and practice." *The Anabaptists*, 176–177.

[225] Hubmaier, *Dialogue with Zwingli's Baptism Book*, Pipkin and Yoder, 181. Hubmaier continued: "For God wants to have from us only his law and his will, not our stubborn heads or opinions. God is more interested in obedience to his words than in all our sacrifices and even the self-devised church practices, as we have it in all the divine writings of the prophets, the twelve apostles, and the saints, 1 Sam. 15:22; Eccles. 4:17. The greatest and right honor that we can offer to God is to keep his Word and live according to his will, not according to our laws and opinions."

must first break apart.... How beautiful is the friend of God that is the Holy Scripture, in which Christ dwells, lives, and rests; and there is no flaw in it."[226]

Source Theories for Hubmaier's Thought

Although Hubmaier's commitment to Scripture cannot be doubted, he certainly was influenced in other ways as well. Though these other influences are secondary, they are still important for placing Hubmaier in the proper context. In tracing the roots of certain Anabaptist convictions, especially free will, the influence of Desiderius Erasmus on Anabaptism, for example, has gained more scholarly attention in recent years. Abraham Friesen, in *Erasmus, the Anabaptists, and the Great Commission*, points to this trend, saying: "In the last thirty years or so the theme of Erasmian influence on the early Swiss Anabaptist movement has grown exponentially."[227] Specifically, Thor Hall has examined Erasmus' influence on Hubmaier and another Anabaptist, Hans Denck, who also had some influence on Hubmaier, in the matter of human free will.[228] Erasmus' influence on Hubmaier does seem to be fairly significant. There is evidence that he actually had met Erasmus in Basel and had great respect for the eminent humanist.[229]

---

226 Hubmaier, *Dialogue with Zwingli's Baptism Book*, Pipkin and Yoder, 229.
227 Friesen, *Erasmus, the Anabaptists, and the Great Commission*, 22.
228 See Thor Hall, "Possibilities of Erasmian Influence on Denck and Hubmaier in Their Views on the Freedom of the Will," *Mennonite Quarterly Review* 35 (April 1961):149–170. Torsten Bergsten writes: "In general the Anabaptists acknowledged the freedom of the will. According to Hans Hillerbrand this emphasis was due to the influence of Erasmus." Bergsten, *Balthasar Hubmaier*, 13.
229 See Bergsten, *Balthasar Hubmaier*, 73. Also Kenneth Davis writes: "There is little doubt that by late 1522, Hubmaier was a convinced Evangelical Reformer, in a broad sense; somewhat more Erasmian than Lutheran. He had been greatly influenced by Christian humanism and especially by Erasmus personally." And again, commenting on Hubmaier's overall influence from humanism, Davis states: "One must recognize, however, that this influence does not refer to humanism in general but primarily to the ideals and piety associated with Erasmian Christian humanism. Hubmaier even noted a discrepancy between what Erasmus taught personally and what he was willing to put in writing. It caused him to express some antipathy toward Erasmus' character but not toward what Erasmus taught." *Anabaptism and Asceticism*, 102.

Pipkin and Yoder remark that Hubmaier's *Freedom of the Will* "was evidently influenced by Erasmus and bears similarities to many concerns of Hans Denck."[230] At the same time they hold that even when the influence is most obvious, "Hubmaier maintains his own perspective."[231] Hans-Jürgen Goertz also argues for this reading of the dependence of Hubmaier on Erasmus: "Although Hubmaier was inspired by Erasmus, he also differentiated himself from him."[232] Pipkin and Yoder note further that "the clearest dependency of Hubmaier on Erasmus is in the selections of Scripture to be used in the treatise."[233]

Another of the considerations regarding influences on Hubmaier's doctrine of free will was his fellow Anabaptist Hans Denck (1495–1527). Between Erasmus and Denck, Bergsten sees Denck's influence as having the greater impact on Hubmaier.[234] George Huntston Williams cites Denck as a clear influence on Hubmaier concerning free will, especially in his second treatise on free will.[235] However, Walter Moore contends that, "One may reasonably doubt George Huntston William's assertion that Hubmaier 'learned from Denck to modify his Zwinglian view on predestination and free will.'"[236] However, Edward Furcha, a Denck scholar, sees in this particular link with Hubmaier's *Freedom of the Will, II* "an unmistakable affinity of thought regarding theological essentials despite dissimilarities in emphasis and direction."[237]

On the other hand, William Estep points out that Hubmaier's influence on Denck may have been more pronounced than was the reverse. Speaking of Denck, he writes: "A Lutheran since his Regensburg days, he was soon to find

---

230 Pipkin and Yoder, *Balthasar Hubmaier*, 449.

231 Ibid.

232 Hans-Jürgen Goertz, *The Anabaptists*, 63.

233 Pipkin and Yoder, *Balthasar Hubmaier*, 449.

234 See Bergsten's discussion of Hubmaier and Denck in *Balthasar Hubmaier*, 354–358.

235 See Williams, *The Radical Reformation*, 248. Also Williams and Mergal, eds. *Spiritual and Anabaptist Writers*, 131, n. 9.

236 Walter L. Moore Jr., "Catholic Teacher and Anabaptist Pupil: The Relationship between John Eck and Balthasar Hubmaier," *Archive for Reformation History* 72 (1981): 95.

237 Edward J. Furcha, ed., *Selected Writings of Hans Denck* (Pittsburgh: Pickwick Press, 1975), 1.

himself numbered with the Anabaptists due to the influence of Balthasar Hubmaier, also of Ingolstadt and Regensburg. It is entirely possible that Hubmaier was responsible for Denck's conversion to Lutheranism in the first place."[238] Thor Hall connects both men with Erasmus, because of the similarity of their arguments on free will (and dissimilarity with other arguments of their time) and asserts that "a certain influence on the part of the major champion for the freedom of the will over the two Anabaptist leaders is highly probable."[239] Moore claims, though, that Hubmaier was not influenced to *change* his essential view of free will by Erasmus or Denck but drew material from them to undergird his already firmly held position learned from his Catholic mentor, nominalist theologian John Eck.[240]

The role of nominalism in regard to Hubmaier's free will doctrine comes into play primarily in his use of the theological construct which differentiates

---

238 Estep, *The Anabaptist Story*, 111. Estep states that Denck was probably baptized by Hubmaier although this has been questioned by other scholars. *The Anabaptist Story*, 112.

239 Thor Hall, "Possibilities of Erasmian Influence on Denck and Hubmaier in Their Views on the Freedom of the Will," 170. Hall notes twelve points of "affinity and agreement" between Erasmus, Denck, and Hubmaier: 1) Man's freedom stems from his creation by God; 2) Man's freedom is the basis of his responsibility to God; 3) Man has fallen, perverting his powers of will and knowledge; 4) God's revealed will must be followed, his hidden will to be left a mystery; 5) God wills all to be saved; 6) Rigid distinction between foreknowledge and predestination; 7) A point of contact in man enabling him to respond to God's grace; 8) The individual is responsible to accept God's offered grace; 9) Fallen man not able to do anything good without God's grace; 10) Responsibility for rejecting grace lies in the will of man; 11) God's relation to man is conditioned upon the response of man at any moment; 12) Moral change and obedience is expected of those who freely accept God's grace. These points do make a strong case for influence on Erasmus' part, but they are too general in some areas. Point eleven especially is problematic as it seems to point to the possibility of loss of salvation, a belief that Hubmaier repudiated. Instead Hubmaier sees the believer as one who "wholly believes that Christ has forgiven him his sins through his death and has made him righteous through his resurrection before the face of God our heavenly Father." Hubmaier, *On the Christian Baptism of Believers*, Pipkin and Yoder, 100.

240 Moore, "Catholic Teacher and Anabaptist Pupil," 95.

between two wills of God, the hidden and revealed. Windhorst writes, "The nominalistic distinction between God's absolute power, and his power regulated and bound by itself, turned out to be one of the most profound and consoling impulses of his Anabaptist theology, for by it he saw both a merciful God and the order for the congregation revealed in the New Testament."[241] Others, such as Werner Packull, have viewed this distinction in God's will in Hubmaier's theology as the employment of scholastic categories and so name him a kind of scholastic Anabaptist of the nominalist strain.[242] Walter Moore has also investigated the effect on Hubmaier of nominalist thought, the position that he learned as a student of John Eck. He concludes, concerning Hubmaier's doctrine of free will, that "Hubmaier maintained throughout his theological pilgrimage the position that he learned as a student of John Eck at Freiburg and especially at Ingolstadt."[243]

Consideration of the possible influence of fellow Anabaptist Hans Denck, who tended toward Spiritualism, concerned with the "inner light" of the Holy Spirit, calls for an examination of the influence of another medieval ideology for Hubmaier, that of Mysticism. Mysticism, closely related to Spiritualism, comes into play with Hubmaier's idea that the spirit of man remains upright even after the fall, a similar concept to the mystical idea of the spark or 'little fire' in man.[244] Hubmaier even occasionally utilized this kind of mystical terminology. In treating the disparate scholarship concerning the influences of Mysticism in Hubmaier's anthropology, Bergsten writes:

---

241 Christof Windhorst, "Balthasar Hubmaier: Professor, Preacher, Politician," 154.

242 See Packull's book, *Mysticism and the Early South German-Austrian Anabaptist Movement, 1525–1531,* Studies in Anabaptist and Mennonite History (Scottdale, PA: Herald Press, 1977). Also see George Huntston Williams discussion of Hubmaier's free will doctrine in *The Radical Reformation,* 336.

243 Moore, "Catholic Teacher and Anabaptist Pupil," 95. Nominalism's influence for Hubmaier's human free choice doctrine will be discussed further in a later section on Hubmaier's trichotomous anthropology which posited three wills, body, soul, and spirit, within man.

244 See, for instance, the introduction in Williams and Mergal, *Spiritual and Anabaptist Writers,* to the selection of Hubmaier's *On Free Will* found there.

According to Baur, Hubmaier strongly emphasized the external authority of the Scriptures, and one cannot find any trace in him of a doctrine of the inner light, characteristic of Hans Denck and his followers. Similarly Hegler, Sachsse, and Köhler have underlined the fact that Hubmaier, unlike Denck and other Anabaptists, was not influenced by the thought forms of mystical Spiritualism. Schulze admits with his teacher Köhler that Hubmaier maintained the Reformation tenet of *sola scriptura*, and yet one can find in his theology the doctrine that the human spirit, in contrast to the body and soul, was not subject to the Fall. Here, according to Schulze, is a point of contact between Hubmaier and the world of mysticism. Emil Händiges pointed this out as early as 1921. According to him, it could be taken for granted that in his teaching about free will Hubmaier had drawn heavily upon the German mystics, who had greatly influenced both his theology and that of Denck. More recently, George Hunston [sic] Williams has pointed out that Hubmaier's teaching on free will approximates that of the Spiritualists. Theobald sees a closer resemblance between the concepts of Hubmaier, Erasmus, and Denck in this regard.[245]

Alvin Beachy equates Hubmaier's trichotomous anthropology, wherein the spirit remains erect after the Fall, exclusively with medieval Mysticism, whether he employed mystical ideas consciously or not.[246]

---

245 Bergsten, *Balthasar Hubmaier*, 39.

246 See discussion, appendix H, in Beachy, *The Concept of Grace in the Radical Reformation*, 200ff. Beachy writes: "The parallels between the mystical anthropology, endowed with soteriological resources, and the anthropology of Balthasar Hubmaier have now been firmly established. The mystics and Hubmaier presupposed the existence of some region or faculty in human nature that had escaped the ruinous consequences of the fall. The relationship between these two anthropologies is so close that the attempt to deny influence of the first upon the second would be vain as well as foolish." This rather overstates the case simply because similar ideas do not necessarily involve influence. In the case of Hubmaier, no overt direct connection exists in his writings showing influence from the mystics in his anthropology. The purpose of such a strong statement, then, seems to have more to do with Beachy's thesis concerning Mysticism's influence on Anabaptism than with Hubmaier's theology.

It must be stated, however, that the similarities between Hubmaier and mysticism, though notable in regard to the idea of the spirit as that which remains of the good in man, cannot be traced to any direct Mystical derivation.[247] Hubmaier does not appeal to any Mystic writers to buttress or authenticate his arguments on free will in the human. As has been noted, Hubmaier's primary concern was to appeal to Scripture for his authority. As Gunnar Westin affirms:

> Hübmaier's understanding of the Bible as the only conclusive authority for faith and life was presented as early as the second disputation in Zürich, 1523 . . . . From this time on, Hübmaier pressed the claims of this conviction in preaching and writing in order to convince others of its logic and its primacy. . . . Expressions such as the "inner word," or "inner light," as used by the mystics, were not employed by Hübmaier.[248]

To label Hubmaier as one who was strongly influenced by Mysticism, then, seems more obfuscatory than enlightening. In contrast to some scholars' acceptance of the idea that Hubmaier had mystical leanings[249] is John Rempel's assessment of Hubmaier's theology. Rempel claims that "the strong bias of his theology was an opposition to the very idea of spirit as inwardness. Its goal

---

[247] George Huntston Williams has pointed to Johannes Tauler as an indirect source for Hubmaier in noting that one of Tauler's mystical sermons contains similar ideas. Williams, "German Mysticism in the Polarization of Ethical Behavior in Luther and the Anabaptists," *Mennonite Quarterly Review* 48 (July, 1974): 273. Alvin Beachy opts for Jean de Gerson as a primary influence, although indirect, for Hubmaier, labeling Hubmaier's anthropology "Gersonian." The similarities are interesting but not as extensive as one might imagine. Even Beachy refers to them as "remains" and "traces" of Mysticism in Hubmaier's anthropology. *The Concept of Grace in the Radical Reformation*, 201. Hubmaier does show familiarity with Gerson in that he mentions him in passing one time, but he never cites Gerson as a source for his own thought.

[248] Westin, *The Free Church Through the Ages*, 98–99.

[249] For example, Franklin Littell writes that "Hubmaier's predilection to mysticism forbade his conceding more than earthly authority to the congregation." Littell, *The Origins of Sectarian Protestantism* (New York: Macmillan, 1964), 17. Littell does not explain what he means here.

was to find an innovative way of speaking about spiritual reality as external."[250] From this perspective the primary tenor and aim of Hubmaier's theology is seen not as mystical but as practical. Gunnar Westin agrees: "The main features of his ideas are as follows: the position of prominence was given to the Scriptures, the highest authority in matters of faith; there was an insistent demand on a Christlike life (faith *and* works); great thought was given to the doctrines of the church (congregations) and the sacraments."[251]

A contrast to the importance laid upon externals as necessary indications of internal spiritual matters by Hubmaier was his contemporary, the Spiritualist Caspar Schwenckfeld (1489–1561), who called for a moratorium on the Lord's Supper until the relevant arguments could be sorted out. The Spiritualists held that the truth of God was spiritual, an inward quality, de-emphasizing outward things.[252] As Neal Blough writes, "The Spiritualists posited a dualistic framework in which the inner and outer reality must be kept apart."[253] Based on this dualism, Schwenckfeld held that because of the bickering among Christians over the meaning of the Lord's Supper (and other ceremonies) there should be a "stillstand" or suspension of the sacrament. Schwenckfeld saw these disputes as abuse of the sacrament and wrote, "we admonish men in this critical time to suspend for a time the observance of the highly venerable Sacrament."[254] Though Schwenckfeld's concern was for peace among the brethren, the Anabaptist leader Pilgram Marpeck (d. 1556)

---

250 Rempel, *The Lord's Supper in Anabaptism*, 89.

251 Westin, *The Free Church Through the Ages*, 98.

252 See Donald F. Durnbaugh, *The Believer's Church: The History and Character of Radical Protestantism*, 76. Another part of Schwenkfeld's Spiritualist theology, according to Durnbaugh, was that the true church was "the invisible church; any attempt to organize a church was futile." With this view of the church a 'standstill' of its ceremonies is clearly consistent.

253 Neal Blough, "Pilgram Marpeck, Martin Luther, and the Humanity of Christ," *Mennonite Quarterly Review* 61 (April 1987): 205.

254 From a circular letter written by Caspar Schwenckfeld, Valentine Crautwald and the preachers and pastors of Liegnitz in April 1526; quoted in Peter C. Erb, "The Life & Thought of Caspar Schwenckfeld von Ossig," *Christian History* 8 (1989): 15.

interpreted this call as from "erring spirits" and "alien preaching."[255] Marpeck wrote in *A Clear Refutation*, "I fear that these spirits lack the true knowledge of Christ; otherwise they would speak differently. They preach a different gospel than Paul, who prescribed that in the Lord's Supper believers should proclaim the Lord's death until He comes."[256]

Along with Marpeck, Hubmaier's stress on God's Word and on the outward substantiating of the truth of the gospel in baptism, the Lord's Supper, church discipline, and a holy life in discipleship, distances him significantly from the Spiritualist camp, who were influenced by medieval mysticism to a much greater degree. William Placher observes that Schwenckfeld, conversely, "did not really mind suspending the ceremony, since he cared about inner spiritual realities, not outward forms."[257] Regarding these issues, Christof Windhorst has written a fine summary of Hubmaier's life and thought:

> On March 10, 1528, Hubmaier was burned at the stake in Vienna as a rebel and heretic. His wife was drowned in the Danube three days later. The fighter for immortal truth became the best witness for the earnestness and strength of his theology and faith through his martyrdom. His teaching on baptism and the Lord's supper lived on in Anabaptism. Thus the truth that he knew could not be executed with him. It is certainly regrettable that his concept of a Christianity which suffered at the hands of the world, but which was nevertheless responsible for that world, so carefully worked out in theory and practice, found no acceptance in separatist Anabaptism. Not until recently have the Baptists thought of this outstanding theologian and practitioner as being among their Reformation fathers, a man who, as a scholar and preacher, was successful and was, in the places where he worked, able to accomplish reforms that radically changed the worn-out fabric of church and society in the sixteenth century. He was, therefore,

---

255 Pilgram Marpeck, *The Writings of Pilgram Marpeck*, ed. William Klassen and Walter Klaassen, Classics of the Radical Reformation (Scottdale: Herald Press, 1978), 51.

256 Marpeck, *Writings*, 51.

257 William C. Placher, *A History of Christian Theology: An Introduction* (Philadelphia: Westminster Press, 1983), 193.

doomed to run into decisive opposition of the guardians of the old ways . . . . The peculiar charm of his personality most likely does not lie only in the outward dramatic course of his life, but rather much more in his theology, which determined and formed his life from the inside. In many ways this theology has continuity with late medieval thought. It picked up impulses from all the various Reformation theologies. With the help of these it consistently took inherited thought further and so developed a thoroughly independent Reformation and Anabaptist theology. The result is that he cannot be assigned clearly to any camp of the Reformation period. The sum of his theology, faith, and life was the irrevocable insight that all of this had to be seen and verified in a Christianity that was active and world-changing.[258]

Thus, Hubmaier's theology resulted in an active Christianity composed of believers who covenanted together as the church to serve one another and evangelize the world. His theology aimed toward a visible believers' church whose members were committed to discipleship and holiness, not toward a contemplative inward experience. Hubmaier's theology, in this broader context, does not resemble mysticism. It is not ruminative in essence, but actively sacrificial.

The key similarity in mystics like Meister Eckhart (c.1260–1328), Johannes Tauler (c.1300–1361), and Jean Gerson (1363–1429) with Hubmaier is that they all posit a ground of contact within man and his will which is "endowed with soteriological possibilities."[259] However, as far as Hubmaier is concerned, the initiative in salvation is all from God through his Word and the Holy Spirit. But the mysticism of Eckhart, Tauler, and Gerson calls for a theology in which "the initiative in salvation belongs to human rather than to divine action."[260] This cannot be stated to be true of Hubmaier. All of the initiative is in the gospel and the word of God in Christ. Man is free to believe or to reject this good news. He is unable to initiate anything concerning sal-

---

258 Windhorst, "Balthasar Hubmaier: Professor, Preacher, Politician," 155–156.
259 Beachy, *The Concept of Grace in the Radical Reformation*, 187.
260 Beachy, *The Concept of Grace in the Radical Reformation*, 187.

vation, only to respond to God's grace. Hubmaier is forthright about this in his emphasis on the new birth in Christ:

> Now we are once born, but in original sin and wrath, as Paul laments to the Romans and Ephesians, also David, Job and Jeremiah, Rom. 7:5; Eph. 2:3; Ps. 51:7; Job 3:1. Accordingly we must be born again or we cannot see the kingdom of God, nor enter it. We must be born of water and Spirit, that is, through the Word of God, which is water to all who thirst for salvation, which Word is made alive in us through the Spirit of God, without whose working it is a killing letter, Jer. 20:14; John 3:5, 4:14, 7:48; 2 Cor. 3:6; Rom. 8:13; Ps. 51:12; Deut. 8:3; Matt. 4:4.[261]

It is clear that, for Hubmaier, it is God's initiative, through the preached Word of the gospel of Christ in concert with the Holy Spirit, by which salvation comes to man and confronts him with the choice to believe or reject God's overture.

According to Hubmaier the very gospel Word is what empowers or enables man to choose since it restores that freedom in him, providing the "power to become the sons of God." This can be contrasted with the mystical approach, for instance of Meister Eckhart. For Hubmaier, the spirit remains upright even after the Fall in his three-fold anthropology, but it is captive to the flesh and darkened by sin. Yet this spirit is what allows Hubmaier to posit free will in man since the Fall, and thus functions as a receptive element in man to receive the gospel message, to choose or reject God's Word in Christ. Hubmaier makes no stronger claim for the human spirit than this. On the other hand, Meister Eckhart wrote:

> Therefore, I say, if a man turns away from self and from created things, then–to the extent that you do this–you will attain oneness and blessedness in your soul's spark, which time and place never touched. This spark is opposed to all creatures, it wants nothing but God naked, just as he is. It is not satisfied with the Father, or the Son, or the Holy Ghost, or all three Persons so far as they preserve their several proper-

---

261 Hubmaier, *Freedom of the Will, I*, Pipkin and Yoder, 431.

ties. I declare in truth, this light would not be satisfied with the unity of the whole fertility of the divine nature. In fact I will say still more, which sounds even stranger: I declare on all truth, by the eternal and everlasting truth, that this light is not content with the simple, changeless divine being that neither gives nor takes; rather it seeks to know whence this being comes, it wants to get into its simple Ground, into the Silent Desert, into which no distinction ever peeped of Father, Son or Holy Ghost.[262]

This kind of mystical approach, in which the spirit or "spark" of the soul seeks God on its own, is not found in Hubmaier. Two key ideas for Eckhart were, first, for divine knowledge one must be detached in thought and see all reality as from within the Godhead, in other words, from the standpoint of divine subjectivity. Second, Eckhart believed that every person possesses a nonintellectual knowledge of God (divine spark, *Füncklein der Seele*) in his soul, making communion with God and participation with the divine nature possible by renouncing individuality. These ideas are not expressed anywhere in Hubmaier's writings. The context for Hubmaier is *always* a scripturally grounded focus on the gospel of Christ by which man receives grace and enters into obedient discipleship.

What, then, is one to make of all the claims as to influences and sources for Hubmaier? Certainly, like any human writer, Hubmaier was influenced by the individuals and ideas to which he was exposed. The question is whether the theories reviewed here are helpful in understanding Hubmaier. While some source analyses are only marginally useful, one of the most helpful is Bergsten's assessment of the relationship between Erasmus, Denck, and Hubmaier. He sets the affirmation of free will by these men in a useful contextual perspective: "In their defense of free will, Erasmus, Denck, and Hubmaier shared a basic common premise, i.e., their opposition to a one-sided Lutheran emphasis on divine omnipotence and the moral impotence of man."[263] Beachy writes in a similar vein:

---

262 Meister Eckhart, "The Spark and the Ground," in *Teachings of the Christian Mystics*, ed. Andrew Harvey (Boston: Shambhala, 1998), 93.
263 Bergsten, *Balthasar Hubmaier*, 357.

In Denck's thought then, there are three primary reasons why one should hold to a doctrine of the freedom of the will, as opposed to the bondage of the will: (1) such a doctrine alone safeguards the absolute and eternal goodness of God, (2) such a doctrine is the only safeguard for the personal and completely voluntary character of Christian-salvation, (3) such a doctrine alone will confront man with the responsibility of exercising the freedom in which he was created by God and prevent him from shifting the blame for his own faults from himself to God.

Balthasar Hubmaier formulated his doctrine of the freedom of the will in a very different manner from that of Hans Denck; yet the reasons he gives for rejecting the doctrine of the bondage of the will are essentially the same.[264]

This basic estimate assists greatly in understanding Hubmaier's doctrine of free will, especially since opposing the disputed Lutheran ideas associated with the doctrine of the enslaved will is the stated purpose of his writings on free will in the preface of *Freedom of the Will, I*.[265]

Hubmaier was one of the only Anabaptists willing to use Scholastic categories, especially his appeal to two facets of God's will, *voluntas absoluta* (the absolute will or hidden will) and *voluntas ordinata* (the ordained or revealed will). However, his use of this construct was not foundational for his theology of free will, but utilitarian. He used such constructs as aids to clarify and bolster what he saw as the overwhelming presence of the idea of human free will in Scripture. Accordingly, the portrait of Hubmaier as an independent thinker and Anabaptist Reformer, who was no doubt influenced by many sixteenth-century thought currents, but whose primary delimiting source was Scripture, is the preferred view for this study. Having examined

---

264 Beachy, *The Concept of Grace in the Radical Reformation*, 49–50.

265 Walter Moore insists: "In all likelihood the controversy between Erasmus and Luther provided the occasion for Hubmaier's writings of 1526/27" Moore, "Catholic Teacher and Anabaptist Pupil," 95. Hubmaier lists the Lutheran doctrinal formula he opposed in these documents as "We believe; faith saves us," and "We can do nothing good. God works in us the desire and the doing. We have no free will." *Freedom of the Will, I*, Pipkin and Yoder, 427.

a few of the various conjectures concerning the possible determinative precursors for Hubmaier's thinking, a review of his works from the perspective indicated is in order.

HUBMAIER'S DOCTRINE OF FREE WILL

Hubmaier's vexation with the notion of the bondage of the will originated with those in his region whom he perceived as using the issue as an excuse for moral permissiveness.[266] In Hubmaier's day (at the time of the writing of *Freedom of the Will*, Calvin was only 17 years old), Luther was the Reformer who most persistently touted a form of Christian determinism by his denial of human free will. Heiko Oberman explains that "for Luther, man is *not* the mule that, stupefied by ignorance, cannot decide between two haystacks—education could help that mule. No, the condition of man does not depend on the breadth of his education but on his existential condition as 'mule,' ridden either by God or the Devil, but with no choice in the matter, no freedom of decision, no opportunity for self-determination."[267] Hubmaier was aware

---

266 "In Nicholsburg, Hubmaier dedicated himself to converting a Lutheran congregation to Anabaptism, to accommodate the stream of Anabaptist refugees who were constantly arriving. In less than a year, Nicholsburg had become one of the movement's centers, with a population of some 12,000 Anabaptists." John Driver, *Radical Faith: An Alternative History of the Christian Church*, ed. Carrie Snyder (Kitchener, Ont.: Pandora Press, 1999), 189. Hubmaier was dealing with those in his city who were still under the influence of Luther's doctrines, especially the bondage of the will, which for Lutherans was inseparable from *sola fide* and *sola gratia*.

267 Heiko Oberman, *Luther: Man Between God and the Devil*, trans. Eileen Walliser-Schwarzbart (New York: Doubleday, 1992), 219. In addition, Oberman states concerning *De servo arbitrio* that, "Luther was unquestionably being provocative: 'Free will in man is the realm of Satan'; 'God Himself does evil through those who are evil.' His response to Erasmus seems to have deteriorated into contempt for man and a profanation of God. And yet, as ill structured as it is, it is not in the least a failure; it is ruthlessly direct and clear. Were these the only pages of his writings to have survived, we could deduce

of Luther's view of free will and had read some of Luther's works. He was concerned about those in his own city who were pushing this same type of determinism, which some apparently took as license for moral negligence.[268] His assault on Luther's ideas was accomplished through his polemic against those near him who were denying the freedom of the will.

Hubmaier had a pastoral interest in these matters. He did not want to see people succumb to a lazy or worldly, and ultimately despondent, sort of Christianity. As he writes in his *Apologia*:

> If we then become children of God there is no doubt that we can serve, honor, and praise our Father out of love and without being compelled by necessity. Anyone who teaches differently misleads many people into indolence and despair through such ideas; for if all things happen by necessity, why should I do much praying, fasting, and giving of alms; if God will have me, it will take place by necessity, but if he does not want me, then all my works are vain. Here one sees now very clearly what great harm and evil have grown out of this false doctrine . . . . But as Adam put the guilt on Eve, and Eve on the serpent, so we would also like to make a fig leaf apron for our malice, put the blame on God, toss our sins off of ourselves and put them on him, which is a great blasphemy, which will not help us escape divine punishment.[269]

---

from them the total scope of Luther's thinking." *Luther: Man Between God and the Devil*, 212.

268 "With his two treatises on the freedom of the human will, Hubmaier entered into one of the hotly debated contests of the Reformation era. The two primary contestants in the debate were Erasmus with his 1524 *De libero arbitrio* and Luther with his answer to Erasmus of 1525, *De servo arbitrio*. Hubmaier himself first addressed the issue in his *Christian Catechism*. Bergsten suggests that it was the pastoral concern of Hubmaier that caused him to address the issue. The denial of the freedom of the will had led to development of tensions in Nikolsburg which he felt were based ultimately on half-truths deriving from a perversion of the biblical perspective. The result was that one might conclude that since it is God who works in us the willing and the doing, there is no reason for Christians to attempt to live the disciplined Christian life." Pipkin and Yoder, *Balthasar Hubmaier*, 426.

269 Hubmaier, *Apologia*, Pipkin and Yoder, 534.

As Alvin Beachy writes, "Hubmaier attributes the low state of morals to two emphases in the Magisterial Reformation, which he says are in themselves but half-truths. . . . Hubmaier says in the preface that it is for the purpose of rooting out such tares . . . that he wrote his book on free will to show 'how and what man is in and outside of God's grace and what he can do.'"[270]

In writing on free will, Hubmaier affirms the grace of God and the impotence of sinful man, yet contends that, in order to complete the picture, one must also affirm the Christian's freedom and ability to do good. In his work, *On Fraternal Admonition*, Hubmaier lamented the sorry state of morals in the evangelical community and claimed the reason was the lack of balanced teaching:

> People had learned no more than two points, without any amelioration of life. The one point, that they could say: 'We believe. Faith saves us.' Second: 'We can do nothing good of ourselves.' Now both of these are true. But under the mantle of these half truths all kinds of iniquity, unfaithfulness, and injustice have completely taken over, and fraternal love has meanwhile become colder among many.[271]

Hubmaier is not denying the first two truths, merely pointing to the need for the proportionate truths of human freedom and responsibility. These principles tended to get short shrift during the Reformation thanks to the Augustinian soteriology of the Magisterial Reformers. This is an important point for understanding Hubmaier. He is not calling for a contradictory view on the subject of human inability regarding salvation, as in Pelagianism (of which he and other Anabaptists were accused), but for a balance.

Hubmaier never denied the Reformation axiom that men come to salvation only through God's grace by faith but believed it to be foundational. The first three theses in Hubmaier's *Eighteen Theses* are quite telling in this regard: "1. Faith alone makes us righteous before God. 2. This faith is the knowledge of God's mercy, which he has shown us by offering his only begot-

---

[270] Beachy, *The Concept of Grace in the Radical Reformation*, 50.
[271] Hubmaier, *On Fraternal Admonition*, Pipkin and Yoder, 375.

ten Son."[272] The third thesis creates the balance, which Hubmaier considered fully biblical: "3. Such faith cannot be idle, but must break forth in gratitude toward God and in all sorts of works of brotherly love toward others."[273] Hubmaier simply and essentially desires to affirm that men, in true human freedom, are called to choose Christ (faith) and then to obey Christ (works of love). He avows over and over that this obedience is not to be attempted in human strength but by *faith in Christ*. The following is a sample of this idea, which is scattered throughout Hubmaier's writings, concerning faith and the weakness of human strength: "But whatever God commands, he gives the power and strength to *those who believe* and who will it, that we may do it without compulsion, for therein is the finger of God., Exod. 8, that all things are possible to the *believer*, Mark 9:23."[274]

The point here is that the ability to do good, to obey the command, only comes through the power of God in Christ. Hubmaier states in *Freedom of the Will, I* that "as soon as Christ says to a person: 'Keep my commandments. Leave evil and do good,' from that hour on the person *in faith* receives power and strength to will and to do such. Yes, all things are now possible to the believer in the one who strengthens him, Christ Jesus."[275] This is an especially biblical idea and is the theological context for the doctrine of human free will in Hubmaier's thought. Hubmaier makes clear that those "who will it . . . without compulsion" are equated with "those who believe." The idea of faith here, for Hubmaier, is that of a choice to trust, manifested in obedience to God's Word.

The power of God's Word is a theme Hubmaier advances again and again. The power of the gospel, of the truth, is what sets the Christian free to obey:

> But out of the power of the divine sent Word, which is the power to salvation for all believers; thence is all our sufficiency, John 1:14; Rom. 1:16. For Christ did not speak as a human being or as the scribes and

---

272 Hubmaier, *Eighteen Theses Concerning the Christian Life*, Pipkin and Yoder, 32.
273 Ibid.
274 Emphasis added. Hubmaier, *Apologia*, Pipkin and Yoder, 553.
275 Emphasis added. Hubmaier, *Freedom of the Will, I*, Pipkin and Yoder, 444–445.

Pharisees, but as an authority, Matt. 7:29; John 7:14ff.; Luke 1:32. Therefore we are again often admonished in the Scripture to remember, observe, and pay attention to those things which pertain to God, Prov. 3:3; Ecclus. 3:21; Phil. 4:8.[276]

This is a significant truth which Hubmaier felt was missed by many in the Reformation period when they emphasized the Augustinian idea of irresistible grace with its deterministic connotations for theology. Hubmaier is claiming that, once the Christian receives the Word of Christ and trusts His truth, God gives him the power to live an amended life. The holy way of living for a Christian disciple is exemplified by the Lord Jesus *and* empowered by Him, the living, indwelling Christ in the born-again believer.

The amended life is a key principle in Scripture, especially respecting the idea of repentance. Hubmaier believed that this indispensable feature of Christianity was being left out, especially in the Lutheran doctrine of grace and the bondage of the will. To show Hubmaier's response to this imbalance, an extended passage, one of many like it, will be quoted. In the second part of his *Freedom of the Will, II*, Hubmaier responds to arguments from his opponents who denied free will and to the Scriptures that they cite to do so. Here Hubmaier brings other biblical passages to bear for a more complete perspective:

> Now once again my good friends cry out over the housetops against me: "Do you hear, do you hear? It is not of willing. It is also not of running." [Romans 9:16] Answer: Yes, for once you are right, if you understand it well as half-judgment. For it does not depend on the willing nor on the running of their own strength. But if God is merciful to us and has offered us mercy through his divine Word, then we can well will and run. Paul testifies to that and says: "The willing is in me," Rom. 7:18. And in another place: "Thus you have to run in order to obtain." "I did not run in vain," Phil. 2:16. "Thus I run and not with uncertainty. I fight thus, not as one who strikes the air, but I tame and castigate my body so that I do not preach to others and be guilty myself," I Cor. 9:26f. Note here once more how Paul wills, runs, fights,

---

276 Hubmaier, *Freedom of the Will, II*, Pipkin and Yoder, 483–484.

strikes, tames his body, and preaches. Dear friends, let those Scriptures stand beside yours, I beseech you, or you will finally have to.

Here, however, they introduce strange glosses and say: "Paul ran," means that God ran in Paul. Samson strangled the lion, that is, God strangled the lion in Samson. Stretch out your hand, that is, God stretches out the hand. The young man kept God's commandments from youth on, that is, God has kept the commandments of God in the young man. All of that, in short, amounts to knocking down half of the Scriptures and to darkening and confusing them in nearly all words with strange glosses. For as the tree, tree, tree in the garden brings forth fruit out of the power of the divine Word when God said: "Every tree shall bear fruit according to its kind," thus shall man, man, man, in the power of the sent Word of God also will and do good, Gen. 1:11.[277]

Again, Hubmaier does not deny the standard Augustinian view of God's grace and man's inadequacy,[278] but understands these as only one side of the truth. The other side, which offsets it, and completes the full account of truth is, of course, human free will and responsibility. Pipkin and Yoder's assessment of Hubmaier's writings on free will affirms this symmetry: "In the course of both treatises Hubmaier makes a study of an unusually large selection of biblical passages in order to prove the freedom of the human will, without at the same time denying the role of grace."[279] Thus, Hubmaier is never found denying the Augustinian concept of original sin and man's desperate need for God's grace. He actually was indebted to Augustine to a certain degree, by way of Luther, for various primary Reformation doctrines like original sin.

Hubmaier likewise affirmed the Reformation commonplaces *sola fide* and *sola gratia*. He merely buttressed them with what he saw as scriptural

---

277 Hubmaier, *Freedom of the Will, II*, Pipkin and Yoder, 482–483.

278 Hubmaier is unequivocal in his affirmation of original sin: "Original sin is not only a weakness or lack, as some write of it, but it is a damnable sin of those who are not in Christ and who walk according to the flesh, it is also the matrix and root of all sins. . . . Anyone who says that inherited sin is no sin tries to give Paul a lesson and teach him what sin is or is not; that is sacrilegious presumption." *Apologia*, Pipkin and Yoder, 540.

279 Pipkin and Yoder, *Balthasar Hubmaier*, 426.

truth concerning discipleship and holiness of life. These Christian virtues derive from the Word-given ability to *choose* the good, Christ and salvation, and then *do* the good in Christian obedience. For Hubmaier, grace is always identified with the Word of God, with Christ and his proffered salvation. Election is thus seen only through the lens of the centrality of Christ and the gospel in the New Testament. As Irvin Horst describes Hubmaier's thought, "Since grace is imparted by the Word (Christ, the Holy Spirit), the freedom it grants in no way conflicts with the sovereign will of God."[280] William Estep summarizes Hubmaier's understanding of these issues:

> Therefore, he became a severe critic of the moral laxity that marked the Lutheran reform. His own moral and ethical sensitivity led him to champion the freedom of the will, for without it he saw no basis for Christian responsibility. Neither the sovereignty of God nor the grace of God nullified for Hubmaier the necessity of an uncoerced response to the gospel. It was the Word and the Spirit that God used to bring salvation to fallen humanity. Once a person through faith had accepted Christ, life could never be the same again. He or she was born again and consequently committed to a life of obedient discipleship. This was not an isolated laissez-faire experience but involved a community of faith, the church.[281]

This new-birth conception of the grace of salvation serves as a corrective to the idea of grace which identifies it with predestination and thus primarily with election, all but consigning Christ's death and resurrection to the status of a secondary consideration.

Thus, Balthasar Hubmaier's aim was genuinely to affirm both sides of the grace and free will issue in regard to the salvation of man, stemming from his study of Scripture. William Estep reads Hubmaier as "arguing that man, although fallen with Adam, still has the capacity to believe in Christ, who alone can save. There is no other way, for this is God's revealed will, according to Scripture."[282] Hubmaier himself writes:

---

280 Horst, *The Radical Brethren*, 131.
281 Estep, *The Anabaptist Story*, 97.
282 Ibid., 95.

> It is to be noted that the Holy Scripture takes up two ... role[s]. Sometimes it puts on the role of God when it takes the completion of all things ... and gives it alone to God .... Sometimes it puts on the [human] role ... and ascribes everything to the human being as if God did nothing at all .... And all this occurs out of the rich grace and goodness of God, who ascribes to us what he does. For there the Scripture says: "The poor will take us into the eternal tabernacle," Luke 16:9. And in another place: "Blessed are the servants whom the Lord finds awake." On the other hand we should ascribe all glory and working to God and recognize ourselves as useless servants and say, "not to us, Lord, not to us, but to your name shall the glory be given, for the pains of this time are not worthy of the splendor which will be revealed in us," Luke 17:7–10; Ps. 115:1. Whoever cannot accommodate himself to the two divisions of Scripture will often stumble. May God keep him from falling. For he will judge many half-truths to be full truths, which is the biggest error in dealing with Scripture.[283]

And so, from Hubmaier's perspective, the importance of what he called a "whole judgment" can be perceived, the scriptural balance of divine grace and human free will for a complete theology.

This symmetry of grace and free will not only corrected the moral negligence Hubmaier felt was a result of unbalanced theology, but also the theological error which made God the author of sin. Hubmaier stated, "He who denies the freedom of the human will, and says it is an empty and useless title in name only and is nothing in itself, calls God a tyrant, blames him for unrighteousness, and gives evildoers much reason to persist in their sins."[284] This was a serious issue for Hubmaier. He equated the concept of the bondage of the human will with the notion that "God must be responsible for all our vices, which is the greatest blasphemy on earth."[285] Hubmaier explained further:

---

283 Insertions added. Hubmaier, *Freedom of the Will, II*, Pipkin and Yoder, 489.

284 Hubmaier, *Apologia*, Pipkin and Yoder, 534.

285 Hubmaier, *Freedom of the Will, I*, Pipkin and Yoder, 429.

If people were deprived of their free will God could never by just judgment condemn the sinner on account of his sins. For if he now were to condemn him for something that is impossible to do and to will, far be that from God. Also this would take away from Christ his legitimate charge that he will make against sinners on the judgment day saying: "I was hungry and you gave me no food, I was sick and in prison and you did not visit me," Matt. 25:42f.; then they could rightfully excuse themselves and say, "It was impossible for us to feed or visit you, we had no free will. Yea, it is on account of your eternal prescience and condemnation that we must now go with the devil into the everlasting fire to fulfill your eternal foreknowledge." From such harmful doctrine it follows that every sinner could lay the guilt upon God and say, "That I stole and robbed was not my fault but the will of God whom no one can withstand," Rom 9:19. Without his will I could not have done it. According to my will I had to do it, for it is captive and bound. Through this error also all the Scriptures would be knocked down that refer to willing and doing, which fill more than half of the Bible.[286]

Ironically, Hubmaier is here trying to achieve the same thing Luther and Calvin were set on accomplishing, to defend the doctrine of the grace of God toward man, though Hubmaier's method was diametrically opposed to the two great Reformers.[287]

---

286 Hubmaier, *Apologia*, Pipkin and Yoder, 535.

287 Henry Vedder, discussing Hubmaier's doctrine of free will, writes: "It is evident that what Hubmaier sought was escape from the paralysing [*sic*] Augustinianism of Luther; and he attempted to work out a theory that should make a reality and not an empty form of the preaching of the gospel. This he believed he had secured by making the spirit an unwilling partner in the sin of Adam, and therefore exempted in a measure from the results of sin. Hence, while the will of the body and the will of the soul are no longer free, the will of the spirit is free. It is only so that the deliverance from his sinful state is possible to man, through the hearing of the gospel . . . . The doctrine taught by Luther and his followers was that in spiritual things the unregenerate man is wholly blind, unable to work the righteousness of God, and his will has become utterly hostile to God, so that he cannot by his own powers give any assistance or co-operation towards his own salvation. He is as a man in the rapids of Niagara,

In summary, it is clear that Hubmaier desired, not to deny God's grace, but to attest to the biblical relationship between God and man by affirming real human free will, allowing man to respond to God' grace in an authentic way. The two main misjudgments he wished to combat in this attempt were the obvious lack of Christian virtue he saw around him, and what he considered to be the blasphemous error of attributing man's sin to God implied in the doctrine of the bondage of the will. He wrote, "These are the half-truths under which we, as under the form of angels, protect all license of the flesh and blame all our sin and guilt on God, as Adam did on his Eve and Eve on the snake, Gen. 3:12."[288] Hubmaier conceived an affirmation of the doctrine of human free will as the solution to these inconsistencies in Reformation theology.

Trichotomous Will in Hubmaier's Anthropology

Balthasar Hubmaier was an anthropological trichotomist. He defended free will in the human being both before and after the Fall. He posited a threefold human will: flesh, soul, and spirit. Before the Fall all three parts of man, Hubmaier calls them "substances," were good.[289] Hubmaier demonstrates from Scripture that man was created with free will. Because of Adam's sin, humankind essentially lost that freedom. "Thus," wrote Hubmaier, "the flesh has irretrievably lost its goodness and freedom through the Fall of Adam and has

---

being swept towards destruction, not only unable to do anything to help himself, but unable even to grasp the rope thrown to him by a friendly hand—nay, not even desiring to be saved, and must against his will be dragged ashore, kicking and struggling against his rescuer to the last. It was thought necessary to teach such a doctrine of the will in order to magnify the divine grace in man's salvation, and to represent man as having any power of co-operation was thought to be a minimising [sic] of God's grace and a bringing back again of the idea of salvation by works. But to Hubmaier it seemed clear that God's veracity and good faith were no less at stake in this matter than the might of his grace. For what purpose are all the invitations of the gospel, if man cannot possibly heed them? . . . Hence the importance, in his estimation, of the preaching of a 'pure, true, clean gospel,' words that flow from his pen so often as to become a sort of formula." *Balthasar Hübmaier*, 193–199.

288 Hubmaier, *Freedom of the Will, I*, Pipkin and Yoder, 429.
289 Ibid., 432.

become entirely and wholly worthless and hopeless unto death. It is not able or capable of anything other than sin, striving against God and being the enemy of his commandments."[290] Here Hubmaier sounds like a good Lutheran. But this is where the distinction between the three components of man comes into play. It is the flesh which is destined for death. The soul is sick unto death because of the flesh, and the spirit, still erect, is imprisoned in the whole mess, and so becomes distorted. The flesh is under the curse of returning to the dust of which it was made. In this way, Hubmaier affirmed original sin. Through the flesh man has lost the knowledge of good and evil, "indeed of wanting and doing the good, and had to pay for this loss with death, so as soon as a person is conceived and born, he is conceived and born in sin. From the first moment already he is up to his ears in sin and from that moment on when he receives life he begins to die and become earth again, Gen. 2:3."[291]

"The spirit of the human being, however," wrote Hubmaier, "has before, during, and after the Fall remained upright, whole, and good. For it has neither with counsel nor deed, will or action, been disobedient in any way in allowing the flesh to eat the forbidden fruit."[292] After describing the human spirit in this way, Hubmaier then described the *soul's* loss of the knowledge of good and evil:

> Adam knew well that the word of the serpent contradicted the Word of God. Nevertheless, he willed to eat of this fruit against his own conscience in order not to grieve or anger his rib and flesh, Eve. He would have preferred not to do it. Thus, since he was more obedient to his Eve than to God, he lost the knowledge of good and evil. So he cannot will or choose good, nor can he not will or flee something evil, for he does not know what is truly good or evil before God, Ps. 14:3; 32:5; 53:2. Nothing tastes good to him but that which tastes and seems good to his Eve, that is, his flesh. For he has lost the right sense of taste.[293]

---

290 Ibid., 433.

291 Ibid., 434.

292 Hubmaier, *Freedom of the Will, I*, Pipkin and Yoder, 429.

293 Ibid., 435–436. Here, obviously, Hubmaier uses Eve as a figure for the flesh.

Hubmaier claims, though, that the spirit in man ate the forbidden fruit against its will, as a prisoner of the body and so remained sound, though captive. But the soul is wounded so that it cannot choose good nor refuse evil. "There is nothing left to it but to sin and to die."[294] The soul is unable to control its "instrument," the flesh, and so finds it impossible to do any good even if the desire and effort are put forth. The spirit, though, can be saved. It is the image of God in man which is still intact.[295]

Therefore, the spirit cannot be snuffed out "for it is originally from God and his image, in which he created us originally, 2 Cor. 3:18; Gen. 1:27; which the old serpent almost blacked out and darkened through sin, Gen. 3:1ff. Nevertheless, it was not possible to extinguish entirely this breath of God in us and it still cannot be done. . . . But God can extinguish it as a punishment so that a person can have eyes, ears and heart and still not see, hear, nor understand, Matt. 13:9; Mark 4:9; Luke 8:8."[296] The punished person is one who has deliberately and stubbornly turned away from God and "sinned against the Holy Spirit . . . They turn their eyes away from God and blame him for not wanting to know them . . . close their hearts and hide themselves and yet complain that he does not knock. . . . And if he knocks, they do not want to open the door; if he seeks them, they do not want to let themselves be found. . . . Nevertheless, the time is coming when they will seek God, but will not be able to find him."[297]

So the soul is dying in the accursed body which threatens to take the whole man, including his spirit, into eternal ruin. "Nevertheless," Hubmaier proclaims, " this Fall of the soul is reparable through the Word of God, Ps. 119:7; which teaches us again what it is to will or not will good or evil, and that after this life through the resurrection of the flesh, the body will become a heavenly, imperishable, noble, and spiritual one for action and fulfillment, 1 Cor.

---

294 Ibid., 435.

295 Hubmaier backs up this concept of the spirit as upright and sound with some questionable exegesis. He claims that in 1 Thess. 5:23, when Paul says, "And may your whole spirit and soul and body be held blameless until the coming of our Lord Jesus Christ," he meant that the spirit is whole while the soul and body are not.

296 Ibid., 437–438.

297 Hubmaier, *Freedom of the Will, I*, Pipkin and Yoder, 436–437.

15:44."[298] So here with the Word of God, free will is restored to man. He sees that he can choose the good and do the good again because of Christ. If he only will acknowledge and believe in Christ it means eternal life. In Christ the soul recovers the knowledge of good and evil and thus its lost freedom to be obedient to the spirit. This is accomplished by God's grace through faith in Christ.

The spark or spirit of man is the conscience of the wounded soul which can be aroused and rekindled by the Word of God, the gospel. Christians have had the full image of God restored, although they are still in the body, which will die. The spirits of non-believers are still enslaved to the corrupted soul and dying body because of sin. The image of God in them is captive to sin and thus needs the Word of God to restore their consciences and give them the opportunity to repent. In Hubmaier's thought, the spirit of fallen man clearly still bears the image of God and is the conscience in man. Hubmaier concludes, then, "to say there is nothing good in man, that is saying too much."[299] In summary Hubmaier writes, "Both flesh and soul are damaged and seriously wounded. Only the spirit has retained its original righteousness in which it was first created."[300]

Hubmaier points out that Paul clarified his statement in Romans 7:18 that nothing good dwelt in him by singling out the flesh. Hubmaier explains: "Paul also said too much when he said, I know that nothing good dwells within me. But he hastens to explain this by adding to this concept: I know that nothing good dwells with me, that is, in my flesh, Rom. 7:18."[301] Whether or not Paul is speaking in this passage about his unregenerate self or the regenerate man he became, the point stands that he notes that his flesh, his sinful nature or carnal self, is his downfall, not his will or desire to do right. Clearly, Paul had a great, though misguided, desire to do God's will even as a Pharisee.[302] The restoration of any ability to *do* good only comes with Christ

---

298 Hubmaier, *Freedom of the Will, I*, Pipkin and Yoder, 435.
299 Hubmaier, *A Christian Catechism*, Pipkin and Yoder, 360.
300 Hubmaier, *Freedom of the Will, I*, Pipkin and Yoder, 438.
301 Hubmaier, *A Christian Catechism*, Pipkin and Yoder, 361.
302 Some commentators believe that Romans 7:14–25 refers to anyone who tries to attain righteousness through the law, whether regenerate or not. John Murray writes: "There are interpreters who take the position that Paul is not here giving a description of normal or actual Christian life but of what follows for any

through His word. This is Hubmaier's point. The desire is in the spirit of the man, but only rebirth through faith in the Word of Christ gives the man the ability to choose and perform righteousness through God's grace and power.

Wilhelm Wiswedel comments on this function of the Word of the gospel in Hubmaier's soteriology:

> In his *Christliche Lehrtafel* Hubmaier speaks of the "inner and outer drawing by God." He does not put them side by side independent of each other, but makes the one the result of the other. The "outer drawing" precedes; it takes place through the public proclamation of the written Word. From it comes the "inner drawing." Thus God has enlightened man also inwardly in his soul, "that it may understand the irresistible truth, convinced by the Spirit of God and the spoken Word, so that one must in his own conscience confess that it is true and that it cannot be otherwise." "The Word of God is water to all those who thirst for salvation and is made alive in us through the Spirit of God, without whose work it is only a dead letter."[303]

The concept here is that through the outward preached Word of the gospel of Christ, together with the inward persuasion of the Holy Spirit, a person is made aware that he can choose the righteousness offered him through Christ's death and continue in that righteousness through the power of the risen, indwelling Christ.

The image of God dwells within fallen man, however feebly, in his spirit. It is that which is able to respond and repent when faced with the gospel, the Word of Christ. Hubmaier, then, clearly equates the spirit of man with both the conscience and the image of God in man. These God-given attributes are

---

man, whether regenerate or unregenerate, who relies upon the law and his own efforts for sanctification. 'The one point of the passage is that it describes a man who is trying to be good and holy by his own efforts and is beaten back every time by the power of indwelling sin. This is the experience of any man who tries the experiment, whether he be regenerate or unregenerate.'" John Murray, *The Epistle to the Romans*, The New International Commentary on the New Testament, ed. F. F. Bruce (Grand Rapids: Eerdmans, 1990), 257, n 19.

303 Wiswedel, "The Inner and Outer Word," 53.

still operative, though captive, in the human being's spirit. Hubmaier wrote: "Likewise all the other Scriptures must be understood that indicate that there is nothing good in man, that is, in his flesh, for God's image has never yet been completely obliterated in us. How can it be evil, for (like the law) it shows and teaches us the good."[304] Thus Hubmaier explained the freedom of the will in terms of the *imago Dei* which contains the conscience and is identified with the spirit of man, before and after the Fall into sin:

> Wherefore one must ruminate these Scriptures, to make an exact distinction between human nature before the Fall, after the Fall, and after the restoration from the Fall through Christ, carefully judging each and making distinctions; thereby one also very easily acquires a true distinction between the free will and the bound will. If before the Fall God's likeness was free and unbound in us, since the Fall it is held captive and the sin of the Fall is damning. After the restoration of the Fall through Christ, this likeness is made free again, although captive in the sinful and a poisoned body; but the curse has been removed from the sin of the Fall insofar as we do not by our own wickedness make it damning again by rebelliously walking in it. Thus Paul teaches us in Romans 8:13. Here you see clearly that the image or inbreathing of God is still in us all, although captive and as a live spark covered with cold ashes is still alive and will steam if heavenly water is poured on it. It also lights up and burns if one blows on it. That is the source of the conscience in the Jews, pagans, and Christians, as Paul writes about it, Rom. 2:15. But Christ restored the quenched spark of flame on Easter Day when he breathed upon his disciples and said, Receive the Holy Spirit, John 20:22. Now Christ has ordered his servants to inbreathe and blow by proclaiming his holy Word, that the wounded soul may be reawakened from sleep.[305]

In salvation the conscience is that which makes the man aware of his sin and drives him to Christ. In a comparison with Luther's theology, Berg-

---

304 Hubmaier, *A Christian Catechism*, Pipkin and Yoder, 361.
305 Ibid., 360.

sten elaborates on Hubmaier's idea that the spirit in man is stirred by the Spirit of God, through the Word of God, to respond and choose God's offer of salvation in Christ:

> Luther is concerned with the righteousness of Christ which is imputed to man—Hubmaier with a change within man which is effected by the preaching of the Word and the work of the Holy Spirit. In Hubmaier the question of the connecting link is important for the work of Word and Spirit. The answer runs: It is to be found in the honest spirit existent in man, the "little fire," and in the ability not actually to do good but to will and to choose it. For Luther, on the contrary, the human will is only "Satan's captive beast of burden" which cannot be set free until the Devil is driven out by the finger of God.[306]

In a sense, then, the spirit of man is a point of contact for the truth of God's Word. God's Word functions to arouse and enliven the spirit so that the man will respond and choose Christ. Robert Friedmann, noting Hubmaier's trichotomous anthropology, observes, "By this tripartite distinction Hubmaier has the tool to blame the soul for its corruption but to exonerate the spirit from all blemish. . . . And this then is the connecting link by which we humans grasp divine grace and divine commandments and become restored to the full image of God."[307]

---

306 Bergsten, *Balthasar Hubmaier*, 354. Bergsten further summarizes Hubmaier's general anthropological views, writing that "man is, indeed, evil by nature and does evil deeds. But he who has been set free by Christ can both desire and do what is good." Bergsten, *Balthasar Hubmaier*, 354. Bergsten states: "According to Hubmaier, this liberation is the work of God and takes place by means of His Word. In his two writings on free will Hubmaier continually emphasizes that man is set free only through the Word sent by God, by which he means the Word that is preached. By this Word fallen man becomes reborn and made alive by the Holy Spirit." Bergsten, *Balthasar Hubmaier*, 351.

307 Friedmann, *The Theology of Anabaptism*, 59. He writes further: "Of course, he [Hubmaier] admits that 'we are poor and miserable sinners,' but through divine grace the original freedom of man has been restored, even if imperfectly. If we surrender ourselves to God in childlike obedience, then we are truly free and able to do God's will, and thus we become disciples of

It is at the point where the spirit of man engages with the Word and Spirit of God (and because of the emphasis on regenerate man's ability to accomplish good in obedience to the Word), that the issue as to works salvation in Hubmaier's soteriology arises. The question whether Hubmaier believed that works were involved in salvation due to his affirmation of human free will has been debated at length by various scholars and is at the crux of the whole Reformation issue concerning free will in man. Estep clarifies and helps dispatch the question at the same time, keying on the concept of faith:

> If one considers the act of believing in itself a meritorious act, then the answer is yes [to the question of works righteousness], but this would impose upon Hubmaier's soteriology a construction that he would not accept. The capacity to choose or reject Christ is, according to Hubmaier, inherent in man. This does not mean that it is any the less of God but it does mean man is something other than an automaton. He is a man made in the image of God with a free will, fallen though he is.[308]

If Hubmaier was influenced by his nominalist training to believe in a works salvation, comparable to that of Gabriel Biel, it does not seem to be very evident in Hubmaier's writings. A contrast with Biel may help illustrate Hubmaier's rejection of works salvation.

Occamist Gabriel Biel (*c*.1420–1495) was characteristically optimistic about human nature and its capacity to will and achieve good. According to Biel, the Fall was a catastrophic event for the human race, an event which necessitated the redeeming intervention of God in history. Still, it was an event which did not extinguish the basic goodness of creation. Confidence in the ineradicable goodness of creation is the theological footing for Biel's particularly cheery assessment of human prospects. For Biel, the resilience of creation, its resistance to damage under the repeated impact of sin, has left less for grace to repair and more for nature to do.

Christ." *The Theology of Anabaptism*, 59–60. Also see Rollin Armour's summary of Hubmaier's anthropology, as it correlates with his soteriology in *Anabaptist Baptism*, 32–33.

308 Insertion added. Estep, "The Anabaptist View of Salvation," 48.

Despite his optimism, Biel describes the human situation grimly enough. Human beings are deprived of the gracious gifts of God, particularly the gift of stabilizing grace, and wounded in their natural powers by indomitable concupiscence. Sinners not only need to be pardoned for their sins but also to be healed. They are not merely offenders; they are victims of a contagion which no human remedies can purge. That does not mean they have lost their reason or their free will, but only that both have suffered damage. They have also retained the use of conscience and *synderesis*; that is, they have a natural inclination away from evil and toward what is good. Even the infected will, apart from all supernatural assistance (excluding the assistance of the *concursus dei generalis*, the natural cooperation of God with creation), is capable of loving God supremely, at least for a flitting moment of time.

For Biel, that capacity for loving God more than one loves wife or family or goods or self has never been lost, though it has been wounded. Sinners are psychologically inhibited by their sin. It is now difficult to love God, whereas it was easy before the Fall. Sinners must summon up their inner resources, turn a deaf ear to the voice of concupiscence, and by sheer force of will do what for Adam and Eve was a spontaneous, unforced, unselfconscious act. But it still can be done. Sinners can still produce human affection for God, which is the fulfilment of the law, even though they cannot induce in themselves the love that justifies. This unconditional love of God for his own sake, is identical in the sinner with the moment of contrition. But God is not obligated to heal the effects of sin simply because people direct love toward Him. They still must be saved.

God gives grace to men and women who use the capacities which they have (reason, free will, conscience, and *synderesis*). McSorley writes, "This is the doctrine of the Ockham-Biel school that fallen man, by his natural powers of reason and free will, without the aid of any divine help other than God's general concursus, can prepare or dispose himself for justification. According to this teaching a sinner, by doing that which he is capable of doing (*facere quod in se ist*) by his own natural, fallen powers, without any special preparation of the will or illumination of the mind by the Holy Spirit, can merit the grace of justification."[309] In other words, Biel teaches that sinners can receive

---

309 McSorley, *Luther: Right or Wrong?*, 190.

grace by perfect obedience to the inner meaning of the law, which is to love God, and of which man is capable. What makes this gospel good news rather than bad is that sinners can do what they should.

Hubmaier is much less optimistic than Biel about the ability of fallen man to love God supremely and thus follow the inner commands of God, thereby winning God's grace which overcomes sin. In fact, this nominalist teaching involving a process of extreme effort to love God, and hence to gain grace as a reward, does not appear in Hubmaier's writings. Instead, it must be said that Hubmaier's focus in promoting the free will of man is on the human choice to receive the grace of God in Christ, and to produce the fruit of good works resulting from that new birth in grace. William Estep writes that "it is difficult to detect a direct dependence upon Nominalism in Hubmaier's theology. If Gabriel Biel's doctrine of justification, which is at once *sola gratia* and *solis operibus*, finds its way into Hubmaier's soteriology, it certainly does not come out as 'justification by works alone' as it apparently did for Biel. For Hubmaier's frame of reference was no longer scholasticism but the Bible."[310] For Hubmaier, grace alone, found in the gospel, is what saves. Men simply are free to receive it and then are given the power to live worthily, according to the commands of Christ, as disciples. No human merit is involved.

This approach of Hubmaier's is a far cry from the call for human effort encouraged by Biel as a necessary partner in accompanying God's grace for salvation. Biel declared: "Though the passion of Christ is the *principal* merit on account of which grace is infused, the kingdom opened, and glory granted,

---

310 Estep, "The Anabaptist View of Salvation," 49. Estep implies, further, that Hubmaier's soteriology was constructed mainly from his study of Scripture and not from his Nominalist training. He writes that, for Hubmaier, the Bible was "the most obvious source of his theology and the final court of appeals. Therefore, one is forced to ask, Are the Nominalist parallels in Hubmaier due to the persistent influence of the Catholic theology in which he was so well schooled or to the Scriptures upon which he relied so completely?" Estep seems to be saying that just because Hubmaier appears to make use of ideas that are similar to some particular Nominalist ideas he would have received in his training, it does not mean that his theology is Nominalist or Catholic, and that those ideas are not scriptural. Whereas the justification by works conclusion of Biel's Nominalism must be rejected as unbiblical.

yet it is never the *sole and complete* meritorious cause. If we do not add our merits to those of Christ, the merits of Christ will not only be insufficient, but nonexistent."[311] As opposed to this idea, in his *A Christian Catechism*, Hubmaier made it clear that no merit on man's own behalf, in his own power, was effectual for his salvation:

> *Leonhart*: But after all, the Scriptures contain many verses that clearly indicate that doing good and evil is in our power and will, as Christ says, "If thou wilt enter into life, keep the Commandments," Matt. 19:17.
>
> *Hans*: Yes, that is true. But these Scriptures do nothing more than to reveal how man was created by God in the first place, how he lost his freedom through sin, and how he is reborn through the Word sent to him. There is a vast difference between being and having been. We were, to be sure, free before sinning; but after sin we were not free until we were made truly free by the death and resurrection of Christ. One who falls and is crippled was straight before, but he is no longer straight until the physician helps him so that his lameness no longer handicaps him. Likewise, although there is still something in us of God's likeness in which we were initially made, Gen. 1:27, still this likeness has been dimmed, captured, and bound by Adam's disobedience. We are thus mired there until Christ makes us free; that is, he renders flesh, sin, death, devil, and hell harmless. Here there is need to pray earnestly and to cry without ceasing to Christ with the apostles: Lord, help us! Lord, we are perishing! Lord increase our faith! On the other hand, we find just as many Scriptures that reveal to us our human weaknesses, incapabilities, and lameness so that we—yes, in spite of our best performance of the divine commands—are unprofitable servants, and so that all our righteousness can be likened to the garments of a defiled woman, Luke 17; Isaiah 64:6. . . .

---

311 Gabriel Biel, *Prepared Epitome and Collection on the Four Books of Sentences* 3.19.1.2.5 and *Sermons on the Festivals of Christ* 2G; quoted in William C. Placher, *A History of Christian Theology: An Introduction* (Philadelphia: Westminster Press, 1983), 168.

> *Leonhart*: How does it happen then that God at many places in the Scriptures promises a reward for our works?
>
> *Hans*: That is due to his gracious kindness. He ascribes these to us as if we had done him a great favor out of ourselves and of our own [strength], whereas he, of course, has no need whatever of us and does not wish our service except for our own benefit. Then let God call it a reward, but woe to you if you should consider it a payment. Consider all God's dealing with you as pure grace. There is nothing that God's grace cannot tolerate or observe less than presumptuous merits of our own, as Paul teaches in Romans 3 and 4.[312]

It is clear, then, that Hubmaier's idea of the spirit of man as a point of contact for divine grace cannot be described as involving any ability to merit God's grace through a great effort to love Him, as in Biel, but should be seen as the bearer of the *imago dei* in man, which allows man to choose to receive or reject the gospel as it comes to him through preaching and by the Spirit of God. Interestingly, Robert Macoskey, in describing this concept in Hubmaier's thought, identifies Hubmaier as a moderate Calvinist:

> In his discussion Hubmaier stresses that Christ died for all men; that God desires the salvation of all men and that each individual sinner needs the assistance of God in making the right decision. It is the Holy Spirit who inspires and God who "exerts" himself in the soul of the believer. Hubmaier leaves it to man to provide a receptive posture for this divine activity. Today we might classify him as a moderate Calvinist.[313]

While this description sounds more mechanistic and Calvinistic than Hubmaier usually was in his writings, it does shed light on Hubmaier's view that God's grace is received and surrendered to by man because it *is* grace, a free offer, which must be accepted instead of forced or it would not *be* grace.

---

312 Hubmaier, *A Christian Catechism*, Pipkin and Yoder, 359–361.

313 Macoskey, "The Contemporary Relevance of Balthasar Hubmaier's Concept of the Church," 107.

THE CENTRALITY OF THE DOCTRINE OF HUMAN FREE WILL IN THE THEOLOGY OF BALTHASAR HUBMAIER

According to Hubmaier, authentic free choice after the Fall is God's doing since He offers to man the power to receive the good, the great alternative to sin and death (Christ), Who is accepted by faith in the word of the gospel. Man, of himself, can only do evil unless God offers the way of faith, trusting God's grace for salvation. The embodiment and fulfillment of that grace is Christ Himself and his death, burial, and resurrection. Hubmaier summarized his view of human free will, before and after the original Fall from grace, in the following passage:

> Here you see, reader, how God created the human being so free that he was at first able without new grace to remain in his inborn innocence and righteousness unto eternal life. He could also forfeit this grace through disobedience, which is what happened. As a result, through the Fall, grace and freedom have been darkened and lost to such a degree that the human being does not know any longer what is good or evil without a special and new grace of God. How can one will to do good and avoid evil if one cannot will anything good, unless one has recognized it beforehand. However, after the restoration, the human being has acquired and again received such grace, health, and freedom through the merits of our Lord Jesus Christ that one can now again will the good and do it, indeed against the nature and will of the flesh in which there is nothing good.[314]

The option to choose the good only comes through good news about Christ, it does not reside in man himself to do good *without* Christ. The choice is to receive the good and the ability to do it, which are both found in Christ, by faith. This is an important distinction and appears to encapsulate Hubmaier's thought regarding free will and unmerited grace.

On the other hand, if people have no real choice between good and evil and must only do evil from their very nature, as in a system of double predestination, how can God judge sin? Even the Fall loses some of its theological impact since it was a controlled event, much as everything else afterward, in the view of a deterministic theology such as extreme Calvinism. If a man, because of the Fall, does not actually turn away from the goodness of God by

---

314 Hubmaier, *Freedom of the Will, I*, Pipkin and Yoder, 443.

an act of will (which is sin), but was never even able to choose goodness, how can God condemn him? To put the choice before fallen man, who really has no choice, and then condemn him for doing the evil he could not help but do, would be deceptive. As Hubmaier said: "It would be a false god that would offer two ways, knowing that we would necessarily have to take the one way. But he is faithful."[315] This faithfulness, to Hubmaier, comes from God in the form of Christ and the gospel, the wonderful option opened to man by God's mercy, grace, and sacrifice.

Discipleship, for Hubmaier, is the choice to continue in the good works which are the fruit of new life in Christ. This submission to God after salvation, by following the commands of Christ, was crucial to Hubmaier's theology of baptism and church discipline. The Christian in true repentance and surrender has committed himself to a new life of good works of love, to be a true follower of Christ. Hubmaier made clear again and again that these works were not accomplished from human strength, but that obedience was still demanded of the Christian. As Abraham Friesen writes, concerning the Anabaptists in general, "discipleship—entailing obedience to all of Christ's commandments—was based on a life-transforming experience resulting from faith in the risen Christ."[316] It seems that Hubmaier was simply trying to clarify and promote the concept of sanctification via discipleship. As the apostle Paul wrote, "work out your own salvation with fear and trembling." Hubmaier took this kind of passage very seriously.

Hans-Jurgen Goertz characterizes Hubmaier's view concerning the Christian's ability to do good works as 'synergism' but is careful to note that the synergistic relationship between God and man begins only in the new birth and, as Hubmaier would contend, only through the continued grace of God. Goertz writes: "This synergism, however, did not relate to the process between fall and rebirth, but rather to the period between man's rebirth and perfection, and well accorded with many New Testament passages, as Hubmaier pointed out, especially in his second work on freedom and in his 'Account of the Faith' (1528)."[317] Hubmaier described the condition of

---

315 Hubmaier, *Apologia*, Pipkin and Yoder, 533–534.
316 Friesen, *Erasmus, the Anabaptists, and the Great Commission*, 108.
317 Goertz, *The Anabaptists*, 63.

the Christian regarding grace, freedom, and good works, as a result of new birth, as follows:

> For the gospel is the power of God unto salvation for all believers. . . . And as soon as Christ says to a man (Matt. 19:17): Keep my commandments; leave evil and do good—from that very hour the man receives through faith the power and strength to will and to do the same. Yea all things are possible to a believer, by him who strengthens him, namely, Christ Jesus (Phil 4:13). We could adduce here all Scriptures (Rom., ch.1; Heb., ch. 4; Isa, chs. 46; 55; Jer., chs. 6; 7; 23; Jonah ch. 3; Amos, ch. 8) in which the power and working of God's Word is shown. So we know of a surety that God originally made all things good, and especially man, in spirit, soul, and body. But by Adam's disobedience this goodness in us was in respect to the soul wounded; in respect to the spirit, it was impeded and obscured by the darkness of the body; and as for the flesh, it was completely ruined. If we are to be free again in respect to the spirit and healed in respect to the soul, if the fall of the flesh is to be harmless, this *must, must, must* take place through a rebirth, as Christ himself says, otherwise we shall never enter the Kingdom of God. God now of his own will begets us, as James says, by the Word of his power, that we should be anew the first fruits of his creatures. In this Word, which Peter calls incorruptible seed, we become anew free again and sound, so that absolutely nothing corruptible is left in us. Thus Christ says: The truth shall make you truly free. And David says: he sent his word and healed me; and in another place: Quicken me, O Lord, according to thy word. Now it follows indubitably that from the power of the divine Word in believers must come real freedom, real health and real life. Else we must disregard half the Bible. Far be that from us![318]

It is observable here that it is essentially a New Testament view which emerges as Hubmaier's perspective rather than a nominalist or scholastic "works salvation" theology.

---

318 Hubmaier, *On Free Will*, in *Spiritual and Anabaptist Writers*, ed. Williams and Mergal, 129–130.

Two Wills of God

God's foreknowledge (as well as providence, divine grace, and sovereign will) is a genuine theological quandary when juxtaposed with human free will. Does God's knowledge of the future eliminate the choices of free beings because they become necessary by virtue of being foreknown? Thomas Oden offers an answer:

> If it were asserted that God's knowledge of future events completely destroys the efficacy of the self-determining influences God foresees, that would constitute a fatalistic negation of human freedom. For that would be tantamount to asserting that there is only one will in the universe, the will of God, and no other wills exist. That is an extreme view, contrary to Christian teaching about creation, human freedom, self-determination, and human dignity.[319]

For many thinkers over the years, human free will and the foreknowledge or providence of God are two concepts that, theoretically, inevitably undermine one another. One concept must be ascendant, to the impingement or even elimination of the other, in order to make sense of them. They are seen as mutually exclusive to some degree. But this is a false dilemma, as Norman Geisler writes: "The Bible is a balanced Book. It affirms both God's sovereignty and man's free choice. It teaches both that God is in complete control and that humans can choose to receive or reject salvation. Unfortunately, however, there seems to be an incurable human propensity to go to one extreme or the other."[320] Many theologians have ratified only one side of the equation, consequently neglecting or canceling the other, as Luther and Calvin arguably did with human free will by insisting that God's sovereignty and foreknowledge are a sort of fatalistic force.

---

319 Thomas C. Oden, *Systematic Theology*, vol. 1, *The Living God*, 73.

320 Geisler, *Chosen But Free*, 143–144. Geisler affirms that, for him, the Bible is in proper balance concerning God's sovereignty and human freedom and "that there is no contradiction in the co-working of sovereignty and free will. We can be assured that (1) God is in control and that (2) we have been given the ability to choose." *Chosen But Free*, 144.

THE CENTRALITY OF THE DOCTRINE OF HUMAN FREE WILL IN THE THEOLOGY OF BALTHASAR HUBMAIER

The historical origin of the problem may be found in Augustine. His own opposing views of grace and free will were employed on different occasions in his writings as weapons against various heresies. This incongruity continued into the Middle Ages and was bequeathed to the Reformation era, becoming its "great debate." Ernst Winter elaborates: "Medieval thought developed a complex theology of free will. Preeminent among the theologians is *St. Augustine of Hippo* who taught the freedom of the will against the Manichaeans, but the necessity of grace against the Pelagians. This two-fold apologetic gave rise to later interpretation differences, of which the Erasmus-Luther controversy is just one example."[321] Part of Hubmaier's answer to the dilemma, from the sovereignty of God side of the equation, was to posit two facets of God's will, the hidden and the revealed. Hubmaier's basic argument is that the hidden will of God in election, foreknowledge, and predestination cannot be acted upon.[322] Humankind can only respond to the revealed will of God, which calls all men and women to choose to trust Christ.

Hubmaier explained his basic concept of God's will in its two aspects in *Freedom of the Will, II*:

> Here my dear friends cry out against me, as Job's friends did also against him: "Do you not see how everything stands with God and nothing in our power? What God wants should and must happen." Answer: That is a statement about the omnipotent and hidden will of God who owes no one anything. Therefore he can without any injustice be merciful to whomever he wills or harden the same, save, or condemn. This power or will the schools have called the omnipotent power or will of God, which no one, as Paul writes, may stand against. Yes, God has the right, power, and authority to make of us what he will, a vessel of honor or dishonor, as the potter has power over his clay and we cannot rightly say, "Why do you do that?"

---

321 Winter, *Erasmus - Luther: Discourse on Free Will*, 3.

322 Luther used a similar concept to bolster the opposite claim, that man's will is in bondage. See Heinrich Bornkamm, *Luther in Mid-Career 1521–1530*, ed. Karin Bornkamm, trans. E. Theodore Bach (Philadelphia: Fortress Press, 1983), 445–446.

> Now however, one also finds a revealed will of God according to which he wants all people to be saved and to come to the recognition of the truth. . . .
>
> . . . Paul speaks of this difference of the two wills very brightly and clearly, saying: "who has recognized the mind of the Lord? We, however, have Christ's mind," 1 Cor. 2:16. When Paul writes, "Who has recognized the mind of the Lord?" he is pointing to the hidden will of God, on the basis of which Isaiah also calls our God a hidden God, Isa. 45:15. When Paul says, "We have the mind of Christ," he points to the revealed and preached will of God, which is God himself and which has become human and we have seen his glory, a glory as of the only begotten Son of the Father, full of grace and truth, John 1:14.[323]

This view represents a plausible theological option for sorting out the sovereign will of God, on one hand, and his call to people to come and surrender to Christ for salvation, on the other. It also frames the unalterable judgement of hell in a much more comprehensible way than in the Lutheran or Calvinist systems, which emphasize double predestination. Since God has *revealed* that He wants all to be saved, only those who refuse Him are condemned. In fact, Hubmaier identifies the revealed will of God almost completely with Christ Himself. Those who are saved avail themselves of His Word of mercy toward them in Christ. Others refuse mercy and, hence, forgiveness, leading to final punishment.[324]

Thus, we find a differentiation between the ideas of a revealed and secret will of God to be a very useful construct for Hubmaier and consistent with his soteriology, which stresses both the grace of God and the free will

---

323 Hubmaier, *Freedom of the Will*, II, 472–474.

324 Hubmaier wrote concerning those who reject God's grace: "For it is fair and just that all those be abandoned by God who first already have left God. 'We have healed Babylon but it did not become whole; we will leave it,' Jer. 51:9. Thus Christ also says to Jerusalem: 'How often I wanted to gather you and you did not want it,' Matt. 23:37. Thus Paul says to the Jews: 'The Word of God had first to be preached to you, but since you reject it, we now turn to the heathen,' Acts 13:46." Hubmaier, *Freedom of the Will*, II, Pipkin and Yoder, 476–477.

of man. It also squarely places the responsibility for sin, and thus for reprobation, on the sinner. There is no confusion here about the origin of sin and the complete justice of God in punishing it. There is also an absence of a bullying tone toward anyone who may question how man can be responsible if God wills everything, as in Calvin or Luther—who also used the two-wills interpretation. Though he insisted that the revealed will of God's mercy in Christ—the gospel—must be the one which is preached, Luther still stressed the hidden will, which he identified with double predestination, even going so far as to lay the blame for evil at God's door.[325] Roger Olson elaborates on Luther's thinking concerning predestination and his use of the hidden and revealed wills of God:

> Luther related his doctrine of double predestination—that God foreordains some angels and humans to heaven and some to hell—to God's hiddenness. Such a terrible idea seems contrary to the gospel, yet it cannot be escaped, so Luther believed. As both hidden and revealed,

---

[325] Roger Olson explains Luther's use of the hidden and revealed wills of God which is similar in some aspects to Hubmaier, and diametrically opposed in others: "In the gospel God is all compassion and perfect goodness without any hint of arbitrariness or capriciousness. This is God 'for us.' This is the only side or aspect of God we are supposed to concern ourselves with. God revealed through the gospel opposes sin and evil and seeks to overcome them by defeating sin, death and Satan through the cross. God for us in the gospel is our only business in proclamation. According to Luther we should focus on this God, who is very much like the waiting father in Jesus' parable of the prodigal son. On the other hand, paradoxically, Luther wished to warn us that this is not all there is to God. Behind the waiting Father of loving face and outstretched arms lies the hidden, dark, mysterious God of all-determining power who is the very cause of every evil thing as well as every good thing in nature and history. Even though this dark divine force has little to do with the gospel message, Luther pointed to it as a necessary background to all of history. Nothing whatever can exist or happen apart from God's direct plan and causation. Here Luther's monergism goes beyond even Augustine's. For Luther the devil was both God's enemy and God's instrument, 'The devil is "God's devil."' God works all in all and even in and through Satan and the godless. 'We should know then that in everything bad that happens to us it is God himself who is at work through instruments.'" Olson, *The Story of Christian Theology*, 388.

God has two wills that seem completely in conflict to finite human minds. On the one hand, God wills the salvation of all. On the other hand, God wills to work evil (although it is not evil for him to do it!) and create Satan, cause his fall and use him as an instrument. Without any attempt to smooth out the apparent contradictions in this doctrine, Luther simply spoke of God's hiddenness and urged Christians to acknowledge it while keeping their focus on God's self-revelation in Christ.[326]

Because he rejected human free will, the resultant deterministic view of God required Luther to attribute all things, including evil and Satan, to God as His instruments. This attribution of evil to God was what Hubmaier could not tolerate. How could a righteous, holy, good God be responsible for evil? The answer from the magisterial reformers was generally that we dare not ask this impudent question and risk offending God's sovereignty. But instead of neglecting to ask the question, Hubmaier holds that God's offer of salvation is His revealed will and must be accepted or rejected according to man's volition, thus making man responsible for sin and evil and not God. The secret will, because of its high, ultimate, and mysterious nature, cannot be comprehended, only conceded and respected, and for Hubmaier it is not identified with double predestination but with the completely free, omniscient, and omnipotent nature of God.

In his conception of the hidden will of God, Hubmaier "touches the article of divine foreknowledge, in which the divine majesty gives us to recognize that God knows all things before they happen."[327] He elaborates further on this 'article of foreknowledge' as it relates to God's revealed will in the incarnate Christ:

> For Paul teaches us four points in the Epistle to the Romans, Rom. 9; 10; 11: The omnipotence of God in Pharaoh, his divine foreknowledge of all things in Esau and Jacob, his full power of the will with the clay and the potter, his mercy to the heathen . . . . The first three things are

---

326 Olson, *The Story of Christian Theology*, 388.
327 Hubmaier, *Freedom of the Will, II*, Pipkin and Yoder, 478.

inconceivable to us. The fourth, God has revealed to us through the incarnation of his only begotten Son, Jesus Christ, our Lord.[328]

The notion of the hidden and revealed wills of God is surely a reasonable option for a soteriological interpretation which wishes to affirm two essential and biblical ideas: divine grace and providence together with human free will and responsibility. God's will *is* that man have free will. He calls on man to respond to His revealed will, his mercy offered in Christ, as an acknowledgment of his hidden and mysterious sovereign nature as Holy Judge of all things.

The hidden will is the mysterious side of God's plan that man cannot fathom, and hence should not be investigated. Hubmaier claims that the mistake made by those denying free will is that they have built their soteriology partly on the hidden will of God, which is, by definition, inscrutable to the human being. Hubmaier writes, "Now we will let the secret will of God, which is unnecessary for us to explore, remain in its dignity, Rom. 11:4ff."[329] This appears to be the problem with Luther's use of the two wills. Even though he calls for the focus to be on God's revealed will in Christ, the fact that evil and judgment depend on God, and not on man's free choice, inevitably draws our attention back to God's immutable hidden will in the 'eternal decrees' of double predestination, and thus to the confusion and inconsistency which results when it is contrasted with God's mercy in His revelation in Christ. Thus, for Luther, the use of the two wills construct would seem to confirm the contradiction inherent in his theology instead of alleviating it.

Hubmaier, however, affirms human free will so that individual judgment and pervasive human evil are contingent on the choices of man. He contends: "The Scripture would be clear, simple, and understandable in itself if only our fleshly hairsplitting would not seek more out of it than its simple sense could bear. Without doubt God knew from eternity that Esau and other people would sin. He did not, however, order them to sin."[330] God's hidden

---

328 Hubmaier, *Freedom of the Will*, II, Pipkin and Yoder, 478–479.

329 Ibid., 475.

330 Ibid., 479. It is important also to note here that Hubmaier is clearly differentiating between foreknowledge and foreordination, the conflation of which should be considered yet another mistake in the magisterial reformers' theology, and in subsequent Protestant theology.

foreknowledge and omniscience then has more to do with the fact that He knows the future and controls history rather than being associated with an arbitrary decree for mankind either to salvation or perdition. Henry Vedder described Hubmaier's view in this way: "The benevolent will of God is the will of his mercy—he wills all men to be saved; the permissive will is that those who will not hear Christ he leaves to the consequences of their refusal.... It is blasphemous to maintain that men sin and are lost in fulfilment of a divine decree, and not of their choice."[331]

In the third part of *Freedom of the Will, II*, Hubmaier responds to his opponents, whom, he says, come to him daily with "many Scriptures by which they hope to eradicate completely the freedom of the will of the human being."[332] In his answer to these opponents he differentiated between the hidden and revealed wills of God. He cautioned that neglecting to make this distinction as they interpreted Scripture resulted in a fundamental error:

> The Scripture that says no one may resist his will does not refer to the revealed will of God, but it refers to the hidden will. Where one now confuses and mixes the two wills with one another there soon follows out of that a notable misunderstanding, error, and confusion of Scriptures. Therefore one should wisely divide the judgments in the Scriptures and ruminate truly on them in order to know which Scriptures point to the secret will of God or to the preached.... From that now comes the division wherein one speaks of the hidden and revealed will of God. Not that there are two wills in God, but thus the Scripture serves us and accommodates itself to speak according to our human ignorance so that we know that although God is almighty and can do all things omnipotently, nevertheless, he wills not to act toward us poor people according to his omnipotence, but according to his mercy, as he has sufficiently testified the same to us through his most beloved Son and through all those who point to him in the Old and New Testaments.[333]

---

331 Vedder, *Balthasar Hübmaier*, 186.
332 Hubmaier, *Freedom of the Will, II*, Pipkin and Yoder, 471.
333 Ibid., 472–473.

Here, again, we see Hubmaier's identification of the revealed will with God's mercy in Christ. He denies that this construct of two wills of God is a kind of unbending doctrinal law. Instead, it assists us in understanding the unity of God's nature as omnipotent and loving at the same time. Although God is sovereign in all his ways, He has chosen to reveal his intentions of grace and mercy and restoration toward mankind in Christ.

Summary of Hubmaier's Doctrine of Human Free Will

Hubmaier wished to counteract the one-sided doctrine of the bondage of the will by promoting the doctrine of human free will. He did so because of what he saw as two egregious errors: moral laxness in the church and the attribution of sin to the just God. He employed a tripartite anthropology to emphasize that the spirit of man is still intact, as God's image in man, and as man's conscience, and able to receive the good news of the great alternative in Christ, who restores man's true freedom and health when the individual chooses Him in faith. He utilized a construct which acknowledged the necessity to interpret the Scriptures according to a hidden, absolute will of God, which is unknowable, and the revealed will of God in Christ, to which man is able to respond. In this way God's foreknowledge and sovereign will (including predestination and election) are balanced with the clear and simple call of Christ to come to Him for salvation. Hubmaier writes, "Therefore he turns himself to all people with the offer of his grace and mercy, not saving even his only begotten Son, but giving him for us all into death so that we are not lost, but receive eternal life, Rom. 8:32; John 3:16. God bears this salvation toward us and offers it to us joyfully . . . and draws all people so that they be saved. Nevertheless, the choice lies with them for God wants them, unpressed, unforced, and without coercion."[334]

For this clear expression of the symmetry between human free will and divine grace, Roger Olson assigns Hubmaier preeminent status as a trailblazer and champion of free will in the history of Christian theology. He regards Hubmaier not only as "the first Anabaptist theologian," but also as "the first Protestant thinker openly to espouse belief in free will on the basis of a

---

334 Hubmaier, *Freedom of the Will*, II, Pipkin and Yoder, 475.

work of God in Christ and through the Holy Spirit."[335] Olson notes that, for Hubmaier, free will "is restored by Christ and by the Spirit of God working through the Word of God. Only because they have free will are people rightly held responsible by God and by the church for their decisions and actions. But whatever they do, they cannot boast because any right decision they make or good action they take is enabled only by grace and is not a product of some innate goodness of nature or character."[336]

---

335 Olson, *The Story of Christian Theology*, 422.
336 Ibid., 422.

Chapter Three

Analysis of the Doctrine of Free Will in Respect to Hubmaier's Broader Theology

The purpose of this chapter will be to show how the doctrine of human free will was of paramount importance to Balthasar Hubmaier's theology as a whole. This one doctrine supported a significant portion of the weight of Hubmaier's total theology. This can be seen especially in the doctrines which received his most intense focus. Hubmaier was not a systematic theologian. His theology flowed from a desire to respond to the challenges to scriptural faith and practice he perceived in his time. This makes the claim of the centrality of free will in Hubmaier's thought even stronger in that the very doctrines where it is clearly vital are the concerns about which Hubmaier wrote and spoke the most, and with the most vigor.

The theological doctrines which formed the core of Hubmaier's full theology, and in which free will is distinctly integral, were his views of soteriology, anthropology, faith, good works (discipleship), ecclesiology, baptism, and religious freedom. These are the areas of concentration in Hubmaier's theology which will be examined in the following analysis, showing free will to be central in each. They will be discussed under several headings: the first is a treatment of the Reformation doctrine of justification in Hubmaier's theology. Second will be a comparison of Luther and Hubmaier and their concepts of faith and works. This is the largest portion of the chapter since it deals with the crucial question of soteriology in relation to free will. Next will be an examination of Hubmaier's views on election and free will. The fourth section will cover Hubmaier's ecclesiology, featuring prominently his doctrine of baptism with its implications for the Anabaptist concept of discipleship. Finally, an investigation will be undertaken respecting Hubmaier's stance on religious liberty and its connection with human free will.

HUBMAIER, LUTHER, AND JUSTIFICATION

Balthasar Hubmaier persuasively accentuated man's free will in his theology, and endeavored to defend it, especially in contrast with the Reformation idea of the bondage of the will, in particular as found in Luther. This does not mean he rejected the doctrine of justification by faith. Hans-Jürgen Goertz states: "Hubmaier was in no doubt that forgiveness of sin was promised and granted solely by the Gospel, which was plainly identified with Christ. He was the 'healer and pardoner of sins'; he 'must speak for us, for our souls to be healed'. The crucial point was faith in, and preaching of, the forgiveness of sin, or, in Lutheran terms, justification."[337] Christof Windhorst describes Hubmaier's *Eighteen Theses* in this way: "They contained a clear reformation program: only personal faith as the acknowledgment of God's mercy makes a man just before God and this expresses itself necessarily in 'every work of brotherly love.'"[338]

In the very first article of his *Achtzehn Schlußreden* (Eighteen Theses) Hubmaier writes: "*Der eynig glaub macht vns frumm vor Gott*" (Only faith makes us good before God). Pipkin and Yoder translate this first thesis as: "Faith alone makes us righteous before God."[339] Vedder translates: "Faith alone makes us just before God."[340] Estep renders this first article as: "Faith alone makes us holy [*frumm = Fromm*] before God."[341] He writes, "In the first article there is the familiar *sola fide* ring, but instead of using Luther's term

---

337 Goertz, *The Anabaptists*, 75.

338 Windhorst, "Balthasar Hubmaier: Professor, Preacher, Politician," 147.

339 Hubmaier, *Eighteen Theses Concerning the Christian Life*, Pipkin and Yoder, 32.

340 Quoted in Vedder, *Balthasar Hübmaier*, 69.

341 Hubmaier, *Eighteen Theses*, in *Anabaptist Beginnings*, ed. Estep, 24.

for justification *(Gerechtigkeit)*, Hubmaier employs the word translated 'holy' *(frumm=Fromm)*. By making the change in the familiar evangelical formula, Hubmaier is doubtless attempting to say that saving faith brings about more than a declared righteousness—it produces a new quality of holiness in life."[342]

The fact that it is the first article of the *Eighteen Theses* may be taken to mean that Hubmaier viewed justification by faith as foundational. Yet Hubmaier's soteriology is also balanced (biblically he believed) by the characteristic Anabaptist emphasis on the doctrine of the new birth. Estep summarizes Hubmaier's soteriology accordingly:

> The new birth *(Wiedergeburt)* is a divine necessity if one is to see God. Repeatedly, he declares that it is God's will that all might be saved, but whether or not a person is saved depends upon that person's acceptance of the grace of God offered in Christ. This grace is not of man but of God. When it is accepted by faith in Jesus Christ, one is saved, redeemed, and born again. Henceforth the christian's life, although not sinless, is characterized by obedient discipleship that finds its highest expression in love of God and neighbor.[343]

Hubmaier's emphasis on the new birth reflects his Anabaptist theology, which sees human free will as being foundational in the decision to receive salvation and in the commitment to live a sanctified Christian life, all of which is enabled by the grace of God who gives the power. Cornelius Dyck sees Hubmaier's doctrine of justification, as with most Anabaptists, as an element in what was considered to be a broader theological category, that of regeneration, which requires a choice be made by the believer:

> Regeneration is an inclusive term describing repentance, conversion, and the continuing process whereby the grace of God works an actual transformation in the very nature of the believer. Forensic grace, the declaration of divine justification of the sinner *without the sinner's response in declared obedience*, declared Hubmaier, makes carnal Chris-

---

342 Estep, *The Anabaptist Story*, 197.
343 Ibid., 95.

tians instead of cross-bearing Christians. Humankind is not simply pronounced righteous, but grows in righteousness under the tutelage of the Holy Spirit.[344]

Henry Vedder surmised that Hubmaier may have deliberately omitted using the Reformation term *justification* in order to differentiate himself from the requisite Augustinian underpinnings of the great Lutheran doctrine.[345] However, Arnold Snyder explains that the Anabaptists understood and accepted Luther's elemental doctrine of justification by faith but sought to include the biblical truth that the Christian is made new and manifests this new life in his conduct:

> Although Anabaptists always maintained that we are saved by faith through grace, the similarity to mainline Protestantism teaching was in this first step alone. For Hubmaier as for other Anabaptists, the proper understanding of the faith that leads to salvation was a faith that bore visible fruit in repentance, conversion, regeneration, obedience, and a new life dedicated to the love of God and the neighbor, by the power of the Holy Spirit (i.e. discipleship). Righteousness was not simply imputed to the sinner for Christ's sake, as Luther had maintained; rather being saved meant *becoming righteous* by the power of the risen Christ.[346]

---

344 Emphasis added. Cornelius J. Dyck, "The Anabaptist Understanding of the Good News," in *Anabaptism and Mission*, ed. Wilbert R. Shenk (Scottdale: Herald Press, 1984), 29.

345 Vedder stated: "This omission cannot be explained like many others; the importance that these doctrines assumed in the Reformation period, and the amount of attention given them by all writers, preclude any explanation, on grounds of lack of necessity, inadvertence, and the like, for their absence from the carefully elaborated and deliberately printed words of any man of the time. The omission must be deliberate, calculated, wilful [sic]. An omission of such character can be accounted for only on one ground, that Hubmaier was anxious to mark clearly his divergence from Luther in some matters that the latter reckoned cardinal in the Protestant theology." *Balthasar Hübmaier*, 201.

346 Arnold Snyder, "Beyond Polygenesis: Recovering the Unity and Diversity of Anabaptist Theology," in *Essays in Anabaptist Theology*, ed. H. Wayne Pipkin (Elkhart, Ind.:Institute of Mennonite Studies, 1994) 14.

Estep agrees: "The treatment of the Reformation concept of justification by faith by the sixteenth-century Anabaptists was distinctive. There is no repudiation of the Lutheran doctrine of justification by faith, but rather a new interpretation which attempted to read into the term more biblical and ethical content than they felt Luther ever gave it, without resorting to a soteriology based on a works righteousness."[347]

Eddie Mabry also believes that Hubmaier made use of a separate German word to indicate a difference in his own idea of justification. Instead of an attempt to disassociate himself from Luther, as Vedder postulated, Mabry suggests that "Hubmaier, rather, wishes to set forth a completely different understanding of the doctrine of justification. Therefore, in his debate with Johann Eck in 1525 . . . Hubmaier uses the root *"fromm,"* instead of the word *Rechtfertigung.*"[348] The idea here is that Hubmaier's doctrine of justification represents an attempt to connect the new birth with the concept of being pronounced righteous. Of course, Luther would not deny the new birth, but his concentration was primarily on forensic righteousness accomplished by Christ. As a corollary of imputed righteousness, Hubmaier, along with his Anabaptist colleagues, desired to emphasize that the new believer is actually being made righteous and is thus capable of living righteously as a born-again follower of Christ.

Moreover, Hubmaier believed in original sin, but not within a deterministic system, as with Luther and Calvin, who apparently claimed that those born in sin, and not of the elect, were from that moment doomed for all time by the will of God. Hubmaier believed that man is prone to sin, but he also believed that each individual sins of his own will and is consequently personally accountable, precluding any necessitarianism in regard to sin. Hubmaier writes, "Through this denial of the free will manifold cause is given to the malevolent to lay all their sins and evil deeds on God, saying, 'That I practice harlotry and adultery is the will of God. What God wills must take place. Yes, who can counter his will? Were it not his will, then I would not sin. If it is his will, then I will stop sinning.'"[349] Since his emphasis on original sin

---

347 Estep, *The Anabaptist Story*, 199.

348 Eddie Mabry, *Balthasar Hubmaier's Understanding of Faith* (Lanham: University Press of America, 1998), 44.

349 Hubmaier, *Freedom of the Will, I*, Pipkin and Yoder, 447.

functioned within a framework of free will in man, Hubmaier viewed every person as having the responsibility to turn away from his own sin and seek salvation in Christ.

Along this line, Robert Friedmann cites Hubmaier as an example of the common Anabaptist thinking regarding original sin:

> Of course, as careful Bible readers the Anabaptists knew very well Paul's thesis that all mankind has inherited from its first parents some corruption, some evil tendencies, and an inclination toward disobedience to God, in short "sin." But this inheritance must under no condition be taken as an inescapable fate which cannot be mended. Hubmaier's booklet *Concerning Free Will* (1527) refers expressly to a passage by the prophet Ezekiel (18:4, and 20) that "the soul that sins shall die" (i.e., the soul may either sin or not sin), and he quotes Ezekiel's dictum that "the son shall not bear the iniquities of the father nor shall the father bear the iniquities of the son." This reference to Ezekiel is particularly significant for Anabaptist thought because it removes the fatalistic character of "inherited" sin which became so oppressive in Protestant orthodoxy and so hopeless as to life's possibilities.[350]

Because of his affirmation of free will Hubmaier saw sin as personal and individual. Thus, ultimately, free will for the human has to do with eternity. On a man's answer to the eternal, good God, yes or no, everything else hinges.

With Luther, however, everything in the end appears to depend on God's decrees of deliverance and destruction. As Alister McGrath writes, "Luther explicitly teaches a doctrine of double predestination."[351] Harry McSorley states that his "main objection" to *De Servo Arbitrio* is "that Luther leaves no place for a decision of faith or even for a decision to sin by man."[352] In a sense, then, a deterministic system unintentionally belittles sin (and the individual's

---

350 Robert Friedmann, "The Doctrine of Original Sin as Held by the Anabaptists of the Sixteenth Century," *Mennonite Quarterly Review* 35 (July 1969): 208.

351 McGrath, *Iustitia Dei*, 203.

352 McSorley, *Luther: Right or Wrong?*, 340.

Analysis of the Doctrine of Free Will in Respect to Hubmaier's Broader Theology

responsibility for it), and anything that belittles sin is in danger of belittling the cross. Without free will, the satanic, rebellious, arrogant, darkness of refusing the God of life and love loses its impact, since in the deterministic concept of the unfree will everyone is already predestined one way or another, to salvation or reprobation. If a decisive and ultimate rejection of God—the insistence that even when God is seen for what He truly is, Creator of life and joy and all that is good, the willful soul must still have its own way and exalt itself in its meaninglessness without God (a blaspheming of the Holy Spirit) even when that meaninglessness is clearly known—if this is not what leads to hell, then hell and sin, and the suffering and death of the Son of God on the cross, are all depreciated.[353]

Hubmaier, in asserting human free will, on the other hand, is able to affirm universal atonement achieved in Christ's sacrifice, which can be accepted or rejected. This more biblically attuned theology preserves both the sovereignty and power of God together with His love and mercy:

---

[353] McSorley makes a comparable criticism of Luther's *Bondage of the Will*, in this case concerning the Christian struggle against evil and Satan: "According to Scripture the Christian—not only Christ—struggles against Satan. Thus we find admonitions to resist Satan such as Eph. 6:11 and James 4:7. How can Luther explain such a struggle and such warnings if man's will plays no part in deciding for or against Satan? How can Luther explain the original sin of Satan? According to *DSA* God simply finds Satan's will evil: 'Thus not creating [but] finding the will of Satan evil. . . .' Elsewhere Luther says Satan's sin came from his turning away from God and from his rebellion against God. But he doesn't say that this was a *free* turning away. Did Satan originally have a free will concerning good and evil? If so, does not Luther have to revise his assertion that all things are necessitated as a result of God's foreknowledge? Was God the 'rider' of Satan's will before Satan turned away from him? If so, how could Satan change the direction of his will? Was it God who changed the direction of his willing from good to evil? The questions we have just raised lead us to another criticism of Luther's necessitarian argument for the unfree will. This concept of unfree will makes it impossible for Luther to give a satisfactory explanation of man's responsibility for sin. . . . In contrast to the conviction that there is no responsibility for sin without cooperation of man's free will, Luther developed a concept of responsibility without freedom." *Luther: Right or Wrong?*, 340.

Christ clearly . . . said, "God so loved the world so that he gave his only begotten Son, that whoever believes in him would not be lost but have eternal life," John 3:16. He suffered for our sin and not only for our sin but for the sin of the whole world, 1 John 2:2. He gave himself for redemption of all people, 1Tim. 2:6. He is also the true light that illumines all people who come into this world, John 1:9. And all those who accept him he gave power to become children of God, after that he also commanded them to preach the gospel to all creatures, so that all those who accept it, believe, and are baptized will be saved, Mark 16:15; John 1:12. From this it is easy to conclude that according to his preached and revealed will God does not want to harden, darken, or damn anyone except those who want to be hardened, blinded, and damned out of their own evil and freedom of will. These are exactly the people who, when Christ comes to his own, do not want to accept him, nor recognize the time of their visitation, nor let him in when he knocks, John 1:11; Luke 19:44.[354]

For the Anabaptists, the vital doctrine of justification is plainly interwoven with the free offer of atonement and forgiveness in the simple biblical gospel, as expressed by Hubmaier in *On the Christian Baptism of Believers*:

> The preaching of the apostles was: as God promised to send the world his Word because of sin, as the prophets and Moses proclaimed this promise everywhere, God has now done that and the Word has become flesh, Jesus Christ, our Savior. He died on account of our sin and rose again for the sake of our justification [*frommachung*], so that all who believe in him should not be lost but have eternal life, Acts 2:38; 10:34f.; John 1:14; Rom. 4:25. Thus David says: "God sent his Word and made us whole" [Ps. 107:20]. Christ also says himself: "I have come into this world not to condemn it but that it may be preserved" [John 3:17]. We have hanged Christ on the tree and have crucified him.
> Dear friends, this is not only said to the actual executioners of Christ but to all of us because we are all guilty of his death, Isa. 53:4f. Truly

---

354 Hubmaier, *Freedom of the Will, II*, Pipkin and Yoder, 472.

Analysis of the Doctrine of Free Will in Respect to Hubmaier's Broader Theology

he had suffered our sickness and borne our pains; yet we considered him as a leprous person and an outcast from God. He was wounded on account of our iniquities and crushed because of our vices. Of this Christ himself laments through the prophet Isaiah and says: "But it was you who burdened me with your sins and wearied me with your iniquities. I am the one, I am the one who blots out the sin for my own sake (for it is promised to you), and I will remember your sins never again," Isa. 43:24ff.

From these and similar discourses which the holy apostles and those sent by Christ included everywhere in their sermons, the people were moved to the recognition of their sin. And by that they also heard how Christ had suffered for them, that he paid for them and gave satisfaction for them on the cross. That again gives joy to people, enlivens the sinner, and brings him on the right path, so that he places his faith, hope, and love in God and trusts him for all good, through Jesus Christ, our Lord. Precisely for that reason, and that is the ultimate one, Christ sent out his disciples as God his father had sent him: that as he, Christ himself, said on earth to the believers, "Take heart, rise, go forth, your sins are forgiven you." Likewise his disciples should now represent him henceforth during the time of his bodily absence and guarantee to all believers a sure and certain remission of their sin through him, Jesus Christ, Rom 5:1. Through this the believers came to rest and peace in their consciences, because they knew that through the suffering of Christ they had acquired a graceful and merciful God in heaven, to whom they were permitted to cry: "Father, Father, Rom. 8:15, our Father who is in heaven," Matt 6:9. Whoever wants, let him read all the beautiful sermons of Peter, Paul, Stephen, and others in Acts of the Apostles, together with the presentation of the Scriptures from the Old Testament. He will find it to be so.[355]

This is a clear statement of a substitutionary view of atonement, seen as justifying those who receive Christ's work and Lordship by faith. It is, therefore,

---

355 First insertion added. Hubmaier, *On the Christian Baptism of Believers*, Pipkin and Yoder, 115–116.

no doubt the foundation of all Hubmaier's theology which he plainly regarded as the true teaching given by the Apostles through Scripture. Notice the firm confidence here expressed by Hubmaier that those who preach the gospel are able to declare a '*guarantee* to all *believers*' of 'a sure and certain remission of their sins through him, *Jesus Christ*.'

Hubmaier, Luther, and Faith versus Works

A comparison of the soteriology of Luther and Hubmaier reveals that the key difference is in their respective viewpoints on human free will. Luther wants basically to champion faith over against works while Hubmaier wants to clarify that personal faith will result in Christian works, without denying Luther's essential thrust, justification by faith. Several issues come into play. Because of their differing views regarding free will, Luther and Hubmaier have two distinct views of the nature of faith. This is crucial to their particular theologies with respect to God's grace, as seen on one hand, for Luther, as a mysterious force imbued arbitrarily by God, and on the other, for Hubmaier, as a free offer given by God, to be accepted or rejected. Also, each understands the nature of the integration of Christian obedience with faith quite differently. Hubmaier stresses discipleship while Luther sees the Christian as righteous and sinner at the same time.

The Concept of Faith in Hubmaier and Luther as it Pertains to Free Will

In his overall conception of faith Hubmaier includes free will, a genuine choice left to man. Free will is operative in initial believing faith and in ongoing Christian faith so that human responsibility remains intact. Luther's idea of faith, theoretically, is much more passive. Faith is basically being still and letting God's grace work, initially and in the ongoing life of the believer. Luther, like Hubmaier, distinguishes two ways in which God draws the individual to Himself, the outward and inward. The outward is the gospel message,

Analysis of the Doctrine of Free Will in Respect to Hubmaier's Broader Theology

which although essential is not determinative for Luther. The inward is the drawing of the Holy Spirit within the soul, which is the decisive and mysterious work of God unavailable to the 'ungodly.' Luther argued against human choice playing any genuine role in faith:

> Now take the saying of Christ in John 6[:44]: "No one comes to me unless my Father draws him." What does this leave to free choice? For he says that everyone needs to hear and learn from the Father himself, and that all must be taught by God. He plainly teaches here, not only that the works and efforts of free choice are fruitless, but that even the message of the gospel itself (which is what this passage is about) is heard in vain unless the Father himself speaks, teaches, and draws inwardly. "No one can come," he says, "no one;" and thus that power by which a man is able to make some endeavor toward Christ, or in other words, toward the things that pertain to salvation, is asserted to be no power at all. . . . For God holds out not only one of his good things, but all of them, and even Christ his Son himself, yet not a man follows unless the Father inwardly does something else and draws in some other way; instead, the whole world persecutes the Son whom he holds out to it. . . . But the ungodly does not come even when he hears the Word, unless the Father draws and teaches him inwardly, which He does by pouring out the Spirit. There is then another "drawing" than the one that takes place outwardly; for then Christ is set forth by the light of the Spirit, so that a man is rapt away to Christ with the sweetest rapture, and rather yields passively to God's speaking, teaching, and drawing than seeks and runs himself.[356]

One of the ways Hubmaier differed with Luther (and also Erasmus) was in his conception of faith. Both Erasmus and Luther thought of faith largely as a gift of God, the "doorway to salvation."[357] Hubmaier, however, is clear that faith is

---

356 Martin Luther, *The Bondage of the Will*, in *Martin Luther's Basic Theological Writings*, ed. Timothy Lull (Minneapolis: Fortress Press, 1989), 213–217.

357 Erasmus, *On the Freedom of the Will*, Rupp and Watson, 52. Erasmus wrote: "St. Augustine and those who follow him, considering how harm-

a decisive personal trust in Christ, a purposeful reception of the Father's gifts to men in Christ. This is a key distinction in the relative theologies of Luther and Hubmaier. Trusting faith requires free will before and after conversion. Necessitarian 'gift' faith requires free will in neither case. God opens the door of salvation without the consent of the sinner.

Thus, faith, for Luther, appears not to be a 'hold fast' type of faith in which the human being's response in personal submission is necessary. Instead, it is a faith that is inevitable for those whom God draws in the inward man. Nevertheless, Luther employs language at other times which suggests his concept of faith *is* one which involves the will. Luther's doctrine of faith sounds very contradictory indeed, depending on whether he is discussing the topic of personal trust as such, or whether he is writing of the bondage of the will and the thunderbolt of God's sovereignty. Luther's idea of faith is not actually that far distant from Hubmaier's on the occasions when the Wittenberg reformer is addressing the Christian's personal faith. However, Luther's Augustinian determinism, which wants to guard salvation by *grace*, appears to undermine salvation by *faith* by stripping it of the decision to trust. Luther's description of faith for those who are already Christian is certainly one of deep personal trust, yet if faith is ultimately only an overpowering 'gift' of God, it would seem the Christian is prohibited by the logic of the unfree will

---

ful to true godliness it is for a man to trust in his own powers, are more inclined to favor grace, which Paul everywhere stresses. For this reason, he denies that man liable to sin can turn to amend his life by his own powers, or do anything which will bring him to salvation unless he is moved by the free gift of God to desire those things which lead to eternal life. This grace which others call 'prevenient,' Augustine calls 'operative.' For faith, which is the doorway to salvation, is the free gift of God. To this, charity is added by the more abundant gift of the Spirit, which he calls 'cooperative grace,' which is always present in those who strive until they attain their end, but on condition that at the same time and in the same work both free choice and grace operate; grace, however, as the leader and not as a companion." Erasmus designates the gift of faith as *free* and here defends free choice, although apparently also affirming Augustine's, and thus Luther's, view of faith as essentially identical to grace which are given as a movement of God's power, who must *pry open* the door of salvation.

from any genuine personal (and thus relational) trust. These ideas about the nature of faith are difficult to reconcile.

Luther's inconsistent ideas here seem to lead to a further practical problem for the Christian: on what basis does he strive to be obedient to Christ, to produce fruits of righteousness in his life? As has already been mentioned, the Lutheran reform suffered from moral carelessness due to Luther's strong insistence on Augustinian *sola gratia*. Roland Bainton writes, "Luther had so insisted that man is incapable of contributing to his salvation as to make easy the inference that moral effort is pointless."[358] Thus, a continued trust demonstrated by obedience, while encouraged by Luther, perhaps remained underdeveloped in Lutheran theology. According to Gordon Rupp, however, a common misconception regarding Luther is that he was not concerned about morality. In a discussion of Luther's tract, *Of Good Works*, Rupp writes, "Luther demonstrates how Christian behavior derives from the fact that 'the first, the highest and most precious of all good works is faith in Christ.' . . . He explains how, from the Christian point of view, it makes all the difference whether good works are done in faith, or apart from it."[359] Still, considering Luther's predestinarian views, one might inquire of Luther in this area of his theology as to why, if faith is a gift of God for the elect, the fruit of good works in Christian people is not also in that sense an inevitable 'gift.' Clearly the evidence of everyday life points to the fact that it is not. Actual human experience and the doctrine of human free will are much more compatible, and to Hubmaier more resonant with biblical truth, than an overwhelming, if 'gracious,' monergism. Indeed, the notion of *overpowering grace* could well be placed in the category of an oxymoron.

Plainly, Luther's theology marks a contrast to Hubmaier's at this point. Hubmaier's idea of faith is, because of allowing for human free will, one of personal trust in God's grace provided in Christ, both in conversion and the continuing Christian life. This allows for a full-blown doctrine of believer's baptism, and a believers' church, and a consequent stress on discipleship

---

358 Roland Bainton, *The Reformation of the Sixteenth Century* (Boston: Beacon Press, 1952), 52.

359 Gordon Rupp, *Luther's Progress to the Diet of Worms, 1521* (Greenwich: Seabury Press, 1951), 73.

and an amended life. The new birth in Christ provides the believer with the power to obey and to produce Christian fruit because of the presence of the Holy Spirit. Faithful discipleship is achievable through trust in Christ's work within the believer and manifested in obedience which accords with his or her new life. To Hubmaier, trust without obedience—an amended life—is a sham. Faith without works is dead. A key element in Hubmaier's definition of faith is that trust in Christ precipitates works of love. In his *Christian Catechism* Hubmaier defines faith as trust in Christ for justification and then distinguishes further between two kinds of faith, one which is dead and one which is living:

> *Leonhart:* Show me also a message of the gospel.
> *Hans:* Christ died for the sake of our sins, and arose for the sake of our justification [*gerechtikayt*], Rom. 4:25.
> *Leonhart:* What follows this message?
> *Hans:* Faith.
> *Leonhart:* What is faith?
> *Hans:* Faith is the realization [*erkantnuß*] of the unspeakable mercy of God, his gracious favor and goodwill, which he bears to us through his most beloved Son Jesus Christ, whom he did not spare and delivered him to death for our sakes that sin might be paid for, and we might be reconciled to him and with the assurance of our hearts cry to him: Abba, Father, our Father who art in heaven.
> *Leonhart:* How many kinds of faith are there?
> *Hans:* Two kinds, namely a dead one and a living one.
> *Leonhart:* What is dead faith?
> *Hans:* One that is unfruitful and without the works of love, James 2:17.
> *Leonhart:* What is living faith?
> *Hans:* One that produces the fruits of the Spirit and works through love, Gal. 5.[360]

---

360 Insertions added. Hubmaier, *A Christian Catechism*, Pipkin and Yoder, 349.

Analysis of the Doctrine of Free Will in Respect to Hubmaier's Broader Theology

Good works was one of Hubmaier's major concerns as an eyewitness of the Reformation. While observing reformation theology as it was fleshed out in real life, Hubmaier wrote that he did "bemoan with tears that people have in so many years not learned better than to say: 'We believe, faith saves us'; while in this age brotherly love and loyalty have grown staler and colder in us than ever before."[361] Thus is seen the essential part free will played in Hubmaier's doctrine of soteriology and of Christian discipleship since he called for works of love as the mark of faith. Gunnar Westin provides a synopsis of Hubmaier's theology of faith:

> Hübmaier's theology provided a wide latitude in the operation of man's free will. . . The one who has been born again and who is truly a believing person performs good deeds; the good tree bears good fruit. The Christian life is a testimony of the true faith; otherwise there is no faith. Absolute obedience to the Word of God, faithfulness in life by serving in love, sacrifice unto death— all of these are, according to Hübmaier and other

---

361 Hubmaier, *Apologia*, Pipkin and Yoder, 527. Hubmaier continues in the same passage: "Indeed in the meantime [here is inserted the note: 'I.e., while we say "we believe."'] all vices have been gaining ground, and human audacity is seated in the highest seat of its violent dominion and [continuing] the practice of all vices and wantonness, which I have often and very sincerely bemoaned to God. We still claim to be Christians, truly evangelical, and boast of our great faith, and have never touched the works of the gospel and of faith with our little finger. We are, consequently, as said above, nothing but mouth-Christians, ear-Christians, paper Christians, but not hand-Christians. Concerning these, St. James speaks most rebukingly in his Christian and very profitable epistle when he writes: 'What does it profit, my brethren, if a man says he has faith but has not works? ... If a brother or sister is ill-clad and in lack of daily food, and one of you says to them, "Go in peace, be warmed and filled," without giving them the things needed for the body, what does it profit? So faith, by itself, if it has no works is dead.... "You have faith and I have works." Show me your faith apart from your works, and I by my works will show you my faith. You believe that God is one; you do well. Even the devils believe—and shudder.' James 2:14–19. Yea, I confess on the strength of this article that mere faith does not deserve to be called faith, for a true faith can never exist without deeds of love."

THE CENTRALITY OF THE DOCTRINE OF HUMAN FREE WILL IN THE THEOLOGY OF BALTHASAR HUBMAIER

Anabaptist scribes, the expression of a living faith. One can and must appeal to the converted will of a newborn person and impress the importance of a true Christian life. It was the want of this in the Reformation circles that made the Anabaptists impatient and critical.[362]

Free will is, to Hubmaier, the logical counterpart of the grace of God. Man's response to God's grace is essential because of man's responsibility for sin. It is also essential because of the gracious offer of reconciliation with the Father through Christ which, when accepted by faith, makes the Christian new and results in works of obedience, love, and sacrifice. With this theology, as Torsten Bergsten observes, Hubmaier "certainly sought to bring a corrective to bear upon the Lutheran Reformation."[363]

The point here is not to utterly dismiss Luther's theology, which engendered and nurtured the Reformation with its unprecedented profundity, complexity, and passion, but to provide a background for understanding Hubmaier's theology more clearly. Hubmaier's theology of free will was undoubtedly an attempt to emend the Lutheran deterministic soteriology which was being taught during his time. Although the teachings in Hubmaier's region may not have been exactly as Luther would have taught,[364]

---

362 Westin, *The Free Church Through the Ages*, 99–100.

363 Bergsten, *Balthasar Hubmaier*, 358.

364 Bergsten notes that "Hubmaier writes that his friends and opponents had denied 'very heatedly' the freedom of the will. They had come to him every day with Bible in hand in hope of 'eradicating completely' this freedom. According to Hubmaier, his opponents believed that everything happened by divine decree and that it was God who evoked good and evil in man. The Christian himself could do no good, since it is God who works in him both desire and fulfillment. These arguments and Hubmaier's rebuttal lead to the conclusion that the Lutheran doctrine of the enslaved will had found its way to Nikolsburg in a garbled and misunderstood form." Bergsten, *Balthasar Hubmaier*, 349. A reading of *The Bondage of the Will* shows that these opponents of Hubmaier had understood reasonably clearly Luther's extreme statements and had taken them to their logical conclusion. Luther may have set them within a wider theological framework, but they were ideas which were directly from Luther's work. The view here is that Hubmaier was dealing with Luther's stated views which were widely known and read and that the concep-

Analysis of the Doctrine of Free Will in Respect to Hubmaier's Broader Theology

Luther himself certainly affirms deterministic ideas in his *Bondage of the Will* unreservedly. So much so, that Hubmaier's free will theology, while still affirming God's grace, could be said to be a direct answer to Luther's insistence on (might we say his willful pressing of) the unfree will as a logical result of God's irresistible grace and sovereignty.[365]

As has been mentioned, there is a tension in Luther's theology between the deterministic tendencies in *The Bondage of the Will* and his firm belief in trusting faith as necessary for salvation. These appear to be contradictory sentiments. Philip Watson speaks to this observable inconsistency in Luther. He asks "how can the thought of a 'hidden God,' who predestines both the elect and the damned, be harmonized with that of the Divine love and grace revealed in Christ?"[366] Watson explains the disparity in Luther's theology by pointing out that Luther presumably "did not mean to contradict himself, and we may

---

tion he had of them was *not* necessarily garbled and misunderstood so much as perhaps misused by Hubmaier's opponents.

365 Luther is thorough in his determinism, boldly appealing in the following passage to what he saw as a reasonable and universal sense of the truth of necessity felt by all people: "For all men find these sentiments written on their hearts and acknowledge and approve them (though unwillingly) when they hear them discussed: first, that God is omnipotent, not only in power, but also in action (as I have said), otherwise he would be a ridiculous God; and secondly, that he knows and foreknows all things, and can neither err nor be deceived. These two points being granted by the hearts and minds of all, they are quickly compelled by inescapable logic to admit that just as we do not come into being by our own will, but by necessity, so we do not do anything by right of free choice, but as God has foreknown and as he leads us to act by his infallible and immutable counsel and power. Thus we find it written in the hearts of all alike, that there is no such thing as free choice." Luther, *On the Bondage of the Will*, Rupp and Watson, 244–245. This is one of many such passages in this work of Luther. The use of the word *unwillingly* to describe folks who may reasonably hesitate to affirm determinism is quite conspicuous, and rather telling, considering the context (see the paragraph before this passage where Luther describes his own struggle with determinism). If everything happens according to necessity, Luther's language and arguments begin to be muddled, confused, and contradicted by any introduction of the obvious free choice and willfulness of human nature.

366 Philip S. Watson, *Let God Be God!: An Interpretation of the Theology of Martin Luther* (London: Epworth Press, 1954), 7.

assume that he was not aware of any fundamental incongruity in his various statements, especially with regard to the most central doctrines of the Faith."[367] Luther, according to Watson, was often seeking to meet opponents on their own turf and answered them according to the arguments presented to him. "The result," writes Watson, "is that his own characteristic point of view... sometimes fails to find quite clear and unequivocal expression. In the *De servo arbitrio*, for example, his real intentions are not a little obscured because he adheres so closely to Erasmus's statements of the issue."[368] Therefore, for Watson, the impression that incongruities permeate Luther's thought is "a false impression."[369]

While it can be argued that Luther promoted a deterministic view it must also be said that his motive, even in this, was to promote his idea of 'faith alone.' Bernhard Lohse contends that, "Luther's treatise on the bondage of the will is a very controversial document, however.... In Contrast to many attempted interpretations, we must maintain that the basis of Luther's argument is the certainty of faith."[370] Although Luther's aim was to affirm faith, the deterministic view in *The Bondage of the Will* was one of Hubmaier's primary targets in his attempt to provide a balance via the doctrine of human free will. Certainly, Hubmaier would have been aware of the source of the arguments for the bondage of the will and of Luther's debate with Erasmus.[371] "Walther Koehler is of the opinion that Hubmaier developed his concept of grace in direct opposition to the forensic concept as found in Luther's doctrine of justification by grace through faith alone, as expressed in the *simul iustus et peccator* formula. Grace so understood, says Hubmaier, allows one to change Christian liberty into fleshly liberty and makes carnal Christians rather than

---

367 Watson, *Let God Be God!: An Interpretation of the Theology of Martin Luther*, 7.

368 Ibid., 8–9.

369 Ibid., 9.

370 Bernhard Lohse, *Martin Luther: An Introduction to His Life and Work*, trans. Robert C. Schultz (Philadelphia: Fortress Press, 1986), 68.

371 Bergsten notes: "It is certainly beyond question that Hubmaier knew Erasmus's *Diatribe*. He probably also made use of Luther's reply *De servo arbitrio* while preparing his own pamphlets on free will." *Balthasar Hubmaier*, 353. Gunnar Westin writes: "Hubmaier was acquainted with Luther's *On the Bondage of the Will* (1525)." *The Free Church Through the Ages*, 99.

those who carry the cross."³⁷² As Bergsten comments, "In his works on free will he does not openly oppose Luther any more than in his other writings. Nevertheless, the former do represent an attack on Luther's views concerning the will, and also concerning man."³⁷³

The necessity of affirming God's grace and sovereignty led Luther to assume that faith was primarily passive in relation to grace, and yet he also spoke of belief as if it involved the will of man, as a confidence and trust. As per the latter, Luther writes as to why certain people are elected and others not, sounding very Hubmaierian: "This difference is to be ascribed to man, not to the will of God, for the promises of God are universal. He will have all men to be saved. Accordingly it is not the fault of our Lord God, who promises salvation, but it is our fault if we are *unwilling* to believe it."³⁷⁴ Luther's use of the word "unwilling" in this passage is starkly conspicuous, and puzzling, when considered in light of some of Luther's statements in *The Bondage of the Will*.

For Luther to say that man has no free will regarding spiritual matters unmistakably contradicts this statement, which affirms the responsibility of man for sin based on his decision to believe or not believe. At the least, the statement plainly contradicts Luther's doctrine of double predestination, especially the affirmation that "the promises of God are universal." Philip Watson comments on this passage of Luther's concerning those "unwilling to believe," seeing it as an allusion to human free will: "By most ordinary standards it would not seem unnatural to speak of a real element of freedom here: not

---

372 Beachy, *The Concept of Grace in the Radical Reformation*, 72.

373 Bergsten, *Balthasar Hubmaier*, 353.

374 Emphasis added. Luther, *Letters of Spiritual Counsel*, 130; quoted in Rupp and Watson, *Luther and Erasmus: Free Will and Salvation*, 26. Many similar statements were made by Hubmaier. One of the chief problems with the necessitarian idea of the bondage of the will was that it laid the blame for sin at God's door. Here is a sample of Hubmaier's thought on this: "As death before the Fall could do no harm to Adam, indeed there was no death, so has it become harmless for the entire world through Christ, unless the world does not want something else, as in fact it does not, 1Cor. 15:21; 2 Tim. 1:10; 1 Pet. 3. Therefore it will carry its burden itself, Gal. 6:5. It follows that if not all people are saved, it is not God but we who are guilty of that, for he gave his most beloved Son into death for us all, John 3:16." Hubmaier, *Freedom of the Will, II*, Pipkin and Yoder, 470.

the absolute freedom which belongs to God alone, and not the liberty of the children of God, nor yet the freedom of action man has in relation to 'things beneath him,' but perhaps (if we may put it so) a freedom of responsible reaction to the 'things above him.'"[375]

This discrepancy in Luther's theology has been a puzzler for scholars just as Augustine's affirmation of free will and later embracing of coercion have been.[376] Robert Friedmann writes of the ambiguity in Luther's Protestant conception of faith:

> The traditional Pauline-Augustine theology . . . was revived by Luther and by the Swiss Reformers, Zwingli and Calvin. In its center stands the concern for the salvation of the individual sinner. Certain sections of the Pauline epistles were selected to develop the Protestant "sola fide" theology which teaches in brief that not by good works but by faith "alone" may the sinner be saved – *whereby the idea of faith remains somewhat undefined.* The moral element was toned down by Luther lest the notion of "merit by works" could creep in again.[377]

Timothy Lull, the editor of *Martin Luther's Basic Theological Writings*, suggests that Luther's theology should be viewed as dialectical. Luther, he says, never really gives "a simple yes or no to a question."[378] Lull observes that Luther held passionately strong views that led him to extremes, both in his theology and

---

375 Philip S. Watson, ed., *Luther and Erasmus: Free Will and Salvation*, 26.

376 Heinrich Bornkamm, in his work *Luther in Mid-Career* comments on the critical scholarship treating Luther's *Bondage of the Will*. He does not attempt himself "to undertake a critical examination of the views Luther set forth in his *De servo arbitrio*. His unheard-of passion, his critical daring in defending his theses, the abandon with which he strides along abysses of problems—all this leaves little doubt that this book drew ample criticism . . . . Individual narrators and critics have brought their own manifold religious, theological, and philosophical presuppositions to the task, often despairing of it and more likely finding Luther's pronouncements like a bundle of truly splendid yet contradictory intentions." Heinrich Bornkamm, *Luther in Mid-Career*, 457.

377 Emphasis added. Friedmann, *The Theology of Anabaptism*, 158–159.

378 Lull, *Martin Luther's Basic Theological Writings*, 2.

Analysis of the Doctrine of Free Will in Respect to Hubmaier's Broader Theology

in dealing with his polemical targets. "This makes Luther a lively person to read and study," writes Lull. "But the impression persists that he is unfair, unbalanced, and not a steady guide to the subtle distinctions of which much of theology consists."[379] Of Luther's doctrine of the bondage of the will, Lull writes: "While Luther generally was trying to revive the Pauline/Augustinian doctrine of grace, there were moments . . . when he seemed to express himself so extremely on the subject that all dimensions of human freedom were denied."[380]

The idea of belief, in the above passage from Luther's *Letters of Spiritual Counsel* (he wrote: "it is our fault if we are *unwilling* to believe"), certainly appears to include a willing trust and its logical opposite, willing disbelief. If there are those who are "unwilling to believe" then the other category must consist of those *willing* to believe. This is Hubmaier's point. But this willing belief is still founded upon Christ as the object of belief, with His effectual and merciful gift of salvation, not upon the willing itself. It is not the willing, in and of the man, which is trusted for salvation; the willing *is* the believing, the choice to trust Christ. Perhaps it is a matter of semantics when it comes to the issue of human free will.[381] For Luther the accent is on free *will*, the ability of men to achieve what they would. For him this simply cannot apply to spiritual things. He wrote:

> The very name, Free Will, was odious to all the Fathers. I, for my part, admit that God gave to man a free will, but the question is, whether this same freedom be in our power and strength, or no? We may very fitly

---

379 Lull, *Martin Luther's Basic Theological Writings*, 2.
380 Ibid., 152.
381 Beachy writes of two definitions of grace (see note 413 below), Anabaptists who emphasized ontological change, and Magisterial Reformers who emphasized the forensic standing of man before God in justification: "The emphasis upon good works as the fruit of grace in the Radical Reformation led to the accusation of 'work's [sic] righteousness' by the Magisterial side. On the other hand, the emphasis upon forensic justification by the Magisterial Reformers often led the Radicals to denounce them as peddlers of 'cheap grace.' That the two sides of the Reformation were in effect working with two different concepts of grace was not, I think, clear to the participants in the struggle of the sixteenth century." *The Concept of Grace in the Radical Reformation*, 5.

> call it a subverted, perverse, fickle, and wavering will, for it is only God that works in us, and we must suffer and be subject to his pleasure. Even as a potter out of his clay makes a pot or vessel as he wills, so it is for our free will, to suffer and not to work. It stands not in our strength; *for we are not able to do anything that is good in divine matters.*[382]

For Hubmaier the accent is on *free* will, the ability of a man to choose for or against Christ. For him this is absolutely essential, not as a work but as a grace from God to be able to receive, and submit to, the message concerning the only hope for salvation. Roger Olson places this idea in broader theological terms, "What Hubmaier was proclaiming as the basis for free will is what other theologians call prevenient grace—the resistible grace of God that calls, convicts and enables."[383] Those who resist, who do not want Christ, are under judgment. So for Hubmaier the ultimate import of the gift of free choice is whether or not one chooses Christ, the exclusive offer of salvation from God. Hubmaier asserts:

> As one is saved in his own faith and not in that of someone else, so also are such people condemned in their own unbelief, for which condemnation they themselves are guilty and not God. For God has often desired to gather them with his Word like a hen her chicks, but they of their own volition have freely and wickedly refused, nor do they recognize the day of their visitation. Therefore they cannot blame it on God, as he himself says, The condemnation is thine, O Israel; only in me lies your salvation, Hos. 13:9.[384]

---

382 Emphasis added. Martin Luther, *Table Talk*, trans. William Hazlitt (London: Fount, 1995), 130. It should be noted that Luther's assertion that free will was "odious" to *all* the Fathers is demonstrably inaccurate. Even Augustine, one of Luther's primary sources from the Patristic era, admitted to free will in man, although he apparently changed his mind later. Chapter one of this monograph cites several key Church Fathers as having affirmed free will in man as essential to moral agency, and thus responsibility for sin, and also essential to faith and thus reception of salvation. See discussion on Irenaeus above.

383 Olson, *The Story of Christian Theology*, 422.

384 Hubmaier, *A Christian Catechism*, Pipkin and Yoder, 363.

Analysis of the Doctrine of Free Will in Respect to Hubmaier's Broader Theology

The finality of this choice, to believe or reject God, reflects the narrow way which Christ claimed Himself to be.

Luther sees the notion of free will in terms of works done in man's own strength in order to please God. He says rightly that this is impossible. The whole point of the sinner's need for salvation from God is that, because of his sin, he is incapable of saving himself. But when Luther rejects free will entirely, seeing it as man's attempt to right himself, he seemingly forfeits the biblical idea of a personal, decisive response to God to receive grace through faith in Christ. This muddles the concept of faith in Luther's theology. It is often unclear what the nature of faith may be for the person at the point of conversion in terms of personal belief. It is characterized largely as an unfathomable agency which God mysteriously bestows rather than an active trust in Christ on the part of the believer, which involves personal submission and commitment to gospel truth. As Kenneth Davis writes: "Parallel with the Anabaptists' rejection of any definition of the content of faith which would divorce it from good works and conduct was their conviction that the Magisterial Reformers were also ignoring the necessity of repentance in their doctrine of salvation. They maintained that the Magisterial Reformers were preaching forgiveness without requiring the intent of amendment of life."[385]

Faith, then, for Luther, cannot involve human decision, for that would make it a work according to his definition of free will. For Luther this was a very personal conviction based on his own religious experience.[386] He says

---

385 Davis, *Anabaptism and Asceticism*, 123–124.

386 A. C. McGiffert comments on this experiential aspect to Luther's thought concerning salvation and the bondage of the will. He goes so far as to say that, for Luther, personal experience of salvation inspired, and thus, in a sense, overrode his theological interest in God's sovereignty: "Luther was thus a thoroughgoing predestinarian; but his predestinarianism was not a theological or metaphysical affair. It is true that in his desire to do away with all human merit, and show the sole activity of God in the salvation of man, he was led to present his predestinarian convictions in theological form, to give them theoretical support in a doctrine of the absolute and unconditioned will of God, taken directly from scholasticism, and to draw from them deterministic conclusions of a very extreme type. But none of this is of the essence of the matter, and it should not be made the starting-point in interpreting his thought. His belief in predestination was the fruit of ex-

that he promised God he would do better, only to fail so many times that he quit promising. He was convinced that he could not be righteous of his own power, his 'will.' Thus the primacy of the grace of God in Christ was liberating to him. He only had to possess faith in God's power. Luther reported his personal struggle toward faith (grace) in the following manner:

> I have often been resolved to live uprightly, and to lead a true godly life, and to set everything aside that would hinder this, but it was far

perience, not of speculation. This is made abundantly clear, for instance, by the fact that while he frequently asserts, in the most categorical fashion, the absolute bondage of the human will, and declares that all our deeds, evil as well as good, are directly caused by God, he yet recognises man's freedom in matters which do not concern his salvation. Evidently his controlling interest was not to safeguard the divine omnipotence, but to give expression to his own experience of God's controlling power in saving him. Peace came to him, after his long struggle to appease the wrath of God by meritorious works, solely because of his vision of the forgiving love of God in Christ. The peace was God's work, not his own. God had disclosed Himself, and his salvation consisted, not in anything that he did in consequence of the disclosure or under its influence, but in the disclosure itself. He found God gracious, he did not make Him so. The very essence of the experience lay in the fact that God had given it. To resolve it into its divine and human constituents, to mark off the agency of God and the co-operation of man, one from the other, in traditional theological fashion, would have been to take all meaning out of it. Not two separable and distinguishing acts, that of God, and that of man, but the one act of God disclosing Himself as a gracious and forgiving Father, this meant faith, this meant trust, this meant peace and salvation." A. C. McGiffert, *Protestant Thought Before Kant* (New York: Harper, 1962), 29–30. In this way Luther may have ignored his *own choice* to trust God as he himself responded to His revelation. This choice to respond may have gone unnoticed because of his aversion to any suggestion of his own effort being involved in his salvation. This is a construing of faith which has often led to confusion in attempting to understand Luther. For Luther, explicitly, no personal choice, no conscious personal submission to God, seems to be involved. Although the choice to trust and submt seems implicitly and inherently involved here in Luther's conception of salvation (as described by McGiffert), it is so veiled, because of a confusion of the choice in *receiving* grace with human works, as to be imperceptible.

from being put in execution; even as it was with Peter, when he swore he would lay down his life for Christ. I will not lie or dissemble before my God, but will freely confess, I am not able to effect that good which I intend but await the happy hour when God shall be pleased to meet me with his grace.[387]

Any encroachment of free will, which by Luther's definition apparently meant works in pursuit of righteous merit, meant going back to the old frustrating and fearful religious life from which he was freed when he discovered that "the just shall live by faith."

Luther was alarmed by any suggestion that it would be necessary to go back to the impossible attempt to make himself righteous in the eyes of a wrathful God. Luther wrote in *The Bondage of the Will* of his personal aversion to free choice:

> For my own part, I frankly confess that even if it were possible, I should not wish to have free choice given to me, or to have anything left in my own hands *by which I might strive toward salvation*. For, on the one hand, I should be unable to stand firm and keep hold of it amid so many adversities and perils and so many assaults of demons, seeing that even one demon is mightier than all men, and no man at all could be saved; and on the other hand, even if there were no perils or adversities or demons, I should nevertheless have to labor under perpetual uncertainty and to fight as one beating the air, since even if I lived and worked to eternity, my conscience would never be assured and certain how much it ought to do to satisfy God. For whatever work might be accomplished, there would always remain an anxious doubt whether it pleased God or whether he required something more, as the experience of all self-justifiers proves, and I myself learned to my bitter cost through so many years.[388]

---

387 Luther, *Table Talk*, 130.

388 Emphasis added. Luther, *On the Bondage of the Will*, Rupp and Watson, 328–329. Notice that 'striving toward salvation' is here equated with free choice for Luther.

THE CENTRALITY OF THE DOCTRINE OF HUMAN FREE WILL IN THE THEOLOGY OF BALTHASAR HUBMAIER

Since the very idea of human free will, especially as he perceived its use by scholastic theologians (who in fact did add human works to the salvation equation), smacked of human effort to be acceptable to God, Luther flatly and fixedly rejected it, particularly as he leveled his biting polemic against Erasmus. Timothy Lull writes, "Luther feels that lurking behind Erasmus's concern for freedom, merit, and good works is human pride—a desire to have something to offer God that will blunt the enormity of our need for grace. Luther feared that the wrong kind of concern for human responsibility would soon connect with the self-centeredness that is the result of original sin."[389]

In consequence, Luther sees free will as blind and impotent. Bernhard Lohse notes in Luther a distinction concerning the human will which holds that "people are free only in relationship to those things that are under them but not in relationship to those that are above them."[390] However, Lohse points out that: "Sometimes Luther came very close to the view that people have no freedom to choose even in matters that are subject to them and seemed to say that human actions even at this level are directed by God."[391] Thus, although Luther allows for a lower order (touching "the things beneath") or natural free will in man, he asserts that it is impossible for fallen man to attend to spiritual matters, the words of God, of which he can know nothing. He wrote the following retort to Erasmus' definition of free choice, which applied the will to spiritual matters:

> The life or eternal salvation, however, is something that passes human comprehension . . . . This means that unless the Spirit has revealed it, no man's heart would have any knowledge or notion of it, much less be able to apply itself to it or seek after it. . . . On the authority of Erasmus, then, free choice is a power of the will that is able of itself to will and unwill the word and work of God, by which it is led to those things which exceed both its grasp and its perception. But if it can will and unwill, it can also love and hate, and if it can love and hate, it can also in some small degree

---

389 Lull, *Martin Luther's Basic Theological Writings*, 152.
390 Lohse, *Martin Luther*, 66.
391 Ibid.

> do the works of the law and *believe the gospel. For if you can will or unwill anything, you must to some extent be able to perform something by that will,* even if someone else prevents your completing it. Now, in that case, since the works of God which lead to salvation include death, the cross, and all the evils of the world, the human will must be able to will both death and its own perdition. Indeed, it can will everything when it can will the word and work of God; for how can there be anything anywhere that is below, above, within, or without the word and work of God, except God himself? But what is left here to grace and the Holy Spirit? This plainly means attributing divinity to free choice, since to will the law and the gospel, to unwill sin and to will death, belongs to divine power alone.[392]

Thus, for Luther, free will, as it pertains to the things of God, is a fiction. A key to Luther's idea (we might say, misapprehension) of free will is seen here. He does not separate free choice from *the ability to perform something*. In this case free will must indeed be rejected. The performance of either the sinner or the Christian is of no worth, only faith.

But free will does not *necessarily* include performance. It can simply mean a choice or decision to rely on someone else's performance. Man is able to apply himself to the "works of God which lead to salvation," which "include death" and "the cross," by virtue of the substitution of Jesus Christ. The key to Hubmaier's theology of justification is the simple and biblical idea of personal trust in the substitutionary atonement of Christ:

> I also believed and confess that thou has suffered under the judge Pontius Pilate, was crucified, dead, and buried, and all of that for the sake of my sins, that thou mightest release and redeem me from the eternal cross, torture, suffering, and death through thy cross, suffering, anxiety and distress, torture, and bitter dying, and through the shedding of thy rose-red blood. Thy greatest and highest love toward us poor humans is made known therein, that thou has transformed thy heavy cross into

---

392 Emphasis added. Luther, *On the Bondage of the Will*, Rupp and Watson, 172–173. Note that believing the gospel is included in the impossibilities for free will.

an easy yoke, thy bitter suffering into imperishable joy, and thy grim death into eternal life. Therefore I give thee praise and thanksgiving, my gracious Lord Jesus Christ, always and forever.[393]

By accepting Christ's sacrifice on his behalf by faith, by believing on the efficacy of the person and works of the Son of God, one receives the benefits of His life and work. But he must choose to believe, to turn from his own efforts and submit to God's finished work in Christ, to say yes to God's offer.

Hubmaier confirmed that "sin is forgiven . . . by the power of the internal 'Yes' in the heart, which the person proclaims publicly in the reception of water baptism, that he believes and is already sure in his heart of the remission of sin through Jesus Christ."[394] But this power does not depend on human effort. As Hubmaier wrote, "we discover that from the tops of our heads to the bottom of our feet there is nothing good. . . . Moreover, man can find within himself neither help, comfort nor medicine, wherewith he might heal himself. Therefore he must give up any hope in himself and utterly despair like a man that has fallen into the hands of a murderer."[395] The answer, for Hubmaier, is to give oneself to the ministrations of the Great Physician, that is, trust Christ. He continues:

> So when a man looks into his own heart, and sees himself as he really is, he knows that he is only a worm. . . . So the man lies wounded, and at the point of death, and cannot help himself, the Samaritan must come, that is Christ Jesus, to bring him medicine . . . . He will . . . so far as possible for a wounded man, yield himself to the Lord's will, and call on Him daily for healing and cleansing. So what the wounded man cannot do in his own strength (for he can do nothing) the physician does. For Christ does not reject the sick who would gladly take the prescription and follow the direction of the physician. But when he is not able to follow through, he recognizes it is his illness which is at fault and he holds

---

[393] Hubmaier, *Twelve Articles in Prayer Form*, Pipkin and Yoder, 236.
[394] Hubmaier, *On the Christian Baptism of Believers*, Pipkin and Yoder, 118.
[395] Hubmaier, *On the Christian Baptism of Believers* in *Anabaptist Beginnings*, ed. Estep, 95.

himself guilty but at the same time he desires grace in the firm belief that God will give it to him, and not allow such sickness to cause eternal damnation. For he has trusted himself over to the physician, Jesus, and cast his sins upon Him to be healed. . . . man must inwardly, in his heart, give himself to a new life according to the rules of Christ, the physician who has healed him and atoned for his sins in whom he has that life. Thus, Paul confesses openly that it is not he who lives, but Christ who lives in him, and who is that life and outside of Christ, he confesses that he is vain, worthless, dead, and a lost sinner.[396]

Clearly, Hubmaier affirms the grace of God in Christ as the only effective medicine for sin to make one righteous. He denies that man's efforts to save himself are of any worth, but he affirms that a Christian submits to Christ, the great Physician, of his own free will.

Another of the problems with Luther's view of the will is that it perceives the will as completely at the mercy of outside forces. The will is dominated either by God or the Devil. Thus, seemingly, the will functions in man only as the capacity to be dominated. This idea excludes the biblical call for a response to God by men, to turn to Him. Harry McSorley explains:

> Instead of the biblical categories of man's (free) obedience to sin or to justice and man's *obedient* servitude to God (justice) or to Satan (sin), which presuppose the possibility that man can disobey God or can, with God's help, turn from sin to God (not simply *be* turned) and which therefore necessitate admonitions both to those who obey sin and those who obey justice, instead of the patristic categories of God's efficacious, liberating grace and man's *liberum arbitrium*, we find in *DSA* [*De Servo Arbitrio*] only categories of a struggle between God and Satan to see who shall control and hold captive man's purely passive will, passive in the sense that it can make no free decisions whatever. Here we find no divine call to conversion, no admonition to steadfastness in justice or to avoidance of sin, no struggle of man with Satan, no personal dialogue which presupposes a free response such as

---

396 Hubmaier, *On the Christian Baptism of Believers* in *Anabaptist Beginnings*, ed. Estep, 95-96.

we find in Scripture, but only a domination of man's will by God or Satan without any free, personal action of man. We find only a struggle between God and Satan, only an unalterable, necessary *velle* of good or evil depending on whether the will is "ridden" by God or Satan.[397]

McSorley concludes that, "Luther correctly emphasizes the biblical doctrine that the sinner is Satan's captive and is not free to escape. But . . . he overlooks the biblical teaching that man's liberation from Satan's captivity involves man's decision of faith and obedience, never forgetting that this decision is itself absolutely dependent upon the liberating grace of Christ."[398]

Hubmaier's view is that the gospel restores the knowledge of good and evil and thus restores man's ability to choose the good through the grace of God in Christ, who has offered his own death and resurrection, His very Self, as the good for man's salvation. It is up to the person to choose Him by faith. Thus, the nature of faith in Christ is unique in that it is the one area where man can utilize his free choice so that it results in effectual grace and salvation, because the work is all done by God in Christ. Leonard Verduin elaborates on the nature of belief as including option:

> The option posed in authentic Christianity is not an option between salvation-by-obedience and salvation-by-faith. Rather, it is the option between obedience accomplished *by* man and obedience accomplished *for* man. The Christ of Scriptures is represented as existing in the modality of rectitude, who by His obedience earned salvation and obtained righteousness, a righteousness that is then imputed to all who by the act of faith receive Him. He who knew no sin was made to be sin for us. The option presented in the Gospel is to accept or reject Him and His righteousness.[399]

---

397 Insertion added. McSorley, *Luther: Right or Wrong?*, 338–339.
398 McSorley, *Luther: Right or Wrong?*, 339.
399 Verduin, *Somewhat less than God: The Biblical View of Man* (Grand Rapids: Eerdmans, 1970), 91.

Free will, if defined as attempting to do works to please God, outside of faith in Christ, *is*, as Luther said in *The Bondage of the Will*, nothing "but an empty name." But choosing to trust Christ and His completed payment for sin is not a work.

The gospel of Christ shows God's good love, and the righteousness He offers in the sacrifice of the unblemished offering, Jesus. The alternative is to continue to make the self the final good, and thus turn away from the true good offered in Christ—who was at the creation and is Creator—to a lie. The human creature who willfully refuses the Creator's grace, the giving of His very Self in His Son, must be allowed to suffer the solitary consequences: the second death, the final separation from the Source of good and life, God Himself. As Hubmaier said: "Hell is the eternally painful and unending deprivation of the contemplation of God's face; it has been prepared for the devil, his angels, and all unbelievers who have not performed deeds of mercy for their neighbor. There is nothing there but everlasting fire, outer darkness, weeping and gnashing of teeth, from which may the almighty kind and merciful Father in heaven graciously preserve us throughout eternity through Jesus Christ, his only begotten Son, our Lord, to whom be glory, praise, honor, and majesty always and forever."[400]

Good Works and the Christian Life in Hubmaier and Luther

The decision to trust Christ for salvation involves human free will. So, for Hubmaier, a very strong emphasis is placed on the believer's ongoing freedom to do good works because of the presence of Christ and his power over sin. To trust God for salvation and then to trust Him for the power to live a sanctified Christian life is, for Hubmaier, undeniably sensible, and also biblical:

> The believing and newly born person under the gospel . . . has just as many trials as before, or even more. He finds (however holy he may be) nothing good in his own flesh, just as Saint Paul laments the same with great seriousness regarding the conflict and the resistance of the flesh, Rom. 7:18. Nevertheless the believer rejoices and praises God

---

[400] Hubmaier, *A Christian Catechism*, Pipkin and Yoder, 365.

that the trial is not and cannot be so great in him, but that the power of God in him, which he has received through the living Word which God has sent is stronger and mightier 1 Cor. 10:13; Rom. 8:11.[401]

Thus, for Hubmaier, faith in the power of God for salvation meant, for the believer, to continue in that belief by working toward holiness, despite weaknesses, based on trust in God's grace, not on human effort. Cornelius Dyck neatly encapsulates Hubmaier's idea: "The call to holiness is both a command and a promise; the disciple hears the call of God and obeys, but such a person prays for and receives enabling grace to do it."[402]

Luther's idea of the Christian life as *simil justus et peccator*, both righteous and sinful, was, to Hubmaier, an unnecessary compromise.[403] As is seen

---

401 Hubmaier, *A Form for Christ's Supper*, Pipkin and Yoder, 400–401.

402 Cornelius J. Dyck, "The Anabaptist Understanding of the Good News," 29.

403 Although Luther used this construct of the Christian as sinner and justified at the same time, he did stress that faith and works are linked, so that faith must be shown by its fruit in works of love, just as Hubmaier emphasized. He does this very clearly in his *Preface to Romans*. It is very different in tone and subject compared to *The Bondage of the Will*, although still never affirming free will in man. The idea one might get from reading *Preface to Romans* is that faith within man and grace from God are indistinguishable. This is evidently one of the primary ambiguities in all of Luther's theology, the failure to differentiate between grace and faith. The following passage is illustrative of this confusion and yet also contains an emphasis on works with faith, and even alludes to an ontological change in the believer. Note especially that faith is not spoken of as a human act (although Luther cannot help but use words like 'confidence' and 'trust') but could basically be characterized as a mysterious force and is certainly considered purely a work of God. Indeed, it is difficult to understand the passage if faith is taken to mean personal belief and submissive trust: "Faith is a work of God in us, which changes us and brings us to birth anew from God (cf. John 1). It kills the old Adam, makes us completely different people in heart, mind, senses, and all our powers, and brings the Holy Spirit with it. What a living, creative, active powerful thing is faith! It is impossible that faith ever stop doing good. Faith doesn't ask whether good works are to be done, but, before it is asked, it has done them. It is always active. Whoever doesn't do such works is without faith; he gropes and searches about him for faith and

Analysis of the Doctrine of Free Will in Respect to Hubmaier's Broader Theology

in the passage above, Hubmaier did not believe in Christian perfection. He saw the Christian life as a matter of striving and grappling with sin in obedience and trust, to overcome as much as possible, as in the biblical Pauline picture of the struggle of the flesh and Spirit. Kenneth Davis aptly describes Hubmaier's view: "Only a relative holiness is achievable, or necessary now; the corrupt, sinful flesh, though no longer dominant in the true Christian, remains present and troublesome throughout life and is eliminated or transformed to incorruption only at the resurrection."[404] But Hubmaier strongly affirmed a commitment, based on the power from God present in the reborn believer, to live a holy Christian life. As Beachy observes, Hubmaier conceived of grace "as an act of God, which brings about an ontological change within the believer himself rather than [just] a forensic change in status before God."[405] The "just" is added to this quotation because the view of this study is that Hubmaier understood salvation as an ontological new birth *along with* or *in addition to* the idea of imputed righteousness, not *rather than* or *instead of* imputed righteousness. Hubmaier essentially apprehended the new birth and justification as two *integrated* aspects of the biblical concept of salvation.[406]

---

good works but doesn't know what faith or good works are. Even so, he chatters on with a great many words about faith and good works. Faith is a living, unshakeable confidence in God's grace; it is so certain, that someone would die a thousand times for it. This kind of trust in and knowledge of God's grace makes a person joyful, confident, and happy with regard to God and all creatures. This is what the Holy Spirit does by faith. Through faith, a person will do good to everyone without coercion, willingly and happily; he will serve everyone, suffer everything for the love and praise of God, who has shown him such grace. It is as impossible to separate works from faith as burning and shining from fire. Therefore be on guard against your own false ideas and against the chatterers who think they are clever enough to make judgments about faith and good works but who are in reality the biggest fools. Ask God to work faith in you; otherwise you will remain eternally without faith, no matter what you try to do or fabricate." Martin Luther, *Preface to the Letter of St. Paul to the Romans* in *The Master Christian Library*, (Rio, WI: Ages Software, 2000), 8.

404 Davis, *Anabaptism and Asceticism*, 143.

405 Insertion added. Beachy, *The Concept of Grace in the Radical Reformation*, 5.

406 Verduin addresses this issue in discussing Luther's construction,

This is an important distinction because, once again, Hubmaier proves himself to be neither Catholic nor Protestant, but Anabaptist. Luther reacted against Roman Catholic soteriology which stressed the transformational process in individuals so that God then recognizes them as acceptable by the merit they produce in His grace. He replaced the Catholic merit-based process with a purely forensic righteousness, resulting in a change of standing before God due to Christ's representing the sinner before God as righteous. But Luther's new soteriology seems to have veered at times toward a neglect of Christian works of obedience, accomplished by faith, because of his understandable hesitance to acknowledge works of any kind as a part of salvation. Leonard Verduin writes, "Because Protestant theology felt called to oppose the notion that men's own obedience gives them standing in the presence of God, it developed a blind spot in regard to obedience as the touchstone of one's state of grace."[407] Hubmaier affirms both of these ideas with his emphasis on the necessity of the "foreign righteousness" of Christ atoning for sin along with his emphasis on works as the fruit of the new birth, without which faith is void. In doing so he avoids the error of affirming one or the other of these ideas alone: the Catholic emphasis on transforming grace which tended to emerge as a works righteousness when identified almost entirely with the Roman institution, or the Lutheran emphasis on a purely forensic righteousness which was predisposed to downplay Christian holiness, and the decision and responsibility inherent in submissive faith.

---

simil justus et peccator, insisting that renewal and pardon in salvation must not be separated. This is an apt description of Hubmaier's view: "Luther was so occupied with salvation as *pardon* that the theology of *renewal* remained underdeveloped. Seen in this perspective, Luther's *simil justus ac peccator* (a justified one and a sinner at one and the same time) was unfortunate, to say the least; for the Biblical representation is that pardon and renewal are as warp and woof; they cannot be taken singly; the one does not occur without the other. The old hymn is on the right track when it petitions: 'Be of sin the double cure; save from wrath and make me pure.' The Christian Scriptures portray the restored man as one who is victorious." Verduin, *Somewhat Less Than God*, 64.

407 Verduin, *Somewhat Less Than God*, 76.

Hubmaier, then, articulated a clear expression of the forensic soteriology stressed by Luther together with an emphasis on transformation toward a "walk," or life, in the Spirit which produces the fruit of righteousness:

> Thus Christ also says in John 14:12, "He who believes in me will also do the works I do, and greater works than these will he do." And yet it is known that we do not and cannot do anything, but he must do it through and in us, as it is written in Acts 3:12 and 14:15. . . . Behold and grasp, all you who have eyes and hands, that John sent his disciples away from himself. For in his preaching they do not find anything but law, sin, death, devil, and hell; and he pointed them to the Lamb of God who would proclaim to them evangelical consolation, that is, a certain forgiveness of sins. Until sinners hear this they have no peace nor rest in their consciences. It is just as if one were to tell a sick person for a long time about a good physician. He still is sick until he comes to the physician who heals him and tells him, "Go forth and be whole." So it is with Christ. He has to speak with us, or his messengers in his place; then we are made whole in our souls. Believed forgiveness of sins is the true gospel which cannot be without the Spirit of God, for the Spirit of God makes the Word alive. Faith is a work of God, John 2:69. For by faith the law of sin and of death becomes a law of the Spirit, Romans 8:2. For what was impossible to the law, God has fulfilled through Jesus Christ so that the righteousness demanded by the law might be fulfilled in us who now walk not according to the flesh but according to the Spirit. . . . From this it follows that . . . the person . . . recognizes that he is a miserable sinner, who cannot help himself nor give himself counsel, who does nothing good but that all his righteousness is corrupt and reproachable. For that reason he despairs of himself. He must also be damned eternally, were not a foreign righteousness to come to his help. His awareness and conscience learned from the law, which is knowledge of sin, show this to him . . . . and points him to Christ, that in him he will find discharge of his sins, rest, peace, and security so that he not remain in despair and thus be lost eternally.[408]

---

408 Hubmaier, *On the Christian Baptism of Believers,* Pipkin and Yoder, 105–106.

The inner transformation in the believer, wrought by the grace of God through the work of Christ, enables the Christian to follow the dictates of his new Master because the Master is within Him through the Word and the Holy Spirit. The idea that the Christian is still at the complete mercy of his sinful nature was anathema to Hubmaier and, he believed, the cause of much confusion and permissiveness, much uncalled-for concession to sin in the life of the church. He set forth this challenge: "Granted that Christ has made us free . . . he has made us no less servants of the cross, which he has laid on our backs, saying . . . clearly that we are not flesh Christians but cross Christians, and we are not to follow the flesh but the Spirit . . . for if we act otherwise we turn evangelical truth into human laziness, living faith into a dead letter, the fruitful vine and fig tree of Christ into thistles and thornbushes, and indeed Christian freedom into a devilish servitude, effrontery, and wantonness, of which the Scripture has repeatedly warned us."[409] Yet, always mindful that the power to do good works is not in man's power but is part of the freedom of God's power in man, Hubmaier speaks in this way of God's commands for the Christian:

> God wants to awaken us from sleep with them and give us the heart to resolve to do good and to accomplish this with the hope of divine help, because he asks it of us. Otherwise, we would not dare to be presumptuous in this, for it would be impossible for us in ourselves, without God's drawing which comes through his Word. Therefore we must first beg him and say, "O Lord, give us what you command of us." We would not even dare to say "Our Father," if he had not commanded us to do so.[410]

Hubmaier, while, of course, believing in the confession, repentance, and forgiveness of sin available to the believer, at the same time viewed the commitment to deny the self, and to live for Christ, with the utmost seriousness due to the presence and power of God (the context here is Christ's finished work celebrated in the Lord's Supper):

---

409 Hubmaier, *Apologia*, Pipkin and Yoder, 529.
410 Hubmaier, *A Christian Catechism*, Pipkin and Yoder, 362.

> He also knows certainly that such resistances, evil desires, and sinful lusts of his flesh are not damning for him if he confesses the same to God, regrets them, and does not follow after them, but reigns and rules mightily over the restless devil of his flesh, 1 Cor. 9:27, strangles, crucifies, and torments him without letup; holds in his rein, does not do his will, cares little that that breaks his neck, Exod. 34:20. So every one who is a Christian acts and behaves so that he may worthily eat and drink at the table of the Lord. Know thou further, righteous Christian, that to fulfill the law it is not enough to avoid sins and die to them. Yea, one must also do good to the neighbor, Ps. 37. For Christ not only broke the bread, he also distributed it and gave it to his disciples. Yea, not only the bread, but also even his own flesh and blood. So we must not only speak the word of brotherly love, hear it, confess ourselves sinners, and abstain from sin, we must also fulfill it in deeds, as Scripture everywhere teaches us: Forsake evil and do good, Ps. 37. Brethren, work out your salvation, Phil. 2:12. While we have time let us do good, for the night comes when no man can work. Gal. 6:9. . . . Not all those who say to me Lord, Lord, will enter into the kingdom of the heavens but he who does the will of my Father who is in heaven, will enter into the kingdom of heaven, says Christ, and adds: Everyone who hears my words and does them, he shall be likened unto a wise man who built his house upon a rock. But everyone who hears my word and does it not shall be likened to a fool who built his house on sand. Matt. 7:21-27.[411]

Thus, Hubmaier's Anabaptist version of the mortification of the flesh is practiced by God's power but carried out in the will of the Christian by faith. These are the words of a theologian identified with a group of Christians who were hunted down, tortured, and executed for their beliefs. They are not theoretical or idle words. As Walter Klaassen writes: "The situation surrounding the Anabaptist church called for a strong discipline. In a world that applied all of its pressures to crush the little company of believers one could not be casual about following Christ."[412]

---

411 Hubmaier, *A Form for Christ's Supper*, Pipkin and Yoder, 400–401.
412 Klaassen, *Anabaptism: Neither Catholic nor Protestant*, 32.

THE CENTRALITY OF THE DOCTRINE OF HUMAN FREE WILL
IN THE THEOLOGY OF BALTHASAR HUBMAIER

It is rather obvious that a deterministic theology, which stresses human depravity in the extreme so that even the Christian is barely, if ever, able to rise above it, may tend to produce minimal commitment or effort regarding practical Christian activity. This was evident in the emergent Protestant culture surrounding Hubmaier. On the other hand, the belief that the power of God is brought to bear on the believer to be able to respond to the commands of Christ to be holy is a very clear feature of the New Testament.[413] But Hubmaier did not expect sinless perfection. He had a balanced view of the believer's righteous standing *in Christ* as being perfect even though he continues to be deficient and fallible, while stressing at the same time the importance of obedient works of love:

> In sum: God requires of us the will, the word, and the works of brotherly love, and he will not let himself be paid off or dismissed with words, Matt.

---

413 According to Alvin Beachy, a basic distinction with Luther and Calvin as opposed to the Anabaptists is in their conceptions of grace, and what salvation actually achieves in the believer is the major difference: "The concept of grace which prevailed within the Magisterial Reformation was inseparably linked with predestination and the bondage of the will. Within this framework grace from God's side is the eternal decrees of divine election. From man's side it is God's act of forensic justification wherein the righteousness of the Christian becomes the imputed righteousness of Christ. Where grace is understood in this manner, spiritual health or wholeness is not something that becomes possible within this world. The Christian is throughout life both justified and sinner. He stumbles through this life as one who is half ill and as one who has the promise that eventually he will be well; but the promise of health is not health itself. Luther and Calvin were in essential agreement on this forensic view of grace as expressed in the formula, *simil justus et peccator*. The Magisterial Reformers arrived at this concept of grace by reading Paul through the eyes of Augustine. So understood, justification by grace through faith means a change of status before God, who for Christ's sake regards the sinner as righteous. It does not mean that within this life there is an ontological or metaphysical change in the believer himself. . . . grace is for the Radical Reformers . . . an ontological change within the individual believer. . . . The Radicals did not think that this grace could be earned through any meritorious work. Yet once received, the gift of grace so understood did enable one to rise higher in the scale of Christian perfection than was generally thought possible where the forensic concept of grace prevailed." *The Concept of Grace in the Radical Reformation*, 4–5.

Analysis of the Doctrine of Free Will in Respect to Hubmaier's Broader Theology

14; Luke 8:21; Rom. 8:1; Luke 17; Isa. 64:5ff.; Col. 2:10; Ps. 32:1f; Rom. 4:5; 5; 7; 8. But what innate weaknesses and imperfections constantly are intermingled with our acts of commission and omission because of our flesh, God—thanks to the grace of our Lord Jesus Christ—will not reckon to our eternal condemnation; for in Christ we have all attained perfection, and in him we are already blessed. What more do we lack?[414]

Alvin Beachy observes, "The only good works, according to Hubmaier, are deeds of brotherly love which God has commanded, but these are acts of gratitude in response to God's mercy."[415]

It should be noted, in addition, that the works to which Hubmaier referred were not ritualistic or sacerdotal in any way. The Anabaptists were often accused of legalism, but for Hubmaier works were to be performed out of love for Christ and love for the brethren and were of such a nature as are indicated in the New Testament.[416] These Christian works in no way resem-

---

414 Hubmaier, *A Form for Christ's Supper*, Pipkin and Yoder, 402. This passage also manifests Hubmaier's views on 'perseverance.' Clearly, he does not view the Christian as losing salvation for any failure on his or her part. Christ has done the work of perfecting the believer in God's sight. There is no lack to make up by any works. The works are done from obedience, and gratitude for God's grace. The assurance of the believer is wholly in the risen Christ and his finished work on the cross.

415 Beachy, *The Concept of Grace in the Radical Reformation*, 25.

416 Walter Klaassen devotes a whole chapter to the alleged legalism of the Anabaptists. He compares the Anabaptists with the reform in Geneva, a place from which the allegation of legalism was leveled against the Anabaptists. Here we see the importance and consequences of the affirmation of free will within Anabaptism: "Even with all their talk about law we cannot simply accept the charge of legalism. For no one was compelled to do these things. Those who belonged to their fellowship had quite deliberately entered the circle of disciples upon Jesus' own invitation. These kinds of actions flowed from within and were not imposed from without. No one who regarded their understanding of God's will as legalism was under any compulsion to join them. And if anyone already in their community could not agree he was not forced to conform against his will but was allowed to leave without restriction. It was quite another story in Calvin's Geneva. There, because all who lived in Geneva were considered members of the church regardless of their own words and actions, specific laws governing behavior were en-

bled the kind of legalism that had prevailed in the Catholic system.⁴¹⁷ Ulrich Zwingli tried to accuse the Anabaptists of a kind of factious legalism (and also perfectionism for good measure), but Hubmaier responded by invoking the principle of voluntarism:

---

forced. There were fines for swearing, drinking, coming late for church, speaking disrespectfully of the preachers, failing to attend church, not being able to recite the Creed and the Lord's Prayer. People were subject to these laws and penalties whether they agreed to them or not, and if they did not it usually meant exile with loss of livelihood. That is legalism. But where, as in the Anabaptist fellowships, no one was baptized without the rule of Christ, including the commitment to accept and participate in church discipline, it is not accurate to dismiss the whole thing as legalism. There was discipline, but voluntarily accepted discipline is never the equivalent of legalism." *Anabaptism: Neither Catholic nor Protestant*, 33–34.

417 Klaassen writes, "Luther's concern was to break free of the multitude of things required of the faithful in Roman Christianity to achieve salvation: the prayers, penances, pilgrimages and all that. All Anabaptists joined Luther in rejecting that kind of righteousness by works. But many were not so subtle; they assumed from Luther's words that works also included moral behaviour, and, therefore, that this too was no longer important. Anabaptists clearly and emphatically distinguished between these ceremonial and cultic laws, and the ethical requirements of the Gospel. . . . The former works ought to be abandoned because they were commanded by men and because they could not deliver what was claimed for them. The latter are the expressed will of God and are the expression and fruit of eternal life." Klaassen, *Anabaptism: Neither Catholic nor Protestant*, 30–31. Hubmaier penned a witty opinion (he often employed puns and other humorous imagery in his writings) concerning the system of Romish works: "Until now we have preached much gossip, unnecessary junk, human laws, and legends, and we have said how we can through this or through that work become righteous and be saved, namely through infant baptism, vigils, masses, organs, pipes, ringing, indulgences, images, pilgrimages, brotherhoods, offerings, purgatory, masses, mumbling, growling, and bellowing. But all this is a small matter, if now we only confess and abstain from this trickery [Ger. *Larvenwerck*, lit. 'masquerade'] and call to God with Paul, 'O God, forgive us; we did it without knowing.' The red whore of Babylon with her cup full of laws, school teachings, and fables has made us drunk, blinded, and deceived us. . . . You must believe the Word of God and not them. God alone is truthful, but all human beings are deceitful." Hubmaier, *On the Christian Baptism of Believers*, Pipkin and Yoder, 143.

Analysis of the Doctrine of Free Will in Respect to Hubmaier's Broader Theology

> *Zwingli*: Whoever lets himself be baptized among you must say: You are without sin and thus live and dress as you say they should, all of which is a sect and a faction. You must not force baptism as if it were a monastic vow.
>
> *Balthasar*: You are unfair and unjust to us in all that. *We force no one.* God loves a joyous giver, 2 Cor. 9:7. Each one should eat and drink what God gives, though moderately and with thanksgiving, 1 Tim. 4:4. Each one should dress as he wants, though the clothing should not be offensive. God forgive you and us all.[418]

As Beachy writes: "Hubmaier maintained . . . that before God one is justified by faith alone, and that here all works of merit such as penance, the eating of fish on certain days, unleavened bread, the carrying of palms in religious processions, have been cast out as whey water."[419]

Contrary to a legalistic or meritorious approach to Christian works, Hubmaier describes the manner and motivation for works of brotherly love as the following:

> Let one also confirm himself in gratitude, so as to be thankful in words and deeds toward God for the great, overabundant, and unspeakable love and goodness that he has shown him through his most beloved Son, our Lord Jesus Christ, John 3:16; Rom. 8:32. Namely that he now gives praise and thanks from the heart to God. Further, that he be of an attitude and ready will to do for Christ his God and Lord in turn as he had done for him. But since Christ does not need our good deeds, is not hungry, is not thirsty, is not naked or in prison, but heaven and earth are his and all that is in them, therefore he points us toward our neighbor, first of all to the members of the household of faith, Matt. 25:34ff.; Gal. 6:10; 1 Tim. 5, that we might fulfill the works of this our gratitude

---

418 Emphasis added. Hubmaier, *Dialogue with Zwingli's Baptism Book*, Pipkin and Yoder, 207–208. The avowal that they forced no one was key to the Anabaptists' practical theology, just as free will was essential to Hubmaier's theology as a whole. Zwingli, on the other hand, forced Anabaptists out of Zurich, or into prison where they died, simply for baptizing adult believers.

419 Beachy, *The Concept of Grace in the Radical Reformation*, 25.

toward them physically and spiritually, feeding the hungry, giving drink to the thirsty, clothing the naked, consoling the prisoner, sheltering the needy. Then he will be ready to accept these works of mercy from us in such a way as if we had done them unto him.[420]

Hubmaier affirms throughout his writings that works are never to be seen as attempts to gain salvation but are a faithful and grateful response to God's grace, seeking to benefit fellow believers, and mankind in general. Works of love, then, are marks of trust in Christ, the believer being resolved to follow His commands in worshipful, thankful obedience.

ELECTION, FREEDOM OF CHOICE, AND THE KNOWLEDGE OF GOOD AND EVIL

Hubmaier affirmed that those who choose to believe are saved by the merits of Christ, but those who choose not to believe are left to receive punishment for sins. How did he reconcile this with the doctrine of election? He handles this question, first, by examining it from a broader perspective, positing a twofold division of the revealed will of God, an attracting will and a repelling will:

> Whoever is not satisfied with this answer, namely, that the mercy of God is the cause of our salvation and our wickedness the cause of our damnation, must ask God himself, Rom. 11:11–12. I was not his advisor, nor was I with him in his council. Whoever says that God wills sin does not know what God or sin is. For sinning is always to do or to omit something against the will of God, 1 John 2:5–6. Yes, as one says: "If God does not want it, I will not sin." I say the opposite. Because God does not want such, we sin, for we resist his revealed will, 1 John 3:9–10. The will of God turned toward us is a will of love; his will turned from us a will of punishment, Isa. 55:6–7; Jer. 51:1.[421]

---

420 Hubmaier, *A Form for Christ's Supper*, Pipkin and Yoder, 397.
421 Hubmaier, *Freedom of the Will, II*, Pipkin and Yoder, 469. Hubmaier also appeals to the mystery of God's hidden will in this matter just as

This is the way Hubmaier frames election. The choice is still in the hands of the human. God turns away from those who turn from him and accepts those who accept him. Frank Wray explains Hubmaier's primary aim in featuring and bifurcating God's revealed will:

> Hubmaier's chief purpose appears to have been to place the responsibility for sin and evil squarely upon the shoulders of man without sacrificing the sovereignty of God or denying man's need for grace. To do so, he distinguished between what God can do and what He does do. God owes nothing to anyone, and therefore he could, without injustice, have mercy upon or condemn whomever He wishes. Here is the so-called secret will or plenary power by which God is able to do all things. But God has revealed His will that all men should be saved. God acts toward human beings not according to his omnipotence but according to his mercy. Hubmaier then proceeded to divide God's revealed will into two parts, which he termed the attracting and repelling will. By the former God offers grace and mercy to everyone; but, according to His repelling will, He turns away from those who do not receive Him and leaves them in their blindness and evil. Hubmaier identified this repelling will with God's will of justice and punishment.[422]

Luther and Calvin do, thought in less vitriolic fashion. Ironically Hubmaier is defending election and the freedom of the will while Luther and Calvin defend election and the bondage of the will in this way. Hubmaier writes: "We should not seek higher things than we are, Eccles 3. Nor should we search more powerful things than we. Rather we should always have before our eyes what God has commanded us, and in many other works should not be curious here on this earth with our eyes, Deut. 4; 5. As it is not good to eat too much honey, so also the one who wants to be a searcher of divine majesty will be thrown down by the splendor of God, Prov. 25:16. To want to know outside of Scripture which people God wants to save or condemn is the worst serpent himself who counsels us so that we become gods, that is, naked and bare, Mark 16:16; Gen. 3:7." *Freedom of the Will, II*, Pipkin and Yoder, 470.

422 Frank Wray, "History in the Eyes of the Sixteenth Century Anabaptists" (Ph.D. diss., Yale University, 1954), 31–32.

THE CENTRALITY OF THE DOCTRINE OF HUMAN FREE WILL
IN THE THEOLOGY OF BALTHASAR HUBMAIER

The provision for salvation is given in Christ if one chooses to take it up by faith. Salvation is furnished in Christ by the grace and mercy of God the Father. This is His revealed will, the hidden will being inscrutable. Thus, Hubmaier's doctrine is not in any sense a circumvention or controlling antecedent of Christ Himself, as the Calvinistic concept of eternal decrees in election can appear to be, but is all based upon belief, or unbelief, in the Son of God Himself. He writes, "Whomever God has chosen and selected by his special choice, in order to keep them, concerns the secret God, whose mind we do not know. For deep are his judgments and unfathomable are his reasons, 1Cor. 2:7; Rom. 11:33."[423] Hubmaier argues further concerning God's revealed will:

> As soon as now God turns to us, calls, and admonishes us to follow after him, and we leave wife and child, ship and tools, also everything that hinders us on the way to him, we are already helped, John 1:35ff. That is called his facing and drawing will . . . Whichever people do not accept, hear, or follow after him, the same he turns himself away from and withdraws from and lets them remain as they themselves want to be. That is now called the withdrawing will of God, concerning which David gives information when he says, "O God, do not turn your face from me," Ps. 51:11. So just in this way is God holy with the holy, and withdrawing with the withdrawn. The first will can be called in the Scripture *Voluntas conversiva a convertendo* [The conversive will in relation to the one to be converted]. The second, *Voluntas aversia ab avertendo* [The aversive will in relation to the one to be turned away from], not that there are two wills in God . . . for there is one single will in God, but one must speak about God humanly and with human words, as if he had eyes and ears, face and back, turned to and away from, and that because of our small understanding.[424]

With this line of thinking in mind, Hubmaier also speaks often of the "restoration," by which he means the work of Christ, which has restored the wonderful option for mankind to be reconciled with God based on his sacri-

---

423 Hubmaier, *Freedom of the Will, II*, Pipkin and Yoder, 467.
424 Ibid., 475–476.

fice and resurrection. He describes this "restoration" as the "recognition and power of knowledge, willing, and working" of good. It is the restoration of the knowledge of good and evil, which, Hubmaier says, was lost in the Fall by Adam and Eve. Hubmaier explains the loss of the knowledge of good and evil. Here is found also his definition of human free will:

> Since free will in the human is nothing other than a power, force, energy, or adroitness of the soul to will or not to will something, to choose or flee, to accept or to reject good or evil, according to the will of God, or according to the will of the flesh, which fleshly will and potentiality should more exactly be called an impotence rather than a power or energy. But the soul, through the eating of the forbidden tree lost the recognition of good and evil in the sight of God, which knowledge it certainly had before the Fall, as far as it was necessary and sufficient for a human creature to know. Therefore that same tree was called a tree of the knowledge of good and evil from which God forbade Adam to eat, Gen. 2:17, that is to desire, know, and experience more than is necessary for a human being. For Eve wanted also to know everything that God knows, as promised her by the crafty serpent. "On the day they eat thereof, their eyes will open and they will become as gods, knowing good and evil," Gen. 3:5. Accordingly they were rightly removed and robbed of this knowledge of good and evil by God and have become as a horse and a mule in whom there is no understanding.[425]

Without this knowledge a person cannot know what is good or evil in God's sight and is subject to the will of his flesh. With the loss of the knowledge of good and evil through willful disobedience comes the loss of the freedom to choose and perform good.

If one is blind to the good then one certainly will be incapable of willing the good, much less carrying it out in action. Hubmaier wrote: "Now a person can no longer will something good nor flee evil unless he knows beforehand what is good or evil in the eyes of God."[426] The human being has lost the free-

---

425 Hubmaier, *Freedom of the Will, I,* Pipkin and Yoder, 443.
426 Ibid., 444.

dom to choose good or evil. Since evil has been chosen in the Fall, good has been forfeited. Only a new grace can restore it. Although the spirit of man remains able to desire the good, he cannot do so because of the lost knowledge and power to do good in the soul. Thus only the darkness and punishment of death await. The new grace which restores the health of soul and spirit through Christ, restores the power of the soul to desire and choose and do good in accordance with the Spirit, all through the work of Christ revealed as the Word, drawing men outwardly through the preaching of that Word and inwardly through the Holy Spirit, and making the man whole again.

In this way, by turning to Christ, the will is free again to choose and to do good. The reborn believer commits to do so, trusting the power of God in Christ by a decision of faith. Estep elaborates:

> Thus, Hubmaier reinforces his argument that fallen man does, indeed, have a free will. While that will is certainly limited by his inherited sinful nature from doing good, it still possesses the capacity, even though captive to the flesh, of desiring the good. Through the gospel, God has taken the initiative, first in providing a way of salvation through the atoning work of Christ and second by drawing men to him. This drawing is twofold, outward and inward. God calls men to himself outwardly by the proclamation of his "holy gospel, which Christ commanded to be preached to every creature, . . ." The inward drawing is the work of God who enlightens the soul which is convicted by the Holy Spirit through the preached word and led to confess Christ before men. While God takes the initiative, he cannot make the decision for man.[427]

The knowledge and power concerning good and evil has been restored in Christ and is made manifest in the cross. It is up to the individual to accept it or reject it. He is given the power to do so in the very word of the gospel message, a restored knowledge of God's will given in Christ, the great Alternative. Hubmaier here summarizes this doctrine of the "restoration," highlighting the grace of God:

---

427 Estep, "The Anabaptist View of Salvation," 47.

Analysis of the Doctrine of Free Will in Respect to Hubmaier's Broader Theology

> Therefore this recognition and power of knowledge, willing, and working must happen and be attained by a new grace of the heavenly Father, who now looks at humanity anew by the merit of Jesus Christ our Lord, blesses and draws him with his life-giving Word which he speaks into the heart of a person. This drawing and call is like an invitation to a marriage or to an evening meal. Through it God gives power and authority to all people insofar as they themselves want to come; the free choice is left to them. It is a new birth, a beginning of his creatures, like humanity in Paradise first had been, excepting only the flesh; indeed, it is truly becoming the children of God.[428]

Becoming children of God can only be accomplished by faith in Christ's work. But the choice to believe is left to the person who is confronted by the gracious offer of salvation.

The idea of "restoration" is a key for interpreting Hubmaier, especially his concept of God's grace manifested in Christ. In the restoration, achieved by Jesus Christ and his death for sins, there is displayed the knowledge of good and evil in the very sacrifice of Christ on the cross. The good God gave his Son, who was completely good Himself, to pay the punishment for the sin and evil of mankind. Hubmaier wrote, "Here note and let hear whoever has ears, that we are again made free through the sent Word and truth of God, through his only begotten Son, Jesus Christ."[429] In this knowledge there is restored freedom because the very nature of this restored knowledge involves a choice. There is good on one side and evil on the other. Man's predicament is manifest in that he has no ability to be truly good in himself. That ability has been forfeited in the Fall; he is in bondage to sin, which is revealed in the necessity of the sacrifice of the Lamb of God.

Hence, Hubmaier also examines man's bondage to sin, applying his tripartite anthropology, explaining how each part, body, soul, and spirit, has been affected:

---

428 Hubmaier, *Freedom of the Will, I*, Pipkin and Yoder, 444.
429 Ibid., 439.

> Here one sees truly how the flesh after the Fall can do wholly and completely nothing; and how, as far as good is concerned, it is completely unprofitable and dead, in all its powers incapable of doing good, and is impotent, an enemy of the law, to whom it does not want to be subservient even unto the grave, John 2:16f. Thus did King David so bitterly complain and cry that no health was in his flesh, Ps. 38:4. On that Paul says: "I know truly that nothing good dwells in me, that is, in my flesh," Rom. 7:18; 8:26. The spirit, however, even if it gladly wanted to will and to do right, is imprisoned. It can accomplish nothing other than bear internal witness to righteousness against evil and cry as a captive to God without ceasing, with unspeakable sighs. Thus the soul has fallen among murderers, has been badly wounded by them and lies there half-dead, Luke 10:30. It has no taste or knowledge any more of either good or evil.[430]

Here we see the spirit functioning as the conscience in man, bearing God's good image despite its futility in its bondage to sin and the flesh. It can only be set free to truly function and *do* good by the grace of God. This grace effects the rebirth in the believer by the "restoration" in Christ, as Hubmaier writes: "Therefore there must be true health and freedom in humanity again after the restoration, for God works always in us the willing and the doing, according to the good resolution of the heart, Phil. 2:13. Although the flesh does not afterward want to do so, it must against its own will do what the soul, which is united with the spirit, wants."[431] However, without the restoration the soul is in peril and darkness because it has lost its ability and power to respond to the spirit (conscience) in any effective way.

But the restoration, the coming of the Word of the gospel, provides the new freedom to choose good, and the opportunity to be made good (justified, righteous), because of the good news of Christ's loving sacrifice accomplished on Calvary. This is all appropriated in a decision to trust Christ and to live by faith in Him. The Word of God, the gospel, then, confronts a person with the crucial choice: to elect to *be* good (forensically and ontologically) through the grace of the Father in His Son and His life, death, and resurrection, ac-

---

430 Hubmaier, *Freedom of the Will, I*, Pipkin and Yoder, 438.
431 Ibid., 439–440.

cepted as a gift by submissive faith alone; or to continue to demand his own way, his own advantage, to choose himself above all others including God, in other words, to choose evil. "Yes, God speaks first and gives power through his Word," writes Hubmaier. "Now the human being can also help himself through the power of the Word or he can willfully neglect; that is up to him."[432]

Additionally, Hubmaier employed his three-fold anthropology to explain the choice which every person faces concerning salvation, and the consequences of that choice:

> To summarize: The spirit is whole also after the restoration. The flesh can do nothing at all. The soul, however, can sin or not sin. But the soul which sins will die, Ezek. 18:20. Accordingly, it can well and rightfully say, *propter me orta est haec tempestas*, that is, "it has to do with me." The flesh has received its judgment. The spirit keeps its wholeness. If I now will, then I will be saved by the grace of God; If I do not will, then I will be damned, and that on the basis of my own obstinacy and willfulness. Thus speaks the Spirit of God through Hosea: "The condemnation is yours, Israel; only in me is your salvation," Hos. 13.9.[433]

So those who refuse the gift of salvation offered in the restoration effected by Christ are allowed to choose eternal death, the second death. As Hubmaier wrote, "Since God first created the light, whoever wants to accept it will do so on the basis of the commandment of God; whoever despises it falls into darkness because of the just judgment of God, John 1:5ff.; 3:19. And the talent which he has and does not want to use, but hides in the handkerchief, will therefore

---

432 Hubmaier, *Freedom of the Will, I*, Pipkin and Yoder, 440. In this passage Hubmaier further extolled the power of the Word: "It is the sent Word of God that works such in the soul, as David says: "He has sent his Word and made them whole," Ps. 107:20. Thus Christ says also: "If you remain in my Word, then you are my true disciples and will recognize the truth and the truth will make you free. If the Son makes you free, then you. are truly free," John 8:31ff."

433 Ibid., 442. The Latin *propter me orta est haec tempestas* can be translated as: 'because of me this storm has arisen.'

be simply taken from him."[434] For Hubmaier this judgment comes because of the nature of sin: "For this reason it is said: Sin is done willingly; if it were not, it would not be sin. This willfulness is the theme of those Scriptures in which God rebukes us because we do not want to hear, know, or accept the good."[435]

Hubmaier points to Christ as He who has overcome all that is harmful to the human being and thus has restored the freedom to choose and do good. The soul "has been awakened by the heavenly Father through the words of comfort, threats, promises, good things, punishment, and in other ways prodded, admonished, and drawn, as well as made whole by his dear Son, and enlightened by the Holy Spirit—as the three main articles of our Christian faith show—by this the soul now again knows what is good and evil. Now it again has obtained its lost freedom."[436] Hubmaier asserts that the person who accepts Christ then has the power to choose good and to reject evil because of the power of God in him made possible in the Word. The soul "can now freely and willingly be obedient to the spirit, can will and choose good, as well as it was able in Paradise. It can also reject evil and flee it. It is the sent Word of God that works such in the soul."[437] "Accordingly," Hubmaier proclaimed, "henceforth every soul that sins will bear its sin itself since it is willingly responsible for its own sin and not Adam, not Eve, not the flesh, sin, death or the devil, for all these things are already captured, bound, and overcome in Christ. To him we say, with Paul, be praise, honor, and thanks for eternity."[438]

Hubmaier goes on to describe those who reject Christ. In this passage we find yet another key doctrinal underpinning for his assertion of human free will, that of the nature of heaven, which is defined as *unforced* delight in God's presence, and promised to those who *freely* believe and *freely* receive it:

> But whoever does not want to come, like Jerusalem and those who have bought oxen and houses and have taken wives–these he leaves out as unworthy of this Supper. He wants to have uncoerced, willing,

---

434 Hubmaier, *Freedom of the Will, I*, Pipkin and Yoder, 440.
435 Ibid., 441.
436 Ibid., 439.
437 Ibid.
438 Ibid., 446.

and joyous guests and donors; these he loves. For God does not force anyone except through the sending and calling of his Word, as also the two disciples at Emmaus did not force Christ to remain with them otherwise than by request and good words, Luke 24:29.[439]

In this concept we also see, emphasized and elaborated, Hubmaier's doctrine of the Word. The Word is the gospel, which is the opportunity in Christ who *is* the Word, to become a child of God by faith. The soul, who is sent this gracious Word, then, is given the power to choose obedience and reject the flesh and sin. This is made possible by Christ, but one must choose: "The soul is now free and may follow the spirit or the flesh. . . . The soul should beware that it not linger too long at this oak of human choice and first at length consider whether it will follow the flesh or the spirit, lest it, like Absalom, who also hung between heaven and earth, 2 Sam. 18:9, be stabbed to death by the slave of sin, that is, by the flesh, with three wounds: of consent, word, and deed."[440]

Hubmaier showcases the importance of God's revealed will in the Word of God Who became flesh. He, His words and sacrifice and resurrection, is God's revealed Word to us. We must listen and respond to these, first and foremost, not allowing unexplainable decrees of predestination, for instance, to usurp the supremacy of the gospel. This is because Christ has vanquished all that might injure a person because of sin. Thus the individual is now accountable for his own decision concerning Christ. If he refuses Him, the harvest of his sin remains to be reaped by the soul alone since the salvation Christ has offered has been rejected. Hubmaier described this offer of salvation in terms of his tripartite anthropology while scorning the notion of the Fall as excusing sin:

> Here one grasps with both hands how Christ has made the Fall of Adam wholly innocuous for us and incapable of condemning, and how he crushed the head of the old serpent through the seed of the woman, Gen. 3:15, how he took away the sting and made its poison no longer lethal to us, 1 Cor. 15:30f. Thus, henceforth, no one may decry Adam or Eve nor excuse or gloss over his sins with Adam's Fall since everything which has

---

439 Hubmaier, *Freedom of the Will, I*, Pipkin and Yoder, 444.
440 Ibid., 440.

been lost, wounded and had died in Adam has been sufficiently restored, healed, and made healthy. For Christ with His Spirit has acquired for our spirit from the heavenly Father that the prison is not harmful to our spirit. And with his soul he has acquired for our soul that through his divine Word it is again taught and enlightened as to what good and evil is. Yes, also by his flesh he earns for our flesh that after it has become ashes it may again be resurrected in honor and be immortal, 1 Cor. 15:22.[441]

Hubmaier perceived here that, for the believer, all has been accomplished through Christ, so that the penalty of sin "is unharmful to him, for it is fulfilled through Christ, who is the Alpha and Omega, the beginning and the end of the fulfillment of divine commandments. In him is our perfection. If the commandments of God are fulfilled, says Augustine, those other things not fulfilled by us are forgiven us."[442]

Because of the perfection of Christ, then, believers also know they are elect and predestined, but all of this is founded on faith in Christ alone. This is Hubmaier's brand of *sola fide*, grounded solely on the revelation of God in Christ, the incarnate Word:

> Whoever God has chosen and selected by his special choice, in order to keep them, concerns the secret God, whose mind we do not know. For deep are his judgments and unfathomable are his reasons, 1 Cor. 2:7; Rom. 11:33.
>
> Nevertheless, it is certain and sure that the crucified Christ wants all people to be saved and come to the recognition of the truth, 1 Tim. 2:4.
>
> We should listen to the incarnated God—thus speaks the voice of the heavenly Father out of the clouds—and not concern ourselves with researching and investigating further God's omnipotence, omniscience, and eternal foreknowledge, predestination, providence, or reprobation, lest we become gods like Adam and Eve, Matt. 17:5; 2 Pet. 1:17; Luke 9:35; Rom. 11:33; Gen. 3:5.

---

441 Hubmaier, *Freedom of the Will, I*, Pipkin and Yoder, 446.
442 Ibid., 441–442.

> It is crazy foolishness of ours that we desire to know the secret will of God, and we despise his known will.[443]

As is evident, Hubmaier does not have an intricate doctrine of election. He simply acknowledges that God knows all and that man cannot know the future as God does, thus he should pay attention to what God clearly reveals, that He requires of us faith and love: "Yes, it is thus, that God knows all things truly, necessarily, and unchangeably from eternity. Which one of two opposites he knows [elect or reprobate], however, is still unknown to us. . . . In the articles concerning faith and love we are sure and certain which choice God wants to have from us, John 20:27-29."[444]

Although Hubmaier does not explicitly state that election is based on God's foreknowledge, this last passage would seem to indicate that this probably was his view. The willing submission or willful rebellion of each individual, in regard to Christ, is known to God, but not to men. Roger Olson states, "Hubmaier also claimed that God's election and predestination are based entirely on his foreknowledge of which individuals will respond to grace and how. He was adamantly opposed to unconditional predestination—the monergism of Augustine, Luther, Zwingli and Calvin."[445] Along these lines Hubmaier wrote: "That would be a perfidious God who would invite all people to a supper, offer his mercy to everyone with exalted earnestness, and would yet not want them to come, Luke 14:16ff.; Matt. 22:2ff. That would be a false God who would say with the mouth, "Come here," but would think secretly in the heart, "Stay there," Isa. 55:1; Matt. 11:28; John 1:12; Luke 15:22."[446]

Hubmaier relegates the doctrine of God's foreknowledge to the category of the secret will of God, which should not, and indeed *cannot*, be the basis of a doctrine of salvation. Instead, he points over and over to the revealed will of God in Christ, contending that this must be the will to which the believer responds in faith and obedience. For Hubmaier the hidden will, His omniscience and sovereign power and providence, belongs to the doctrine of God

---

443 Hubmaier, *Freedom of the Will, II*, Pipkin and Yoder, 467.
444 Insertion added. Ibid., 468.
445 Olson, *The Story of Christian Theology*, 422.
446 Hubmaier, *Freedom of the Will, II*, Pipkin and Yoder, 465-466.

proper, not to soteriology. Any other approach to soteriology, such as double predestination, which inclines toward deterministic fate, is, for Hubmaier, to make a 'god out of every cherry pit.' He wrote, "Therefore there should be no dispute concerning the omnipotence of God, as to what and how much is possible to God, but of his known will which he has revealed to us by the Scripture, or we will in the last analysis make a special god out of every single cherry pit, Rom. 12:2. Whoever denies the freedom of the will in the human being to whom God sends his Word and who has not sinned against the Holy Spirit, denies, overthrows and rejects more than half the Holy Bible, Matt 12:32; Luke 12:10; Heb. 6:6; 10:31."[447]

HUBMAIER'S ECCLESIOLOGY: BELIEVER'S BAPTISM

For Hubmaier, Baptism, instead of being an initiation into 'Christendom,' is the outward sign of inward personal faith in Christ. "The baptism of Christ," writes Hubmaier, "is a public and outward confession or oath of faith, that is, that the person inwardly believes the forgiveness of his sins through Christ, for which reason he lets himself be enrolled and outwardly dedicated among Christians, and that he wants to live according to the Rule of Christ."[448] This was a completely different proposition than the prevailing idea of the major Protestant reformers, who, comparing baptism with Israelite circumcision, made of it an admission into the 'community of believers,' mostly for infants. This community was identified with Christian society as a whole, assigning to baptism the power of regeneration. For the Anabaptists, *believer's baptism* was the external sign and affirmation of the individual's internal decision to

---

[447] Hubmaier, *Freedom of the Will, II*, Pipkin and Yoder, 471. For an example of what we might call 'cherry pit theology' see Millard Erickson, *Introducing Christian Doctrine*, 2nd ed., 126 ff., in which he discusses the movement of various fingers.

[448] Hubmaier, *Dialogue with Zwingli's Baptism Book*, Pipkin and Yoder, 209.

trust Christ and purposefully identify with the local body of believers. This formula inevitably involves freedom of choice.

Leonard Verduin refers to sixteenth century societal Christianity—Christendom—as a "culture religion" which precluded individual choice in the matter of its constituency:

> A culture-religion must of necessity be or become optionless religion–for a culture is the spiritual heritage of a total people. A culture-religion must find a way of including all in one and the same category, if not vitally and enthusiastically then academically and nominally. . . . In Christendom all members of society are held to be regenerate; all are said to be believers; all are assumed to be converted; all are allegedly "in Christ." And they are all of these things without any real exercise of option. And this by plan. For a culture-religion cannot tolerate a composite society, one that consists of men in the modality of lostness and of men in the modality of savedness; all must, by hook or by crook, be herded together in one and the same compound. A culture-religion cannot take the risk that is contained in the idea of membership-by-choice. It cannot sponsor a Church that a person *joins*; for wherever there is joining there can also be non-joining. Christendom (that is Christianity after it has been transformed into a culture-religion) had to usher in a Church to which one belonged apart from any exercise of option on his part. It did. In Christendom one *belongs* without the exercise of option. When Christendom was launched, *christening* was invented. Christening is what Christian baptism becomes after it has been stripped of decision-making. . . . As Martin Luther put it in his day, "If men were to *come* to baptism, the number of baptized ones would be appreciably less." In Christendom, that is, when Christianity had become a culture-religion, a baptism . . . which a man *comes to* has to make room for a baptism that is *brought to* man. But implied in the change-over is the loss, at least the drastic reduction, of option. With . . . Christendom the Christian insight that man is by definition a creature of option went into partial eclipse.[449]

---

449 Verduin, *Somewhat Less than God*, 91–94.

In this context, the Anabaptists found themselves at odds with all of sixteenth-century society since their commitment to believer's baptism and a free church, principles they saw as scripturally derived, assumed a composite society, as in New Testament times, not a monolithic Christendom.

As opposed to the "Christendom" concept of ecclesiology, Sydnor Stealey remarked that Hubmaier, "properly emphasized baptism as the door to the church and showed that the true order in baptism is this: (1) the Word, (2) hearing, (3) faith, (4) baptism, (5) good works. . . . He recognized too that infant baptism tends to uniformity without faith, that uniformity tends to enforced conformity, and that enforced conformity is tyranny."[450] So, for Hubmaier, the baptizand enters the waters of baptism "in order to manifest to other believers in Christ his heart, mind, faith, and intention, he *joins* their brotherhood and churches, so that from now on he might interact with them and they again with him as with a Christian. Therefore, he accepts and gives a public testimony of his internal faith and lets himself be baptized with water."[451]

Though Luther and Zwingli had in early days flirted with the idea of a voluntary church, these Magisterial Reformers found it impossible to maintain their state-supported reforms without infant baptism and its attendant societal ideal, Christendom. Hubmaier, however sought to view baptism only from the perspective of Scripture, and was ruthless in this appeal. He wielded the clear content of the Bible concerning believer's baptism as a sword, effectively shredding the scriptural qualifications and glosses, along with appeals to Old Testament law and church tradition, of the Magisterial Reformers' defense of pedobaptism. As Verduin writes, "In the sixteenth century the strife between the Reformers and the Anabaptists was at heart a struggle between proponents and opponents of Christendom; the Reformers were resolutely committed to Christianity as a culture-religion and the Anabaptists were as resolutely opposed to it. The Reformers feared a composite society and the Anabaptists feared a non-composite one."[452]

---

450 Sydnor L. Stealey, "Balthasar Hubmaier and Some Perennial Religious Problems," *The Review and Expositor* 40 (October 1943): 419.

451 Emphasis added. Hubmaier, *On the Christian Baptism of Believers*, Pipkin and Yoder, 117.

452 Verduin, *Somewhat Less than God*, 95.

Analysis of the Doctrine of Free Will in Respect to Hubmaier's Broader Theology

Gunnar Westin makes it clear that the very idea of believer's baptism undercut the Magisterial Reformers' left-over Roman Catholic 'Christendom' concept of society and ecclesiology: "It should be underscored emphatically that when Hübmaier denounced the sacrament of infant baptism and published his arguments for the baptism of believers in the summer of 1525, in an attack on Zwingli, he blazed a new trail. Acceptance of his arguments would have led to the overthrow of the national and territorial church organization, which Luther and the Reformed theologians carried over from the Catholic Church."[453] In his defense of believer's baptism, Hubmaier refuted charges of schism and anarchy leveled by those who sought to uphold a sacral and territorial Christian society via infant baptism:

> They further introduce a much more ungrounded, fictitious, and untrue complaint, saying: "One would thus make factions and sects, thereby abolish the government, and no longer be obedient to it." . . . But injustice is being done to us; we do not make factions and sects but act in this matter according to the Word of God. Neither angels, devils, nor human beings will ever be able to refute that, although some rage still so much and publish against it. Thus one sees very well in their writings that they prefer to obscure and darken the clear, bright, and plain baptismal Scriptures so that one does not see their error and stumbling. One recognizes their touch which does not resonate at all on the harp of Christ. May God grant us not such obscuring or glossing but the clear simple understanding of his living Word: *that* is something. In addition we confess publicly that there should be a government which carries the sword, that we want and should be obedient to the same in all things that are not contrary to God, and the more the same is Christian the more it desires from God to rule with the wisdom of Solomon so that it does not deviate either to the right nor to the left against God. Therefore we should also seriously and with great diligence pray to God for it, so that we may lead a peaceful and quiet life together in all blessedness and uprightness.[454]

---

453 Westin, *The Free Church Through the Ages*, 100–101.

454 Hubmaier, *On the Christian Baptism of Believers*, Pipkin and Yoder, 97–98.

THE CENTRALITY OF THE DOCTRINE OF HUMAN FREE WILL
IN THE THEOLOGY OF BALTHASAR HUBMAIER

In his balance here Hubmaier was a man completely ahead of his time. His view of how the Christian relates to society is how most modern evangelical Christians see it.[455] This seems clearly to be a result of his determination to view all these things in accordance with a simple and natural understanding of Scripture.

Conversely, Robert Torbet comments on the Magisterial Reformers' use of Scripture regarding their ecclesiology:

> While Luther and Zwingli virtually admitted that there was no justification in the Scriptures for a mixed membership, that is to say, of both regenerate and unregenerate members, both leaders failed to apply the principle of the authority of the Scriptures consistently. By retaining the practice of paedobaptism and the union of church and state, they

---

[455] Howard Snyder writes: "In the sixteenth century it was difficult to conceive of the Church as a people distinct from the rest of society or as a specific community separate from the world. Such a conception of the Church was so revolutionary as to be heretical and so threatening as to appear politically subversive. Largely for this reason, those who did go so far as to affirm the right and necessity of the Church to be a separate, distinct community of God's people—the Anabaptists—died by the hundreds for their faith. It is certainly more than coincidence that the contemporary rediscovery of Anabaptism has paralleled a new emphasis on the Church as community and as a people." Howard A. Snyder, *The Community of the King* (Downers Grove: Inter-Varsity Press, 1977), 35-36. Snyder further clarifies his understanding of the Protestant reformers' view of the church: "Neither Luther nor Calvin saw the Church as identical with the state or with society in general. They even admitted a certain tension between the Church and society. But they did not conceive of the Church as a sociologically distinct, self-conscious community existing in evident tension with surrounding society, that is, as a counterculture." Snyder, *The Community of the King*, 196. The general idea of a counterculture (and sociologically distinct) model of church in relation to society certainly dovetails better with the New Testament church, with modern conservative evangelicalism, and, of course, with the Anabaptism of the sixteenth century than the total cultural and governmental unity, 'Christendom' model, enforced in the territorial Protestant reform of the Magisterial Reformation, a leftover from medieval Roman Catholic society which had been dominant in Europe for so many centuries.

continued an ecclesiastical system which inadvertently perpetuated the evils of an unregenerate church membership. It was for Anabaptists like Hubmaier . . . to withstand Zwingli on this point at the peril of their lives.[456]

John Rempel concurs: "What took Hubmaier decisively beyond the reformation at Zurich was his understanding of faith and of the church. Faith as a willed response of obedience and church as the voluntary pact of those who had come to faith."[457] Gunnar Westin also characterizes Hubmaier's ecclesiology as exceptional in comparison with the territorial reformers, who continued with the old Constantinian system: "The greatest sensation which Hübmaier created was his concept of the congregation (church) and the sacraments, especially baptism. . . . The church is a congregation of true believers (*Sonderkirche*) which are separated from the parochial congregation of the national Church, upon which both Zwingli and Luther established their Reformation churches."[458]

Hubmaier's congregational view of the church also led to an emphasis on discipleship, based on the belief that the Christian has the freedom to do good works in his new life in Christ. Hence, his understanding of the church as a community of believers in voluntary association entailed a call for fraternal admonition. Hubmaier viewed the believer's consent to receive this brotherly admonition, in association with baptism, as a commitment to fellow members of the church to live by the rule of Christ. He follows Matt. 18 as the simple order of admonition. The purpose was to maintain the holiness of the life of the church. This was Hubmaier's simple New Testament answer to what he saw as the besetting weakness of Protestantism: worldliness. Hubmaier lamented: "For we all want to be good Protestants by taking wives and eating meat, no longer sacrificing, no more fasting, no more praying, yet apart from this one sees nothing but tippling, gluttony, blaspheming, usury, lying, deceit, skinning and scraping, coercing, pressing, stealing, robbing, burning, gambling, dancing, flattery, loafing, fornication, adultery, rape, tyranny, strangling, murder. Here

---

456 Torbet, *A History of the Baptists*, 515.
457 Rempel, *The Lord's Supper in Anabaptism*, 53.
458 Westin, *The Free Church Through the Ages*, 100.

all the frivolity and insolence of the flesh finds free play; here the luxury of this world has the place of honor, rules, jubilates, and triumphs in all things."[459]

Hubmaier believed the Protestant propensity to permissiveness stemmed partially from the practice of infant baptism. He asserts, "Where water baptism is not given according to the order of Christ, there it is impossible to accept fraternal admonition from one another in a good spirit. For no one knows either who is in the church and who is outside."[460] Again the crucial role of human free will for Hubmaier's theology is clearly seen in that believer's baptism, based on a personal choice of faith, manifests itself in a clear demarcation between the church and the world. This makes fraternal admonition conceivable since, for Hubmaier, part of the baptismal pledge was a commitment to surrender to brotherly rebuke, of one's own free will, out of love for Christ and His church. The following is a section involving discipleship and fraternal admonition in the baptismal pledge Hubmaier wrote in his *Form for Water Baptism*:

> "Will you henceforth lead your life and walk according to the Word of Christ, as he gives you grace: So speak":
> "I will."
> "If now you should sin and your brother knows it, will you let him admonish you once, twice, and the third time before the church, and willingly and obediently accept fraternal admonition, if so speak":
> "I will."[461]

To Hubmaier, without scriptural baptism, resulting in a believers' church, "we are scattered to the winds, like sheep without shepherds, without a pasture, without markings, neither knowing nor being able to recognize who has *let himself* be marked as a sheep of Christ, or who *chooses* to remain as a wild buck outside the flock of Christ."[462] Note the language of human free will here, which underlies Hubmaier's ecclesiology.

---

459 Hubmaier, *On Fraternal Admonition*, Pipkin and Yoder, 376.
460 Ibid., 385.
461 Hubmaier, *A Form for Water Baptism*, Pipkin and Yoder, 389.
462 Emphasis added. Hubmaier, *On Fraternal Admonition*, Pipkin and Yoder, 385.

Analysis of the Doctrine of Free Will in Respect to Hubmaier's Broader Theology

Cornelius Dyck describes the difference between the Magisterial Reformers and the Anabaptists concerning the connection between a holy life and their theology, particularly with regard to ecclesiology:

> Sixteenth-century Anabaptist witness often began at the point of personal morality. To follow Christ meant to adopt a disciplined, almost ascetic style of life. . . . In Germany, Luther's emphasis on salvation by faith instead of works had lifted the controls of the medieval penance system. Private conscience and civil law were to take its place under the gospel. "The Word will do it," he believed. But the Word was interpreted as teaching the impossibility of escape from sin, making grace people's only option. And so, half jokingly, Luther once said, "sin bravely" in order that grace may abound. Medieval work-righteousness was to be abolished forever.
>
> The biggest obstacle to holiness, however, was the Reformers' acceptance of the medieval social structure, which made church and state coterminous. Neither Luther nor Zwingli could bring themselves to the founding of a church of believers only, though both considered it. In his *German Mass* of 1526, for example, Luther wrote: "They who seriously want to be Christians and want to confess the Gospel in word and deed, these ought to inscribe their names in a book and assemble in a house by themselves for purposes of prayer, the reading of Scripture, the administration of baptism, the reception of the sacrament and to engage in other Christian activities . . . but I neither can or may as yet set up such a congregation; for I do not as yet have the people for it. If however, the time comes that I must do it, so that I cannot with a good conscience refrain from it then I am ready to do my part."[463]

Hubmaier regarded the failure of the Reformers to form a believers' church, with a commitment to Christian holiness, as the result of a faulty, half-developed theology in which the necessity of all things became an excuse for sin. Luther sounded as if he were making excuses when he considered how the Anabaptists viewed his reform: "When they look at us and see the offensive

---

463 Dyck, "The Anabaptist Understanding of the Good News," 26–27.

defects with which Satan distorts our churches then they deny that we are a Church and they are unable to lift themselves over this. . . . but it does not offend God, seeing that for the sake of faith in Christ He excuses it and forgives."[464] Luther is here clearly admitting the troubling, problematic worldliness of his own group.

Hubmaier returned to his lamentation concerning Protestant laxness, squarely placing the blame on a theology devoid of the truth regarding the freedom and responsibility of man:

> Here no Christian deeds shine forth from anyone. Brotherly love and faithfulness is utterly extinct. Yet all of this (as painful as it is to say it) comes to pass behind the facade of the gospel. For as soon as you say to such "evangelical" people: "Brother, it stands written, forsake evil and do good," immediately he answers, "It stands written, we can do no good. Everything comes to pass according to the providence of God and necessarily." They think that thereby sin is permitted them. If you say further, "It stands written, they who do evil shall go into eternal fire," John 5:29, immediately the reach for a fan of fig leaves, Gen. 3:7, to cover their vice with, and say, "But it stands written: faith alone saves us and not our works."[465]

This is clearly a shot taken at Luther's doctrine of the bondage of the will. As we have seen, it is not that Hubmaier rejected *sola fide* but that he perceived the necessitarian teaching which undergirded Luther's theology as unbalanced at this point, in need of the word of James, "faith without works is dead." Cornelius Dyck concisely encapsulates Hubmaier's view: "His emphasis on freedom of the will was central to personal and communal accountability, without which there can be no discipleship."[466] Arnold Snyder writes: "For Hubmaier and the Anabaptists the biblical model of Christian community

---

464 Martin Luther, *Works*, St. Louis ed., Vol. 5, col. 747; quoted in Leonard Verduin, *The Reformers and Their Stepchildren*, 126.

465 Hubmaier, *On Fraternal Admonition*, Pipkin and Yoder, 376.

466 Cornelius J. Dyck, *Spiritual Life in Anabaptism* (Scottdale: Herald Press, 1995), 86.

was the community of yielded, regenerated, faithful, baptized, committed and obedient believers. The anchor of Anabaptist spirituality was this community, formed by the spiritual and water baptism of believers, maintained by fraternal admonition and nurtured by the Supper of the Lord (celebrated as a memorial) and by communal worship."[467]

The Lord's Supper, then, confirms the mutual dedication of love to Christ and to brother in Christian discipleship. As Hubmaier wrote, "We conclude that the bread and wine of the Christ meal are outward word symbols of an inward Christian nature here on earth, in which a Christian obligates himself to another in Christian love with regard to body and blood. Thus as the body and blood of Christ became my body and blood on the cross, so likewise shall my body and blood become the body and blood of my neighbor, and in time of need theirs become my body and blood, or we cannot boast at all to be Christians."[468] John Rempel makes clear that this emphasis on service to fellow believers is not works salvation: "Lest one assume, however, that behind this ... doctrine of the Holy Supper stands a theology of good works, it is necessary to recall that Hubmaier is unequivocal about the initiative of God's grace in saving humanity. That imitation of Christ's love which Hubmaier enjoins is possible only by grace and by the presence of the Spirit."[469]

Life in the believers' community was so essential to the Anabaptists, and to Hubmaier, that they recognized the practice of the ban for church discipline, based on Matt. 18, as imperative for the purity and unity of the church. Fraternal admonition and the ban were always to be motivated by love for the purpose of joyful restoration. Hubmaier warns, "let every Christian take heed to himself that such remonstrance and sharpness of the word might flow forth out of love and not from envy, hate, or wrath."[470] Hubmaier writes that the ban is "not for petty offenses as our papists have been doing, but for an offensive sin; and it is done for the good of the sinner, that he may exam-

---

467 Snyder, "Beyond Polygenesis," 15.
468 Hubmaier, *Several Theses Concerning the Mass*, Pipkin and Yoder, 76.
469 Rempel, *The Lord's Supper in Anabaptism*, 56–57.
470 Hubmaier, *On Fraternal Admonition*, Pipkin and Yoder, 378.

ine himself, know himself, and desist from the sin."[471] If the sinner repents, the church "receives him again with joy, as the father did his prodigal son."[472]

Aware of the potential abuse of the scriptural injunction to dissociate from those who remain in sin, Hubmaier made it clear that the ban was to be pressed only in matters of serious and ongoing public sin: "For the Christian church bans no one unless he has first been found guilty of a scandalous sin or public vice."[473] In analyzing Hubmaier's thought concerning the ban, Jaroslav Pelikan notes, "It was essential to remember, however, that those whom the church banned by this process had in fact excommunicated themselves, and that so solemn a condemnation was to be reserved for truly grave offenses, 'not for [stealing] six shillings' worth of hazelnuts."[474] Clearly, none of these scriptural ideas concerning church discipline are possible without an underlying recognition of human free will. Those believers who choose to sin willfully and egregiously must be disciplined for their own sakes and for the church's.

Robert Friedmann, in examining Hubmaier's thought on the ban, observes a correlation with his position on free will:

> The two subjects actually belong together: the recognition of man's freedom of decision on the one hand, and the necessity of disciplining this will by means of the ban on the other hand. In the tract on *Brotherly Admonition* (or *Punishment*) emphasis is laid on the loving intent in all this disciplining. Its justification, however, is seen in the baptismal pledge (*Taufergelübde*) of all those who constitute the true church. In other words, church and discipline belong together.[475]

To Hubmaier, baptism was the outward expression of inward surrender to Christ and thus also represented a responsibility to the body of believers, which included submission to church discipline and the ban. This kind of personal pledge could never be made by an infant. Babies cannot decide

---

471 Hubmaier, *A Christian Catechism*, Pipkin and Yoder, 354.
472 Ibid.
473 Hubmaier, *On the Christian Ban*, Pipkin and Yoder, 411.
474 Pelikan, *The Christian Tradition*, vol. 4, 319.
475 Friedmann, *The Theology of Anabaptism*, 145

Analysis of the Doctrine of Free Will in Respect to Hubmaier's Broader Theology

to commit themselves in this fashion. As Roger Olson writes: "If anything is clear in Hubmaier's theology it is his passionate belief . . . that authentic Christian life begins with a free decision made by the individual in response to God's gracious act in Jesus Christ. Such a free and personal response of the will cannot happen within an infant."[476]

Only those who had heard the Word and freely confessed faith, who understood and believed the gospel, were to be recipients of baptism. G. W. Bromiley notes that even Ulrich Zwingli "went so far as to concede to Balthasar Hubmaier, the pastor of Waldshut, that normally baptism ought to be preceded by instruction."[477] Hubmaier insisted that the biblical *ordo salutis* was "(1) word, (2) hearing, (3) faith, (4) baptism, (5) work."[478] Thus it was

---

476 Olson, *The Story of Christian Theology*, 421. Olson concisely outlines Hubmaier's baptismal theology in the following account: "According to the New Testament pattern, he argued, 'no one should be baptized with water unless beforehand he confesses faith and knows how he stands with God.' Speaking for all Anabaptists, he wrote, 'Thus we confess openly that we were not baptized in childhood' and 'infant baptism is a trick which is invented and introduced by human beings.' According to Hubmaier, baptism is simply a public testimony of previous conversion and regeneration by God's Spirit and must follow them or else it is not genuine baptism at all. That is why he and other Anabaptists rejected the term rebaptism for their practice of baptizing mature believers who had been 'washed' as infants. For them that practice was not rebaptism but the first genuine baptism. . . . The overall context of Hubmaier's theology makes clear that in this he included conversion and regeneration on the basis of repentance and faith. It is the 'internal baptism' and absolutely must come first. Water baptism 'is an outward and public testimony of the inner baptism in the Spirit, which a person gives by receiving water, with which one confesses one's sins before all people.' This is the ceremony by which a new believer enters into the fellowship of the church and pledges to live life for Christ. . . . It is not a sacrament, nor does it convey a gift of faith or grace. Yet it is necessary because Christ commanded it as outward testimony and pledge and the church needs it to know who properly belongs within its fellowship and who does not." *The Story of Christian Theology*, 420-421.

477 G. W. Bromiley, ed., *Zwingli and Bullinger*, The Library of Christian Classics (Philadelphia: Westminster Press, 1953), 119.

478 Hubmaier, *On the Christian Baptism of Believers*, Pipkin and Yoder, 129.

crucial in Hubmaier's ecclesiology for the believer to have made his own personal choice of faith, submitting himself to Christ before baptism and to the church's discipline in the baptismal pledge. With infant baptism, church discipline as a free will agreement between believers was impossible. The result of the Magisterial Reformers' denial of free will in the human, and affirmation of pedobaptismal regeneration as the foundation of a territorial state church, was a disturbing ethical leniency in the German and Swiss Reformation, and state-supported legalism in Calvin's Geneva.[479]

---

479 Leonard Verduin gives examples of the Magisterial Reformers' attempts to deal with the embarrassing fact of the moral laxness, what Verduin calls "conductual-averagism," in their territorial Protestant churches, as compared to the success of the Anabaptists' clear moral commitment in emphasizing free will discipleship: "It is apparent that the undeniably good way of life of the Stepchildren was an uncomfortable fact to the Reformers – so that they sought to escape it. In this mood Henry Bullinger wrote: 'Those who unite with them will by their ministers be received into their church by rebaptism and repentance and newness of life. They henceforth lead their lives under a semblance of quiet spiritual conduct. They denounce covetousness, pride, profanity, the lewd conversation and immorality of the world, the drinking and the gluttony. In fine, their hypocrisy is great and manifold.' The Reformers, in an attempt to get away from the mortifying fact that the Stepchildren were actually succeeding in their onslaught against conductual-averagism, resorted to the argument—an old one—that the good works were nothing but bait with which the devil baited his hook so as to catch a lot of fish. Bullinger, for example, wrote that the exemplary lives of the Restitutionists 'are hypocrisy, for . . . even Satan can transform himself into an angel of light . . . . he who wishes to catch fish does not throw out an unbaited hook.' After granting that the Restitutionists, Pilgram Marpeck and his wife, were 'people of devout and blameless lives' he added: 'But this is an old trick of the devil, with which he has in all churches, form the days of the Apostle Paul, sought to catch his fish.' . . . No one squirmed more painfully in view of the unwelcome fact that the Restitutionists were successfully attacking conductual-averagism than did Martin Bucer. He was constantly urging the magistrates to greater rigor in the use of the sword, saying with a glance at the Stepchildren: 'Their most pointed argument is always this that we keep house so badly; with this argument they lead astray many people. God help us, so that we may one day be able to take this argument away from them, yes from our own conscience and from the Lord our God. Of a truth it is getting to be high time that on the day of Saint Catherine we deal seriously with

Analysis of the Doctrine of Free Will in Respect to Hubmaier's Broader Theology

For the Anabaptists, baptism was a sign of faith, the hearing and confessing of belief in the gospel of Christ, and a sign of deliberate solidarity with one's fellow believers in a mutual commitment to trust and obey Christ. Paul Lederach elaborates:

> So important was baptism to the early Anabaptists that Hubmaier said, "Where there is no proper baptism, there is no church." This was not a reference to "baptismal regeneration." Rather, the emphasis was on the essential nature of the new birth and the pilgrim life. Baptism was an open commitment to and confession of both the experience of the new life and of being on the way. Baptism was always entered into freely. No one was coerced. It was received on the basis of one's own desire.[480]

It is not difficult to draw from this statement a noticeable foundational commitment to human free will in Hubmaier's theology as it is associated with his concept of baptism. Rollin Armour confirms Hubmaier's emphasis on free will

---

the matter of our housekeeping … for if this is not considered and remedied all our counsels against this rod of the Lord will be in vain.' At another time this Reformer complained: 'The magistrates are rather coarse and carnal men and the preachers are very neglectful; many of them frequently get drunk. Since the lords and council-men are that kind of people … they drive the poor people away with their wild way of life [*mit irem überbolderen*]. The plain man cannot bring himself to recognize the Church of Christ among such wild persons, and, to distinguish correctly between doctrine and life.'" Verduin, *The Reformers and Their Stepchildren*, 110–111. On legalism in Geneva see above, note 416.

480 Paul Lederach, *A Third Way: Conversations About Anabaptist / Mennonite Faith* (Scottdale: Herald Press, 1980), 82. Commenting on Hubmaier's work *On the Christian Baptism of Believers*, Cornelius Dyck writes: "It is an analysis of the major biblical texts on baptism as taught and practiced by John the Baptist, by Christ, and by the apostles. He concluded that everywhere baptism followed after some kind of preaching or instruction, and after faith in the message heard had been expressed. The book does not deal with rebaptism, since he considered the infant baptism of the Roman Catholic Church not to be baptism by biblical standards. The simplicity, clear biblical basis, and blunt statement of the case make this sixty-eight page booklet a classic." Cornelius J. Dyck, *An Introduction to Mennonite History*, 3d ed. (Scottdale: Herald Press, 1993), 52.

as it connects with faith and baptism: "The significance of this view for believer's baptism is perfectly clear: baptism manifests one's faith, a faith attained by one's *voluntary* response to God and now confessed with the aid of the Spirit. This view would be standard for the Anabaptist movement."[481]

Hubmaier decried pedobaptism because the infant is incapable of embracing faith in Christ, or exhibiting it in baptism, by their own volition. Therefore, infant baptism based on a *prospective* decision of faith is yet another misapprehension of the biblical mandate concerning baptism according to Hubmaier:

> Here in particular let every Christian consider and judge how one can baptize the little babies as long as neither word, preaching, nor faith have preceded. . . . But that one alleges to baptize infants on the grounds of a future faith is really a mocking casuistry, for under no circumstances was that the institution of Christ. He says, "Teach all nations, and then baptize them in the name of the Father, and the Son, and the Holy Spirit." One does not know whether at a later time it will be the will of the child or not.[482]

Here we see again how important the decision of the will in faith is to Hubmaier. Arnold Snyder describes the significance of baptism for Hubmaier and the Anabaptists, which was based on a freely chosen submission to Christ: "The inner call of God's Spirit, or the 'baptism of the Spirit' as Hubmaier called it, demanded an outward and visible response from those who had been inwardly called and who had freely accepted the call. Water baptism signified that the inner yieldedness to Christ had already taken place (the water was the 'covenant of a good conscience'); it signified that the believer was now yielding to the Body of Christ on earth (the church); and it signified a willingness to suffer all for Christ and the brother and sister."[483] Baptism, then, is the public commit-

---

481 Emphasis added. Armour, *Anabaptist Baptism*, 33.
482 Hubmaier, *On the Christian Baptism of Believers*, Pipkin and Yoder, 118.
483 Snyder, "Beyond Polygenesis," 14.

ment of the will as it has been yielded to Christ and thus the believer enters into fellowship with others who have made the same decision.

Contrary to Hubmaier's idea that the decision of faith precedes baptism, an utterly passive, irresistible-gift-faith theory allowed Luther to affirm infant baptism, even though his earliest suppositions inclined toward adult baptism. Roger Olson states that, "Luther and Zwingli both defended infant baptism on the ground that faith is a gift of God and not a contingent, free decision. Their monergistic views of salvation form at least a part of their foundations for this practice."[484] Luther said that if faith is a gift, then it is not a problem for God to give the gift to an infant.[485] Thus faith, in this view, appears to be

---

[484] Olson, *The Story of Christian Theology*, 421.

[485] See, Luther, *Table Talk*, 181, where he writes: "The Anabaptists pretend that children, not as yet having reason, ought not to receive baptism. I answer: That reason in no way contributes to faith. Nay in that children are destitute of reason, they are all the more fit and proper recipients of baptism. For reason is the greatest enemy that faith has: it never comes to the aid of spiritual things but—more frequently than not—struggles against the Divine Word, treating with contempt all that emanates from God. If God can communicate the Holy Ghost to a grown person, he can, *a fortiori* communicate it to young children. Faith comes of the Word of God, when this is heard; little children hear the Word of God, when this is heard; little children hear that Word when they receive baptism, and therewith they receive also faith." To use the logical construct *a fortiori* after discounting the role of reason in these matters would appear contradictory. In addition, one of Luther's arguments for infant baptism was that the person can come to faith later if faith was not present at the time of baptism (since we can never be sure if anyone really has faith: an argument he uses to accuse the Anabaptists of making baptism a work since they are trying to be 'sure' of faith by baptizing believers which, of course, was not the point). He actually undermines his refutation of free will in matters of faith with this argument: "So here again the Anabaptists are urging on to a work, so that when the people are baptized they may have confidence that everything is right and complete. In reality they pay little attention to faith, but only seem to praise it. For, as we have already said, were they to be sure beforehand of faith, they would never again baptize anyone. [In other words Luther is arguing that the Anabaptists must be sure that belief is present before they baptize since they claim that the Scripture says 'whoever believes' is baptized. Confession is not enough for Luther. This appears to be a specious argument.] If they did not rely on works but earnestly sought for faith,

a mysterious power furnished to infants at baptism. Yet Luther also admits the possibility that one can receive baptism *without* faith, which undermines

---

they would not dare to rebaptize. The unchanging Word of God, once spoken in the first baptism, ever remains standing, so that afterwards they can come to faith in it, *if they will*, and the water with which they were baptized they can afterwards receive in faith, *if they will*." Emphasis Added. *Concerning Rebaptism*, ed. Lull, 361. Note the obvious language denoting the human will in these matters. Accordingly, Luther seems to be implying that there *is* free choice in this case. Also note that "faith in it" refers to baptism, "the water," and thus the concept of baptismal regeneration appears here for Luther. See the *Large Catechism* where Luther writes "Therefore state it most simply thus, that the power, work, profit, fruit, and end of Baptism is this, namely, to save. For no one is baptized in order that he may become a prince, but, as the words declare, that he be saved. But to be saved, we know, is nothing else than to be delivered from sin, death, and the devil, and to enter into the kingdom of Christ, and to live with Him forever." Contrary to Luther's accusation of the Anabaptists, the doctrine of baptismal regeneration makes a work of baptism much more indisputably than did the Anabaptists. If baptism does the work in the infant, then faith in Christ alone is set aside to an alarmingly significant degree. See the *Large Catechism* where Luther writes, "But as our would-be wise, new spirits assert that faith alone saves, and that works and external things avail nothing, we answer: It is true, indeed, that nothing in us is of any avail but faith, as we shall hear still further. But these blind guides are unwilling to see this, namely, that faith must have something which it believes, that is, of which it takes hold, and upon which it stands and rests. Thus faith clings to the water, and believes that it is Baptism, in which there is pure salvation and life; not through the water ... but through the fact that it is embodied in the Word and institution of God, and the name of God inheres in it. Now, if I believe this, what else is it than believing in God as in Him who has given and planted His Word into this ordinance, and proposes to us this external thing wherein we may apprehend such a treasure?" The Anabaptists, reflecting the New Testament, saw baptism as only an outward confirmation, a sign, of the inward conversion of faith which was already achieved and grounded entirely on Christ's work revealed in his Word by the Holy Spirit. Luther continues: "Even if they contradict the Word a hundred times, it still remains the Word spoken in the first baptism. Its power does not derive from the fact that it is repeated many times or is spoken anew, but from the fact that it was commanded once to be spoken." This statement seems to leave no room for the markedly biblical idea of confession of faith *of the believer* as being associated with salvation. Insertions and emphasis added. Luther, *Concerning Rebaptism*, ed. Lull, 361.

its effect, as those citizens who continue in sin and unbelief clearly illustrate. Consequently, faith alone effects salvation, contradicting and attenuating Luther's affirmation of baptismal regeneration.[486] Luther later altered his idea that faith can be given to infants, and instead based the baptism of infants on the faith of the parents, which contradicts the idea of faith as a gift.

These conflicting notions concerning faith and baptism make evident the practical problem in Luther's theology which flows from an insistence on dismissing human free will. Estep remarks on the incongruous nature of Luther's baptismal theology:

> Luther's battle cry, "Justification by faith," became his plumb line for interpreting the Bible. However, due to the persistent Roman Catholic appendages of his theology, he was never able to give this truth consistent expression. Consequently, in Lutheranism there has always been an irreconcilable contradiction between the theology of justification by faith and the theological support of infant baptism.[487]

W. J. McGlothlin concurs. He writes of Luther, "He retained the baptism which he had received in the Catholic church including infant baptism and the doctrine of baptismal regeneration. This was a radical contradiction of his doctrine of justification, but he does not seem to have felt the inconsistency."[488] The faith of a Christian is described by Luther as a warm and personal

486 See Luther, *Concerning Rebaptism*, ed. Lull.

487 Estep, *The Anabaptist Story*, 196–197.

488 W. J. McGlothlin, *The Course of Christian History* (New York: Macmillan, 1926), 112. Here we also see the problem of assurance for the believer inherent in Luther's theology. Since assurance cannot be based on simple faith in the effectual work of Christ followed by confession and baptism, since with double predestination faith is simply a gift in which no decision or choice to submit on the part of the Christian is possible due to the bondage of the will, Luther suggests that the rite of infant baptism becomes the basis of assurance in the life of the believer, even though he admits that faith alone justifies and baptism is bereft of its potency without faith: "Thus we must regard Baptism and make it profitable to ourselves, that when our sins and conscience oppress us, we strengthen ourselves and take comfort and say: Nevertheless I am baptized; but if I am baptized, it is promised me that I shall be saved and have eternal life,

trust in Christ in many of his writings. But in the background is the sovereign juggernaut of God's foreordained will, based on double predestination, which one must not question. Add the baby baptism muddle and what emerges is quite a confused set of beliefs.

Hubmaier's theology appears to be more integrated when considering the interconnection of his concept of faith as a personal decision of trust and commitment to Christ with his insistence on believer's baptism, which serves as the bulwark of his ecclesiology. These ideas both reflect Hubmaier's affirmation of the doctrine of the freedom of the human will, which functions as a binding force in making his views in these areas of his theology consistent. Rollin Armour details the correlation of these pivotal tenets in Hubmaier's theology:

> Hubmaier . . . developed two important theological corollaries to the doctrine of believer's baptism: freedom of the human will, and regeneration of the soul. In both of these he marked out positions which became common to Anabaptism. According to the first, salvation comes to man only after he himself has freely responded to God's offer. Since no infant is capable of this, infant baptism is improper. But the first also leads to the second: the will that is capable of choosing to receive God's grace is reborn by that grace and thereby receives the power to obey the will of God in all things. This being true, baptism serves as the formal means through which the reborn believer commits himself to this life of obedience in fellowship with other believers. Part of the significance of this was that baptism was the public profession of faith and commitment of life. But the other part was that baptism rests, in

---

both in soul and body. For that is the reason why these two things are done in Baptism namely, that the body, which can apprehend nothing but the water, is sprinkled, and, in addition, the word is spoken for the soul to apprehend. Now, since both, the water and the Word, are one Baptism, therefore body and soul must be saved and live forever: the soul through the Word which it believes, but the body because it is united with the soul and also apprehends Baptism as it is able to apprehend it. We have, therefore, no greater jewel in body and soul, for by it we are made holy and are saved, which no other kind of life, no work upon earth, can attain." Luther, *The Large Catechism*, trans. F. Bente and W. H. T. Dau in *The Master Christian Library*, (Rio, WI: Ages Software, 2000), 89.

this view, on the doctrine of regeneration–regeneration conceived as inner renewal, a metaphysical change within the person giving him once again the power of living righteously.[489]

Considering how vital the doctrine of believer's baptism was for Hubmaier and the Anabaptists' ecclesiology, this is certainly a strong argument for the centrality of human free will in Hubmaier's theology as a whole. Roger Olson makes the observation that, "At the heart of Hubmaier's theology lies on overriding concern that governs everything else: individual conversion. . . . Throughout his writings—especially about baptism—Hubmaier presupposed that faith is a free decision to believe the gospel and trust in Jesus Christ and his grace alone for salvation."[490]

RELIGIOUS FREEDOM

Perhaps the greatest contribution made by Hubmaier to public life was his defense of religious freedom as expressed in his tract, *On Heretics and Those Who Burn Them*. Pipkin and Yoder state: "One can argue that this is the first text of

---

[489] Armour, *Anabaptist Baptism*, 56. Armour goes on to discuss baptism in light of this effort to live righteously and notes that Hubmaier acknowledged the difficulties involved with battling against sin, the disciple's life of taking up one's cross and following, even unto death: "Finally, Hubmaier described baptism in a way that included the whole of the Christian life, for not only did it witness to the regeneration already wrought within the heart of the believer, but it signified the struggle with sin that lay ahead of him. Although Hubmaier did not stress the possibility of martyrdom as much as other Anabaptists would, he was sure that the Christian's fight with sin would be difficult and perhaps painful. At that point he contributed an important concept to Anabaptist baptismal thought: the baptisms of water and Spirit would be completed through the baptism of blood in the lifelong battle to conquer evil by the power of the Spirit." *Anabaptist Baptism*, 57. Of course, Hubmaier himself became a martyr for the cause of believer's baptism and genuine personal faith in Christ, and fulfilled his own baptism of blood as he was burned at the stake in Vienna in 1528.

[490] Olson, *The Story of Christian Theology*, 420.

the Reformation directed specifically to the topic of the liberty of dissent."[491] William Estep asserts that, though scholars have held various views on Hubmaier's ideas concerning the Christian and the state, there is "yet a significant difference . . . between Hubmaier and the Magisterial Reformers. It is in this difference that Hubmaier makes his own unique contribution to Anabaptism and the Free Church movement."[492] Hubmaier was ahead of his time in taking a firm stance for freedom of conscience, especially in contrast to the prominent Protestant reformers who embraced political power and violence in the name of Christianity. Of course the Magisterial Reformers overshadow him to this day, though Hubmaier suffered martyrdom for his beliefs rather than siding with religious leaders in positions of power, both Protestant and Catholic, who exiled, imprisoned, tortured, and executed those who differed theologically.

This divergence from the enforced state-church approach of the Reformers, and, contrariwise, from his fellow Anabaptists' appeal for complete dissociation from government affairs, is part of what made Hubmaier's contribution to religious liberty unparalleled in his time. Estep salutes this remarkable originality in his introduction to Hubmaier's *On the Sword*:

> He forged a new pattern in religious configurations between the near anarchy of some Anabaptists and an Erastianism [state control of the church] inaugurated by Luther and perpetuated by Zwingli, Calvin, Cranmer, Knox, Cotton, *et al.* It was Hubmaier, who in the midst of conflicting ideologies was able to see that religious liberty and the separation of church and state did not demand that the Christian withdraw into an isolationist cocoon of noninvolvement in order to maintain the integrity of his faith. To the contrary he saw such involvement as a Christian responsibility. Therefore, this document has special relevance for this day of religious pluralism and freedom.[493]

---

491 Pipkin and Yoder, *Balthasar Hubmaier*, 58.

492 Estep, *Anabaptist Beginnings*, 107. Scholars have presented varying views: from seeing Hubmaier as accepting a state-church similar to Zwingli, to a pragmatic approach, to an Erasmian form of pacifism. See Estep's discussion in *Anabaptist Beginnings*, 107.

493 Insertion added. Ibid., 107.

Analysis of the Doctrine of Free Will in Respect to Hubmaier's Broader Theology

Estep, then, does not equate Hubmaier's view with that of the Magisterial Reformation and its state supported church, as some scholars have. Estep reads Hubmaier as holding that "the state, even if staffed by Christian magistrates, remains secular in nature and purpose, not because God does not exist (secular humanism) but because God has so ordered it in His infinite wisdom and according to His sovereign will."[494]

Hubmaier's ideas on these issues, where politics and secular power intersect with theology and the church, are taken for granted by nearly every freedom-loving individual today, but in his own time Hubmaier suffered the fate of thousands like him when he was burned at the stake for his religious beliefs. In fact, all three of the great Magisterial Reformers were guilty of encouragement of, or direct involvement in, persecution and even execution in one form or another, in the name of stamping out heresy. Roger Olson describes Ulrich Zwingli's role in the sweeping general persecution of Anabaptists:

> In Zurich, Zwingli and the city council passed laws against the Anabaptists and urged the civil authorities throughout Europe to hunt them down and arrest them. Felix Manz, Zwingli's onetime star pupil and protégé, was the first Anabaptist martyr. He was arrested and taken to Zurich for trial. Zwingli consented to the sentence: drowning. This so-called third baptism became the punishment of choice for Anabaptists among both Catholics and Protestants. On January 5, 1527, Manz, the leader of the budding Swiss Brethren movement, was bound and thrown into the Limmat River in the center of Zurich. During the next few years, thousands of Anabaptists were hunted down by the special police know as *Täuferjäger* (Anabaptist-hunters), and many, including women, were executed. Children of Anabaptists were taken away and given to families of officially recognized church bodies.[495]

Zwingli was guilty of imprisoning and torturing Hubmaier himself, along with other Anabaptists, in Zurich's heretic's tower. Hubmaier appealed to Zwingli's conscience, asking him how this could be the right approach: "Stop

---

494 Estep, "Church and State," 271.
495 Olson, *The Story of Christian Theology*, 417.

also the miserable imprisoning and banning of pious brothers, the exiling out of the territory, imprisoning, throwing into the dungeons, putting in stocks and blocks, drowning and the like, all of which [stopping] you may do easily. . . . Aye, my dear Zwingle, do so for the sake of God and the truth, then the cause will soon come right everywhere."[496]

Religious freedom was the logical political extension of Hubmaier's soteriological belief in non-coercion. If man does not have free will, as the Lutherans and Calvinists claimed, then how will he be able to accept Christ's invitation? "For Christ did not come to slaughter, kill, burn, but so that those who live should live yet more abundantly (John 10:10)," said Hubmaier.[497] This invitation to life became the theological and biblical basis for Hubmaier's ideas about liberty of conscience, something he articulated clearly and pow-

---

496 Hubmaier, *Dialogue with Zwingli's Baptism Book*, Pipkin and Yoder, 232–233. Hubmaier wrote, in *A Brief Apologia*, Pipkin and Yoder, 308–309, after he had been in Zwingli's "Heretics Tower, in which one sees neither sun nor moon and lives on nothing but bread and water. . . . in which dead and living people remain lying next to each other and must thus perish," a bold and impassioned appeal to secular leaders to desist from punishing heresy in the following: "I ask, admonish, and warn in the name of Jesus Christ and his final judgment, all those at whose side God has hung the sword, that they not use it against innocent blood, neither through capturing, chasing, beating, putting in the blocks, hanging, drowning, or burning. For truly, truly, I say to them, the martyred and shed blood will cry up to God in the heavens together with the innocent blood of the pious Abel against such Cains, murderers, and blood spillers. He will demand it at their hands and will pour out his revenge over them and their children. For whoever sheds human blood (understand: against the order of divine justice) that one's blood, says God, shall itself also be shed, Gen. 9:6. Whoever takes the sword and uses it shall himself be destroyed by the sword, Matt. 26:52. Therefore, you government, watch what you do (so speaks King Jehosaphat by the Spirit of God to his judges, 2 Chron. 19:6–7). You do not wield a human office but one from God, and what you judge will come over you. Watch that the fear of God be with you and do everything with diligence. With God there is no malice, nor respect of persons, nor covetousness for bribes or gifts. Take heed, take heed, O government, that you not stain your hands and wash them in the blood of the innocent."

497 Hubmaier, *On Heretics and Those Who Burn Them*, Pipkin and Yoder, 62.

Analysis of the Doctrine of Free Will in Respect to Hubmaier's Broader Theology

erfully in a way Luther, Calvin, and Zwingli never approached. As Verduin asserts, "the Reformers were not protagonists of religious liberty. For that we must go to the camp of the Second Front [Anabaptists]."[498] Concerning what was to be done with heretics, Hubmaier wrote: "Yea, we should pray and hope for repentance as long as a person lives in this misery. But a Turk or a heretic cannot be overcome by our doing, neither by sword nor by fire, but alone with patience and supplication, whereby we patiently await divine judgment."[499]

The fact that Hubmaier's position on free will as it relates to salvation is at the root of his argument for religious freedom is another example of the centrality of free will in his thought. William Estep confirms this connection between free will, salvation, and religious freedom in Hubmaier's thought:

> It is strange that so few historians working in the history of the Renaissance and Reformation have recognized Hubmaier's remarkable contribution to the Free Church understanding of church-state relations. Hubmaier's *On Heretics and Those Who Burn Them* was the most creative work on religious liberty the sixteenth century produced. In this

---

[498] Insertion added. Verduin, *The Reformers and Their Stepchildren*, 90n. Franklin Littell also unequivocally denies the magisterial reformers were in any sense to be credited with promoting religious liberty: "Luther and Calvin both thought in terms of complementary territorial and religious institutions, and both were bitterly opposed to any pluralism of religious communities with a given territory. The problems of securing the liberty of preaching, of maintaining a church order, of providing a system of inspection, were variously answered by the Reformers. But they one and all finally came to the conclusion that such discipline as had to be exercised should be in the old medieval way through the magistrates, and not in any 'new' fashion borrowed from the primitive Church. . . . Thus one Reformer after another, however tempted, drew back from the logic of a radical New Testament order. It is surely wrong to attribute to any one of them an attitude of religious voluntaryism which modern countries largely take for granted as a right. The Reformers can hardly be cited to support religious liberty, and were horrified by the implications of the Free Church position." Franklin Littell, *The Free Church*, (Boston: Starr King Press, 1957), 18–19.

[499] Hubmaier, *On Heretics and Those Who Burn Them*, Pipkin and Yoder, 62.

THE CENTRALITY OF THE DOCTRINE OF HUMAN FREE WILL IN THE THEOLOGY OF BALTHASAR HUBMAIER

tract, Hubmaier goes well beyond Marsilius de Padua, Luther, Erasmus, and even Castellio. After redefining the term "heretic," Hubmaier makes a plea for a freedom of religion that includes even the atheist, who, he claims, should not be deprived of his civil rights if he obeys the secular laws of a given state. He also asserts that to persecute anyone for his religion may appear to be a Christian and pious act but in reality is a denial of the incarnation, for as Hubmaier implies, Christ came not to coerce but to invite men to salvation. It was Hubmaier's conviction that faith was not the result of the heretics' tower but only arose out of a heart convinced of the truth in Christ. Hubmaier's motto, found on everything he ever published, "Die Warheit ist Untodtlich" (Truth Is Immortal), was Hubmaier's way of saying, "When you have burned a person who holds to the truth, you have not burned the truth."[500]

When Estep points out that Hubmaier believed that Christ "invites" and does not "coerce" he is articulating a significant principle in Hubmaier's concept of free will as it relates to freedom of conscience. If Christ, who has every right to use his power, does not coerce men to come to salvation, certainly religious leaders and secular powers should not coerce "heretics" to believe any official state-sanctioned dogma.

---

500 William R. Estep, review of *Balthasar Hubmaier: Theologian of Anabaptism*, ed H. Wayne Pipkin and John Howard Yoder, *Journal of Church & State* 32 (Spring 1990): 420. Estep characterizes belief in an uncoerced offer of the gospel (and the necessity of an uncoerced response), along with its inferences for government and church relations, as a key distinguishing mark of the Anabaptist movement, unquestionably setting it apart from mainstream Protestantism: "The ecclesiology of the Anabaptists did have certain implications for the state that were unacceptable to Zwingli and to Luther as well. The Anabaptists saw more clearly than either Reformer that the proclamation of the gospel was predicated upon an uncoerced response. As Hubmaier wrote in 1524 in his *Concerning Heretics and Those Who Burn Them* (*Von Ketzern and ihren Verbrennern*), even the atheist (*Gotssfind*) had a right to his unbelief as long as he obeyed civil law. Hubmaier made the distinction that all Anabaptists made between 'heretics' and 'criminals.' The state, he insisted, had the right to punish criminals but had absolutely no right to prescribe or proscribe a man's religious confession or lack of it." Estep, *Renaissance and Reformation*, 188.

Hubmaier did not, of course, consider himself a heretic. His commitment to Scripture has been documented. The submission of his thought and life to the Bible, said Hubmaier, made it impossible for him to be a heretic because he was willing to be better instructed by anyone who did so from Scripture. He declared, "I may err, I am a human being—but a heretic I cannot be, for I constantly ask instruction in the Word of God."[501] Hubmaier's view of heresy revolved around the authority of Scripture, from which his definition, and thus his tolerance, of heresy were derived. This was a departure from the medieval notion, prevalent in Hubmaier's day, that heretics (also called schismatics) were dissenters from Christian society ('Christendom' with its tradition, rituals, control, and hierarchy). To Hubmaier, the Scripture, the sword of God's Word which the church wielded, must be the authoritative standard in matters of theological orthodoxy. Hubmaier defined heretics as those "who blind the Scripture, and who exposit it otherwise than the Holy Spirit demands."[502] He taught that, "Should they not yield to words of authority or gospel reasons, then avoid them and let them go on to rant and rage (Titus 3:10) so that those who are filthy may become yet more filthy. (Rev. 22:11)"[503] Lest someone deem this approach to be insufficient Hubmaier asserted, "The result of these words will not be negligence but a struggle as we combat without interruption, not against human beings, but against their godless teachings."[504]

For Hubmaier, since man *does* have free will, religious leaders (who are prone to error) should await with patience God's final judgment: "That is just what Christ intended when he said, 'Let both grow up together until the harvest, lest in gathering the tares you tear up the wheat together with it.' (Matt 13:29f.) . . . Who, even though they resist, are not to be destroyed until Christ will say to the reapers: 'Gather the tares first and bind them in bundles to be burned.' (Matt. 13:30)"[505] Thus to condemn and punish heretics in this world is to act against the judgment of God Himself. Hubmaier warned, therefore,

---

501 Hubmaier, *A Brief Apologia*, Pipkin and Yoder, 308.
502 Hubmaier, *On Heretics and Those Who Burn Them*, Pipkin and Yoder, 59.
503 Ibid., 60.
504 Ibid., 61.
505 Ibid.

of the even more horrific error of destroying those who in reality were *not* heretics: "If to burn heretics is such a great evil, how much greater will be the evil, to burn to ashes the genuine proclaimers of the Word of God, without having convinced them, without having debated the truth with them."[506] An argument for the centrality of free will in Hubmaier's theology is all the more convincing as one of its practical applications is observed: a staunch and striking stand for liberty of conscience. This contrasts sharply with the prominent Protestant theologies of the Reformation era, which insisted on a state-supported monolithic Christian society in which no taint of heresy would be tolerated.

Religious leaders of this time, both Catholic and Protestant, asserted that the secular power, to whom they handed the heretics over, was responsible for their deaths. Hubmaier replied, "Nor is it an excuse for them (as they babble) that they turn the godless over to the secular authority, for whoever in this way turns someone over is even more guilty of sin. Every Christian has a sword [to use] against the godless, namely the [sword of the] Word of God (Eph. 6:17f), but not a sword against the evildoers."[507] Here Hubmaier distinguishes between the "godless" or heretic and "evildoers" or criminals, which the state has the God-given responsibility to punish. "It is fitting that secular authority puts to death the wicked (Rom. 13:4) who cause bodily harm to the defenseless," declared Hubmaier.[508] So in Hubmaier's view of state-church relations he clearly differentiates between heretics and criminals and between the sword of the church (the word of God) and the sword of the state (punishment for crime). Therefore he concluded that the sword of government should never be used against heretics. James Stayer writes of Hubmaier: "It was very radical in the sixteenth-century Holy Roman Empire to tell the civil arm to keep out of the manipulation of religion."[509] "Balthasar Hubmaier . . .

---

506 Hubmaier, *On Heretics and Those Who Burn Them*, Pipkin and Yoder, 64.

507 Ibid., 63.

508 Ibid.

509 James Stayer, "The Radical Reformation," in *Handbook of European History, 1400–1600: Late Middle Ages, Renaissance, and Reformation*, vol. 2, *Visions, Programs, and Outcomes*, ed. Thomas Brady Jr., Heiko Oberman, and James Tracy (Grand Rapids: Eerdmans, 1995), 276.

may have been pleading" his own case, notes Stayer, but when he "argued for toleration of religious dissent," he was "also violating the sixteenth-century truism that only religious uniformity rendered a polity governable."[510]

John Kiwiet in his essay, "Anabaptist Views of the Church," notes Hubmaier's positive attitude toward civil authority, military service, and participation in public life. Kiwiet believes it was a "Christ transforming culture" approach, as opposed to most other Anabaptists who were stricter separatists, preferring a "Christ against culture" approach. He defends Hubmaier's model of ministry in Nicholsburg, Moravia, writing that, "He sought the support of [Lord] Leonhard of Liechtenstein in Nikolsburg not because he wanted to create a state church, but because he aimed for order and peace."[511] Gunnar Westin takes the view that Hubmaier's more balanced view of Christianity and the state was a lost theological and social avenue, missed by the majority of Anabaptists:

> The war against the Turks, which was an acute problem in the eastern part of Europe, demanded watchfulness, sacrifice, and man power. When the radical Anabaptists now declared that they would neither participate in any form of war nor pay taxes to the support of war, they were regarded by the ruling powers as traitors. This problem has persisted until the present day. There was a middle way open with Hübmaier and his principles toward the community and the state, but for the strict Anabaptists there was only one way—refusal to have anything to do with the state.[512]

Hubmaier derived this "middle way" concerning the church and the state from what he considered a balanced and natural reading of Scripture.

So, Hubmaier, without rejecting the legitimate God-given role of secular government in society, was able to affirm freedom of belief—liberty of dissent—as a principle of non-coercion due to the central position human free

---

510 Stayer, "The Radical Reformation," 276.

511 Insertion added. John J. Kiwiet, "Anabaptist Views of the Church," in *The People of God: Essays on the Believers' Church*, ed. Paul A. Basden and David S. Dockery (Nashville: Broadman & Holman, 1991), 230.

512 Westin, *The Free Church Through the Ages*, 95-96.

will held in his theology. Non-coercive soteriology and non-coercive freedom of conscience went hand in hand for Hubmaier. Estep elaborates:

> Ultimately, the Anabaptists' movement for religious freedom received its greatest motivation from the conviction that faith cannot be coerced.... No one surpassed Hubmaier in proclaiming eloquently or illustrating graphically—through his own tragic experience—that faith cannot be coerced.... It was Hubmaier's conviction that both church and state suffer when people are tried and condemned for religious reasons....
>
> ... In his abstract of principles, *Concerning Heretics and Those Who Burn Them*, articles 21, 22, and 28 suggest a theological basis for religious freedom more profound than is generally recognized.... Hubmaier argues that faith or lack of it is not within the jurisdiction of secular government. To the contrary, he declared ... that to burn a heretic is in appearance to confess Christ when in reality it is to deny him. Is he not saying that to persecute a person for heresy is to deny the incarnation, for the God revealed in Christ is the God of invitation, not of coercion?[513]

On the other hand, irresistible grace in salvation, as in the later Augustinian model affirmed by the Magisterial Reformers, and coercive church-state power in religious matters supporting a monolithic society, also go hand in hand. When Luther denied human free will, thus eclipsing the role of decision in faith for salvation, he in part also ultimately denied freedom of conscience in society.[514]

---

513 Estep, *The Anabaptist Story*, 261–263.

514 Leonard Verduin describes the dilemma, and evolution, in Luther's thought on coercion: "We see then that the Reformers had to choose between two alternatives, to continue in the tradition of 'Christian sacralism' or to go in the tradition of the long rebellion against that concept. The latter alternative was fraught with very great difficulty. It would mean to go it alone, without the help of the princes. This would expose the reformatory movement to almost insuperable danger—for, over against it stood the Catholic order, armed to the teeth with weapons which, as history had shown for a thousand years, it was

Analysis of the Doctrine of Free Will in Respect to Hubmaier's Broader Theology

Summary

The centrality of human free will in Hubmaier's broader theology is evident in its key features. Free will is central in his *soteriology* since Hubmaier insists on a decision of faith, a human response to God's grace in salvation. Hubmaier's trichotomous *anthropology* allows for the spirit in man, however darkened by

---

not loath to use. . . . Luther had a decision to make, a hard decision. Let no one belittle the extremely cruel nature of the dilemma which he and his fellow Reformers faced. Humanly speaking the only thing that offered any hope was to construct a rival Constantinianism, a new territorial Church, which could then offer the older Constantinianism some formidable competition. . . . But Luther also had his other moments, when he was more in accord with the New Testament. . . . 'Heretics must be converted with Scripture and not with fire!' In these early days, in 1523, Luther gave voice to the following: 'The soul's thoughts and reflections are revealed to no one but to God; therefore it is impossible to compel one with physical force to believe this or that. It takes another kind of compulsion to accomplish this; physical force is incapable of it.' . . . There were moments in which Luther cherished the ancient Restitutionist hope of having some day a Church of believers. He spoke sometimes, to his most intimate friends, about this pipe-dream. But each time he was jerked back into the world of reality and its harsh requirement. Then the other alternative beckoned. . . . The Reformation had crystallized in the pattern of neo-Constantinianism; there was nothing left but to turn the guns on those who had deserted the Reform because of it [such as Anabaptists]. Luther assigned to his associate Urbanus Rhegius the task of leading the attack, telling him to write a book against the *Schwärmer*, as he now began to call them. Rhegius complied, with a volume in which lavish praise is heaped upon Constantine and his successors for the direction they had given. Rhegius endorsed to the hilt the policy of coercing those who stand in the way of sacralism, liquidating them if need be: 'The truth leaves you no choice; you must agree that the magistracy has the authority to coerce his subjects to the Gospel. And if you say, "Yes, but with admonition and well-chosen words but not by force" then I answer that to get people to the services with fine words and admonitions is the preacher's duty, but to keep them there with recourse to force if need be and to frighten them away from error is the proper function of the rulers . . . . What do you suppose "Compelle intrare" means?'" Insertion added. Verduin, *The Reformers and Their Stepchildren*, 72–74.

sin, to accept God's grace, and thus does not eliminate free will after the Fall. For Hubmaier, free will derives from the image of God in man which cannot be obliterated, and, as opposed to a doctrine of total depravity, still functions in fallen man, however weakly. Hubmaier believes that man is able to respond to God's Word and that the very same Word is man's restored opportunity and freedom in the gospel, enabling him to choose the good God through the sacrifice of Christ, but also allowing for the option to reject Him.

Thus, free will becomes key to Hubmaier's concept of initial and ongoing faith in Christ. Free will is necessary in the human response of surrender to God in Christ at conversion. The very nature of this submission is a yielding, in faith, of the believer's will in favor of God's revealed and gracious will in Christ. Thus, a passive faith is invalid, and an ongoing commitment to surrender to the will of God in holy discipleship, issuing in works of brotherly love, essential. Accordingly, free will is central to Hubmaier's *concept of faith* as a decision, a "yes" to God's gracious offer of His only Son and a commitment to continue to trust God, manifested in an obedient Christian life.

Out of this soteriological foundation flows Hubmaier's requirement that *baptism* come after faith, according to the New Testament order. Only one who has decided for Christ in his innermost being can publicly confess this and commit to following Christ in solidarity with fellow believers through baptism. In this way free will was essential to Hubmaier's *ecclesiology*, the Anabaptist doctrine of the voluntary believers' church made up of those who are members through their own choice, made public by submitting to believer's baptism. As Verduin writes, the Anabaptists "were committed to the creation of a Church composed of Christians-by-choice, to take the place of a Church consisting of christians-by-happenstance."[515] To uphold the unity

---

515 Verduin, *The Reformers and Their Stepchildren*, 244. Verduin comments further in his discussion of the element of choice in regard to the ecclesiology of Reformation times, stating that the Protestant reformers were not "willing to be guided by the New Testament" to form their ecclesiology, resulting in a state supported church which operated as a rival to, and which was modeled after, the old medieval Roman Catholic church system. The magisterial reformers' reaction to the Anabaptists, once they fully embraced government force and territorial control over the church, was to reject the idea of a *free* church as wildly dangerous. It represented "the very thing the sa-

Analysis of the Doctrine of Free Will in Respect to Hubmaier's Broader Theology

and integrity of this free church of true believers, church discipline, involving brotherly admonition and the ban, must be exercised. This points to an emphasis being laid on human free will as a reality in church life. Those who choose to remain in obvious sin after believer's baptism are reprimanded and finally banned according to the order of Matthew 18. Those who choose to return and repent are joyfully restored as prodigal sons. Choices are clearly made here by the followers of Christ which affect the church and therefore also witness to human free will.

Finally, in Hubmaier's stance on *religious freedom* it is clear that liberty of conscience derives from the fact that Christ is seen as the final Judge who refuses to coerce but draws men to Him in patient love. No man, therefore, has authority to condemn anyone in this world for individual beliefs. In these matters men must appeal to "the judgment of God (to whom judgment belongs)," seeing that God wills for the heretic that "either they are converted or hardened so that the blind become more blind and all the while both the seduced and the seducer descend further into iniquity."[516] This principle precludes premature human judgment and punishment. If God has allowed for a genuine choice even in eternal matters, certainly no man can presume to take this freedom away by use of physical restraint, torture, or execution. Hubmaier's non-coercive soteriology is consistent with his non-coercive view of religious liberty. Hubmaier stood courageously against persecution and murder of individuals simply for their beliefs, but he was not naive about reality. He knew that his own beliefs made him a target of those to whom he appealed, in vain, for religious liberty. He paid the ultimate price, being burned at the stake in Vienna on March 10, 1528. Three days later his wife, Elsbeth, followed him in martyrdom when she was drowned in the Danube River.

---

cralists [advocates of the union of church and state] want to avoid at all costs." The Anabaptists' "ambition to organize a Church that consisted of followers" was to the Protestant reformers highly "objectionable." Insertion added. *The Reformers and Their Stepchildren*, 244.

516 Hubmaier, *Concerning Heretics and Those Who Burn Them*, in *Anabaptist Beginnings*, ed. Estep, 50.

Conclusion

What the Bible says about human freedom is of paramount importance. The biblical data has been appealed to vigorously in all stages of the debate over this issue through Church history. Combatants from both camps have accused the other of dragging in philosophical arguments and assumptions, thus sullying the pure doctrine of Scripture. This kind of accusation is common fare throughout the history of the Church, appearing in a wide range of theological issues. What one is to make of these denunciations is something of a conundrum. To center theology on Christ is not a cure-all. Many have centered on Christ and still de-emphasized or over-emphasized some doctrines in the name of centering all on Christ. The theologian comes to the issue and to the text with presuppositions. This is a given. Misunderstandings and failures in communication are also rampant in Christian history.

These difficulties come into play especially with such a hot issue as free will. Human nature seems to incline toward identifying one's own opinions or system with the biblical text. The next step, of course, is to excoriate any who disagree as unbiblical at best, unchristian, heretical, and even satanic at worst. Accordingly, much of the rhetoric of the Reformation can be characterized as polemic, and even as unbridled fulmination. One of the appealing features of Balthasar Hubmaier's writing is that it is significantly less polemic in nature. As Sydnor Stealey writes, "Compared to his contemporaries, especially Luther and Zwingli, he was mild and temperate, even sweet-spirited, in controversy."[517] When reading through a quantity of Luther, Calvin, or Zwingli one blushes at certain passages where sheer vitriol or disdain seem to characterize the writing, both explicitly, by the words which are used, and implicitly, by the attitude which this bludgeoning of foes appears to disclose. Revealing this characteristic of Reformation theology does not argue for a simpering sort of collegiality, as modern sensibilities about tolerance might require. The sixteenth century was not a delicate epoch, and the issues were, and are, infinitely serious. The debates were over vital personal religious convictions, not simply 'dialogue' over academic subject matter. But a spirit of antagonism and acidity was often given free rein in the works of the great Reformers.[518]

As has been indicated, a reading of Hubmaier gives a very different impression. Along with a commonsense approach, a dash of humor, and good use of imagery, Hubmaier writes as one appealing to readers he respects. He does not impugn or sweep away whole groups of people to the waste bin of heresy or perdition as Luther and Calvin tend to do. Hubmaier writes of heretics: "Those who are such should be overcome with holy instruction, not con-

---

[517] Sydnor Stealey, "Balthasar Hubmaier and Some Perennial Religious Problems," 410.

[518] An example is the exchange between Luther and Erasmus on free will, here related by Paul Johnson: "The wide dissemination of Luther's deterministic views of salvation, with which he [Erasmus] totally disagreed, forced him to make his own position clear. . . . When Luther published a characteristically rude reply, Erasmus thought it time for a rebuke: 'How do your scurrilous charges that I am an atheist, an Epicurean and a sceptic, help your argument? . . . It upsets me dreadfully that your arrogant, insolent and rebellious nature should have put the world in arms. . . . I would wish you a better disposition, were you not so marvellously satisfied with the one you have already. Wish me anything you will - except your temper.' To Luther, he was now 'a snake', 'a piece of shit', the 'insane destroyer of the church', the 'inflamer of the base passions of young boys'; he told his circle he had seen Erasmus walking 'arm in arm with the devil in Rome.'" *A History of Christianity*, 278. These sorts of invectives are not found in Hubmaier's writings, even when writing against Zwingli, who had ruthlessly imprisoned and tortured him so that Hubmaier even succumbed to a recantation of Anabaptism (which he then publicly renounced).

tentiously but gently, even though the Holy Scripture also includes wrath."[519] On the other hand, the use of convenient designations drawn from heresies of the past, vilification, and appellations of contempt to classify men, flowed all too easily from the pens of the leading Magisterial Reformers. 'Schwärmer,' (self-deluded fanatics, unbalanced extremists), was only one of the names Luther used to lump together all kinds of groups of men and women, including the Anabaptists. Verduin notes: "In his day Luther said that there had gone from his camp *Wiedertäufer, Sacramentschwärmer, und andere Rottengeister.* . . . The term *Rottengeister* was a sort of catch-all, an and-so-forth, to cover the rest of an allegedly evil crew."[520] Thus it may be said of the Magisterial Re-

---

[519] Hubmaier, *On Heretics and Those Who Burn Them*, Pipkin and Yoder, 60.

[520] Verduin, *The Reformers and Their Stepchildren*, 243. Of course, not only did the great reformers use invective and storm and bluster against opponents (Calvin used 'monster,' 'dog,' 'ass,' 'swine,' 'blockheads,' 'madmen,' 'brainless,' 'stupid men,' 'monstrous rascals' and other characterizations to label his opponents, referring to their words as 'vomit,' 'poison,' 'vile,' 'pestilential,' 'plague-spot,' 'abominations,' 'ravings,' and this is but a sampling), the real damage to their reputation, which is often ignored or excused by those in Protestant traditions, is that they were willing to execute and persecute those they villainized with their words, the most pertinent example being Zwingli's torture and imprisonment of Hubmaier. As Harry Loewen asserts, "Both the Zwinglians and Lutherans did not shrink from using violence when it came to supporting their cause. For example, the leading Lutheran princes John Frederick of Saxony and Philip of Hesse, invaded in 1542 the Catholic province of Brunswick, drove out the rightful ruler, Duke Henry, and forced the Lutheran creed upon the people. The Anabaptists were not blind to these inconsistencies. Menno Simons wrote: 'Why do they indiscreetly accuse us of uproar while we are wholly innocent and clear of all uproar and they never pay attention to their own destructive, bloody murdering uproar. Again what bloody uproars the Lutherans have for some years made to introduce and establish doctrine, I will leave to them to reflect upon. Nevertheless we, although innocent, must be accounted the tumultuous heretics and they the God-fearing, pious, peaceable Christians.'" Harry Loewen, *Luther and the Radicals: Another Look at Some Aspects of the Struggle Between Luther and the Radical Reformers* (Waterloo, Ontario: Wilfrid Laurier University, 1974), 106. Calvin, too, used the city council's power in Geneva to exile, imprison

formers that their invective, in that they condemned those who differed theologically as evildoers fit to be punished, and the substance of their writings, in that they made little allowance for (conspicuously obvious) human free will, was at times excessive or imbalanced.

The Logic of Symmetry: Divine Grace and Human Free Will

Luther's concern for *sola gratia* with its outgrowth of deterministic double predestination induces in his theology a weak anthropology (what is man except a complex bag of dirt galvanized now by God and now by the devil). It also seems to engender a misunderstanding of faith, as a 'gift' from God thrust upon completely passive individuals. These elect believers are fortunate enough to have been chosen before they were ever born, and no reason for this arbitrary choice can be given which would be decipherable to human intellect. This may seem to be an extreme extrapolation, yet it is the logical conclusion to some of Luther's convictions about the unfree will, and a reflection of Luther's extreme statements concerning God's omniscience and omnipotence in *The Bondage of the Will*.

Kenneth Scott Latourette summarizes Luther along these lines:

> Luther admitted that natural reason was offended by the doctrine of man's helplessness in sin and by a conception of God which, while holding Him to be good, taught that by His mere will He hardens and damns men whom He has not chosen to save. He confessed that at one time the apparent contradiction had so driven him to the abyss of despair that he wished that he had never been born. Luther stood in awe of the majesty and inscrutable justice of God. God, he maintained,

---

and execute those he deemed heretics or who took a stand against his and his theology's dominance in the canton, thus being marked out as his opponents, the burning of physician Michael Servetus being the most famous example.

is inaccessible to human reason. To Luther there was a paradox even in the self-revelation of God in Christ, that the Eternal and Omnipotent should be seen in a stable and on a cross. Man, so Luther held, does not have free will. Man's will is like a beast of burden. It is ridden either by God or by the Devil and does whatever the one who is in the saddle directs. In the heat of controversy Luther went beyond what he held in calmer moments, but his position was consistent with his basic conviction that none of man's works avails.[521]

Luther of course reveled in certain absurdities which he perceived in the truth of the gospel. He featured these apparent absurdities in what he called the *theologia crucis* in which the weakness of the revealed will of God in the cross pointed up the foolishness of the facade of man's philosophical or meritorious efforts to know God by the strength of his own will. But a theology of the cross can be maintained, in that it focuses on Christ as the stumbling block before mankind, without ejecting free will.

Hubmaier provides just such a balance, believing that man could never be saved by his own works, but affirming the element of decision in the trusting surrender of faith. An important feature of Hubmaier's concept of faith is the idea of surrender or submission to God, a yielding to heavenly authority on the part of the believer which seems frankly inconceivable without free will.[522] Hubmaier writes of this surrender, his own variety of the theology of

---

521 Kenneth Scott Latourette, *A History of Christianity: Volume II: A.D. 1500- A.D. 1975*, rev. ed. (Peabody, MA.: Prince Press, 1975), 724.

522 Yieldedness was a significant idea for Anabaptism in general. Donald Kraybill explains: "The Anabaptists talked of giving themselves up to God's will. This internal spiritual struggle was an attempt to lay aside selfish ambitions and devote oneself wholly unto God. But for the Anabaptists the struggle was not merely an internal spiritual one, it also had external consequences. The notion of discipleship, so central to Anabaptist understandings of Christian faith, meant following the way of Jesus in daily life regardless of the consequences, which might include suffering and persecution. Indeed, the martyr's death was the paradigmatic expression of Gelassenheit [tranquil submission] in which one completely gave oneself up to God's will." Insertion added. Donald B. Kraybill, "Yieldedness and Accountability in Traditional Anabaptist Communities" in *Anabaptist Currents: History in Conversation*

the cross, in the context of his doctrine of baptism. To Hubmaier the confession of Christian faith is "a renunciation that one must address to the devil and his works, so that a person, in the power of God the Father and the Son and the Holy Spirit, may yield himself in such surrender that he is willing with Christ to suffer, die, and be buried, in the faith that he will arise with him to everlasting life, Rom. 6:4."[523] The essence of this theology of the cross is that the believer surrenders his will to God's will as revealed in Christ. But Christ is not what human reason would expect. Instead of conquering by His power He sacrificed his life in weakness and death. To surrender to this kind of God is to admit a deeper need—that of forgiveness of sin—than what human reason is ordinarily ready to admit. Hubmaier writes, "The world does not want to be [seen as] an evildoer, but righteous and just in its own works. It establishes for itself laws, and rules by which it thinks it can be saved and despises the unattractive, plain, and simple rule of Christ."[524]

Creation itself points to the limitations of human reasoning since it is not even clear how God and man can exist together as realities from a purely human standpoint. The age-old metaphysical question of the one and the many, which no philosopher or theologian has yet completely understood, much less fully explained, is part of the reality of existence, created by the Triune God, and must be said to be a "both" rather than an "either/or." It can readily be argued that it is the same with human free will and divine sovereignty. At this point it may be helpful to note the role of theological method when it comes to these sorts of thorny issues. Instead of treating the question of God's sovereignty and man's responsibility, providence and human free will, as an either/or proposition, perhaps based on the biblical teaching, the subject can be affirmed as *both*.

Plainly, theologians must simultaneously affirm seemingly contradictory truths, especially when *both* (as in sovereignty and free will) appear to be abundantly evident in Scripture and in Christian experience. One way to reconcile

---

with the Present, ed. Carl F. Bowman and Stephen L. Longenecker, 269–280 (Bridgewater, VA: Forum for Religious Studies, Penobscot Press, 1995), 270.

523 Hubmaier, *Apologia*, Pipkin and Yoder, 556–557.

524 Insertion added. Hubmaier, *Summa of the Entire Christian Life*, Pipkin and Yoder, 86.

the contradictions may be to consider possible underlying causes of erroneous thinking which may undergird great theological debates. For instance, in the matter of free will and providence, Owen Thomas writes that a relational model for thinking through these ideas, as opposed to a mechanical one, serves much better to harmonize man's choice and God's sovereignty:

> One difficulty in the traditional debates was that the model used was often a mechanical one. The influence of grace and the human will were interpreted on the analogy of physical forces. When this is the case, the problem is insoluble; it is either grace or freedom or a mixture which determines an act. When the model or analogy is that of human personal relations, however, the difficulties can be overcome. The influence of a great and good person upon another person can be exerted in such a way that the freedom of the latter is not overridden but rather enhanced. Thus there is no necessary contradiction between the influence of grace and human freedom.[525]

Reinhold Niebuhr was one of the most outstanding modern proponents of this symmetry of grace or sovereignty and human freedom. He articulated the need for balance in this area, which more properly reflects the biblical tone and data concerning the issue: "The biblical account assumes a divine providence over individual and collective destinies, which establishes meaning on the vast panorama of history without annulling human freedom. The alternative methods of establishing meaning by coordinating historical events into systems of natural or rational coherences, tend to create excessively deterministic or equally excessive voluntaristic interpretations of historical events in which either the freedom or the finiteness of men is obscured."[526]

One of the theological systems which Niebuhr viewed as out of balance was Calvinism, especially any form which emphasizes providence so that it is the only operational factor in human history:

---

[525] Owen C. Thomas, *Introduction to Theology*, revised ed. (Harrisburg, PA: Morehouse Publishing, 1983), 111.

[526] Reinhold Niebuhr, "Freedom," in *A Handbook of Christian Theology*.

THE CENTRALITY OF THE DOCTRINE OF HUMAN FREE WILL
IN THE THEOLOGY OF BALTHASAR HUBMAIER

> It must be admitted that versions of the Christian faith frequently interpret the idea of providence so that the freedom of man is annulled or imperiled and God appears to be an arbitrary despot of the historical drama.... Calvinism has been particularly guilty of the primitive interpretation of the legitimate biblical idea of the sovereignty of a mysterious divine power who is both the creator and providential preserver of the human and historical enterprise.[527]

Niebuhr finds Luther's theology to be lopsided in a similar way: "Luther seems to heighten the Augustinian doctrine in the interest of a greater consistency but at the price of imperiling one element in the paradox, the element of human responsibility. Free-will is denied to the point of offering man an excuse for his sin."[528]

Christian beliefs about creation point to a balance between God's unlimited freedom, expressed in his sovereign will, and man's limited freedom. Free will and grace come in at the very beginning and are actually two aspects we find unified in the character of God as Creator. The creator created the world *freely*. It was not because he needed a world or because he boiled over, so to speak, as a volatile essence, but because He so decided. This free choice to create makes the creation a matter of unqualified benevolence and *grace* and not a necessity. Diogenes Allen explains:

> The ontological difference between God, who is inherently everlasting, and all else, which is contingent, is more fully expressed by the notion that God, who created the universe, created it *freely*. God did not have to create the universe. God felt no external or internal compulsion to create. On the one hand, since God is the source of everything, nothing would be external to God prior to creation to compel God to create. There would be an internal compulsion were God inherently unstable so that a creation might result from a pressure of forces

---

527 Reinhold Niebuhr, "Freedom," in *A Handbook of Christian Theology*.
528 Reinhold Niebuhr, *The Nature and Destiny of Man: A Christian Interpretation*, vol. 1, *Human Nature* (Louisville: Westminster John Knox Press, 1996), 244.

within which compel God to create . . . . There could also be internal compulsion if God were in want or lacking completeness. God then might create a world so that God could be enriched with what is not divine. But the God of the Bible acts *freely* and thus is inherently stable and inherently full, complete, or perfect. The act of creation is thus an act of sheer generosity.[529]

The very fact that there is the non-contingent God and the contingent universe is the first insoluble conundrum that man faces and yet to deny one factor or another is to obliterate the Judeo-Christian view. Mankind must have both if he is to have anything (existence). As A. W. Tozer writes: "Man is a created being, a derived and contingent self, who of himself possesses nothing but is dependent each moment for his existence upon the One who created him after His own likeness. The fact of God is necessary to the fact of man. Think God away and man has no ground of existence."[530]

The same holds for God's sovereignty and man's free will. Both God and man are free, man on a limited basis and contingent upon God (just as humans exist contingently and on a limited basis), God supremely and absolutely. The Calvinist-Arminian controversy places both elements of reality in opposition, one closer to determinism, stressing God's freedom, and the other closer to works righteousness, accentuating man's freedom. Both tend toward extremes which do not jive with Scripture. To reconcile these and arrive at "mere Christianity" is to affirm both, then to demonstrate how Scripture corresponds with experience and with the broader history and nature of man and his world. This, it seems, can be done just as well, and infinitely more helpfully, as any demand that one component of reality or the other must be predominant.[531] Luther's theology appears to insist that God's providence

---

529 Diogenes Allen, *Philosophy for Understanding Theology* (Atlanta: John Knox Press, 1985), 9–10.

530 A. W. Tozer, *The Knowledge of the Holy* (San Francisco: Harper and Row, 1961), 28.

531 Tozer writes: "The attempt to answer these questions has divided the Christian church neatly into two camps which have borne the names of two distinguished theologians, Jacobus Arminius and John Calvin. Most Christians are content to get into one camp or the other and deny either

operate as an irresistible force at the expense of true human freedom and personhood. On the other hand, Arminians may tend to claim that Christians may lose salvation, grounding it logically almost totally on human willing and performance and thus rendering the very concept of a salvation beyond the power of man moot. If one chooses Christ then one may 'unchoose' Him, so to speak, by sinning. This puts an inordinate emphasis on human choice and distorts the idea that faith in Christ is confident trust in the ultimately trustworthy One, the Son of God, who has already achieved all that is necessary for man's eternal salvation.

THE LOGIC OF THE PERSONAL: DIVINE GRACE AND HUMAN TRUST AS FREEDOMS OF RELATION

The Bible states plainly that the salvation offered to men is exceedingly good news because it is accomplished by God Himself, who is faithful and reliable without fail. Faith is the choice to trust oneself to God's faithfulness and *His*

---

sovereignty to God or free will to man.... Here is my view: God sovereignly decreed that man should be free to exercise moral choice, and man from the beginning has fulfilled that decree by making his choice between good and evil. When he chooses to do evil, he does not thereby countervail the sovereign will of God but fulfills it, inasmuch as the eternal decree decided not which choice the man should make but that he should be free to make it. If in His absolute freedom God has willed to give man limited freedom, who is there to stay His hand or say, 'What doest thou?' Man's will is free because God is sovereign. A God less than sovereign could not bestow moral freedom upon His creatures. He would be afraid to do so.... Certain things have been decreed by the free determination of God, and one of these is, the law of choice and consequences. God has decreed that all who willingly commit themselves to His Son Jesus Christ in the obedience of faith shall receive eternal life and become sons of God. He has also decreed that all who love darkness and continue in rebellion against the high authority of heaven shall remain in a state of spiritual alienation and suffer eternal death at last." *The Knowledge of the Holy*, 111–112.

accomplishment of salvation in Christ. A Baptist theologian, Walter T. Conner describes this idea of faith succinctly:

> Faith is the condition of salvation, because the moral relations of the case demand faith. The grace of God that gives salvation must be appropriated by man's faith. Otherwise grace is in vain. But any act not necessarily involved in the moral relations of the case, if made a condition of salvation, would be an arbitrary prescription on God's part. Moreover, faith as a condition of salvation is not an act by which man merits or earns anything. It is the act by which the bankrupt sinner puts all his trust for salvation in Another and in what that other has done for him. It is not an act in which the sinner makes any claims for himself; it is rather an act in which he acknowledges that he cannot help himself and in which he signs away his life to Another. So there is involved in the act of faith the very opposite of any claim to doing anything by which one wins the favor of God; it is an act in which one acknowledges the utter impossibility of doing this and by which one casts himself on Christ and what he has done for his acceptance with God.[532]

So the privilege and responsibility of man, the crown of God's creation, is to make use of God-given human choice to surrender to the Sovereign God and His work and ways revealed in Christ, and thus enter into eternal freedom from sin, death, and the prince of this world. This seems clearly to be the message of the Bible. Hubmaier's theology of free will affirms this truth: "If now a person who has been brought through the Word of God to recognition of his sin confesses himself to be a sinner, and is further taught by the Word of God that he should call upon God the Father for the forgiveness of his sin for the sake of Christ, and if he does that in faith and does not doubt anything, then God has cleansed his heart in this faith and trust and has remitted him all his sin."[533]

---

532 Walter T. Conner, *The Gospel of Redemption* (Nashville: Broadman Press, 1945), 209.

533 Hubmaier, *On the Christian Baptism of Believers*, Pipkin and Yoder, 117.

Here is a clear instance which confirms that, for Hubmaier, faith and personal trust are synonymous.

Hubmaier characterizes faith, then, as when "people believe, trust God, expect all good things from God our heavenly Father and believe that he is our gracious, good, gentle, benevolent, and merciful Father in heaven, who carries, protects, and shields us as a human being [shields] his child, or like a hen her chicks under her wings."534 Hubmaier continues:

> This confidence and sincere trust in God through Jesus Christ, that is, through the favor, grace, and good will which God the Father has for his most-beloved Son Jesus Christ, is exactly true faith. Of this faith all the books which really describe faith thoroughly are full. It is in this faith that we should cry, pray, and call upon God that through the favor and good will which he has for his Son he might also be favorable to us. That is what it means to pray in the name of Jesus. What we ask in this way from the Father in the name of Jesus he will give us. Thereto he has guaranteed and pledged us his eternal living Word which will not fail for eternity. Before that could happen, heaven and earth would have to crumble.535

Hence, for Hubmaier faith is concentrated totally on Christ. The believer enters a relationship with God through a decision to trust God's goodness given in His Son. This relationship with God can only be truly fulfilled voluntarily. If man is compelled, he is automatically diminished in his God-given capacity to reciprocate (being made in God's image), since he is not able to respond freely, and thus authentically, to God in love. This is God's great desire: a human creature who is related to him in submissive love, of his own will, and thus made whole by accepting the mercy of God through faith in Christ. Calvinist and Lutheran doctrine veer toward a view of man as a being on which God operates with His 'grace,' and restores by force of his Sovereign plan and

---

534 Hubmaier, *On the Christian Baptism of Believers,* Pipkin and Yoder, 116.

535 Ibid.

power. And then, only the elect are imbued with this irresistible application of grace and life.

Hubmaier's view recognizes man as privileged to respond to God's redeeming grace in Christ, thus restoring his relationship with God to the ideal God had in mind for human beings in the first place. As Denis Janz states: "The rectification of man's relation to God and to his fellow man is, for Hubmaier, the sum and substance of Christian teaching, the central core from which all else follows."[536] This relational theology includes free will in man, centering on God's loving relationship with man, and emphasizing God's moral requirement for mankind to be loving toward fellow men. Hubmaier's theology, then, serves as an alternative to a necessitarian pressing of God's 'immutable decrees.' What seems to be missing in a deterministic view is a cognizance that God's original plan is *all about* this relationship of grace and generosity offered to mankind. There is a sense in which, in order to preserve the 'grace' of God, He is actually rendered less gracious (in certain facets of traditional Protestant theology) by very rigidly stressing His sovereignty as an inflexible sort of fate. His providence, seen in this logically narrow and exclusive sense, is so smothering as to rule out any other vital players on the scene, including and particularly, man. Everything, and everyone, becomes a cog in the machine of God's decrees and thus the system strays toward a perception of God as energy or force (monergism) rather than as Person.

This kind of deterministic theology obscures the story of the Bible since Scripture paints the picture of God loving and condescending and covenanting with men, over and over, in order to cement a *relationship* with mankind. Indeed, the very doctrine of the Trinity points to a relationship between God and man as being foundational to God's plan. The eternal interrelation between God the Father, God the Son, and the Holy Spirit as reciprocal and free, yet perfect in unity, surely provides a backdrop for God's intention to "make man in our image" and for every succeeding event in God's initiative toward man. His great desire is to be in loving relationship with his beloved creatures, unspoiled by evil and self-absorption. This is forfeited at the first entrance of compulsion because the very nature of a genuine relationship demands that

---

536 Denis Janz, *Three Reformation Catechisms: Catholic, Anabaptist, Lutheran*, Texts and Studies in Religion (New York: Edwin Mellen Press, 1982), 18.

it be mutual. Hence, a truly reciprocal relationship between God and man is impossible unless mankind is free to choose it. The moment the relationship is forced it is no longer of the highest order: a free and correspondent relation of welcoming love, as Jesus said, "I call you friends." Thus, a key element for understanding God's intentions toward man, as in Hubmaier's theology, becomes free will in man, a faculty given by God which enables him genuinely to enter into a loving relationship with his Creator, through the grace given in Jesus, *if he will*.

By including free will in the equation of God's grace, man's dignity is restored, and God's sovereignty is actually enhanced when it is perceived that his highest goal is to reestablish humankind's happy bond with Himself, and thus also restore the true identity and potential of men. This means bearing the fruit of the Spirit, in love directing the self toward fellow human beings by seeking their good. Man is given the gift to be able to choose all of this simply by submitting (a word which by definition must entail free choice) in faith to Christ, allowing the work of Christ to prevail on his behalf. Thus, in a free will theology like that of Hubmaier, faith is chiefly a choice to trust Christ for salvation as well as sanctification.

Man's free will and God's grace, then, are not mutually exclusive but mutually responsive in Hubmaier's theology. God's omnipotent grace working through man's trusting obedience, all made possible in Christ who represents God to man and man to God, bears the fruit of loving works. Hubmaier expresses these ideas in a response he wrote to those who quoted the passage, "However, not I, but the grace of God which is in me," 1 Corinthians 15:10, as proof against free will:

> My dear Eliphas, as you think that not I but the grace of God is working, so I think: with me and not without me. For the Scripture does not say, "I without grace" nor "the grace without me." But it says: "The grace of God with me." Therefore also the saying of Paul should be understood: "I can do all things in him who strengthens me," Phil. 4:13. Farewell: you have good counsel.[537]

---

537 Hubmaier, *Freedom of the Will, II*, Pipkin and Yoder, 487.

Conclusion

Alvin Beachy observes, "Thus, for Hubmaier ... the claim to the experience of grace is nullified if one does not seize the new possibilities that are opened up for him through the grace of God in Christ."[538] As Hubmaier might say, good works are acts of a trusting, obedient, living faith in Christ.

For Luther, however, faith is primarily a 'gift.' It is, necessarily, since man has no free will. Though in practice and in pastoral counseling Luther emphasized faith using language suggestive of choice (a decision to *trust*),[539] Luther's accent on a life of trust for the Christian appears to be at variance with his deterministic theology. He speaks of trust as essential to faith and yet sees faith sheerly as a gift of God, no decision of the individual being involved. Luther is heard to say:

> The very highest worship of God is this that we *ascribe* to him truthfulness, righteousness, and whatever else should be ascribed to one who is trusted. When this is done, the soul *consents* to his will. Then it hallows his name and *allows* itself to be treated according to God's good pleasure for, *clinging* to God's promises, it *does not doubt* that he who is true, just, and wise will do, dispose, and provide all things well.[540]

---

538 Beachy, *The Concept of Grace in the Radical Reformation*, 31.

539 Luther advises, "If you wish to be cured of sin, you must not withdraw from God, but run to Him, and pray with much more confidence than if a bodily need had overtaken you. God is not hostile to sinners, but only to unbelievers, that is, to such as do not recognize and lament their sin, nor seek help against it from God, but in their own presumption wish first to purify themselves, are unwilling to be in need of His grace, and will not suffer Him to be a God Who gives to everyone and takes nothing in return." Martin Luther, *A Treatise on Good Works* in *The Master Christian Library*, (Rio, WI: Ages Software, 2000), 54. This is written to Christians concerning their prayer life, but still shows that Luther's concept of trust sounds very much like one must make a choice in these matters, contradicting his deterministic system of the unfree will. This is but one of numerous examples in Luther's writings.

540 Emphasis added. Luther, *The Freedom of a Christian*, in *Martin Luther's Basic Theological Writings*, ed. Timothy Lull, 602. Notice all the words which presuppose free human choice in this passage. How does the idea of consent, for instance, correspond in any way with the unfree will? See also note 539 above as another example of this inconsistency.

THE CENTRALITY OF THE DOCTRINE OF HUMAN FREE WILL IN THE THEOLOGY OF BALTHASAR HUBMAIER

If this beautiful picture of faith is restricted by a deterministic theology in which free will has no place, then it is only after God irresistibly produces the change within man that he finds this sort of trusting faith operating in his life. With this kind of system there can be no true personal repentance and no true personal trust since the man who has no free will has been given faith whether he wants it or not. In this way Luther's will-in-bondage theology invalidates the idea of faith as personal trust which he expresses here in so fine a fashion.

The human experience unquestionably includes a sense that life on earth is spiritually significant, as persons feel existence to be, from an early age, a moral affair.[541] This sense of the weightiness and importance of choices

[541] Andrew Fairbairn writes, along these lines of the evident significance of free will for human experience (which points to man's spiritual nature), that "the reality of freedom lies deeper than argument. Nature witnesses to it; man blames himself when he does wrong because he believes himself to have voluntarily chosen the worse when he could have taken the better. Law judges a man most severely when it holds him to have freely committed the crime with which he is charged. Responsibility is not a vicarious thing, where a necessitated victim bears the blame of ancestral or social sins; but it means that man is to be judged for a thing or act he himself willed to do. He is tried alike by God and man upon the principle which each individual conscience authenticates—that he whose action is in question did it when he could have done otherwise; and he was bound to do as he could have done. But while freedom is a *sine quâ non* of moral action and implied in all moral judgments, it has here a further significance:—it qualifies the argument from the transmitted experiences of the past. For what a man inherits leaves him still a free man; the judgment he has to bear is for his own act, and not for the acts of his ancestry, even though they may have created in him tendencies which are not easily resisted. These tendencies do not cancel freedom, only condition it; they define the limits of responsibility, but while they may qualify they do not annul it, for its ground stands unbroken. But in doing this his freedom does much more; it lifts man above the chain of physical causation, and makes him the symbol of a being higher than the forces that are governed by mechanical necessity. For since he is free he stands in conduct in the same transcendental relation to the forces and laws of Nature as he does in knowledge to their qualities and objects. His freedom is the correlate of his thought; and as the man who knows phenomena is not one of the phenomena he knows, so the will that can initiate action is not a mere event or link in a series of antecedents and sequents, where each follows the other either without perceived

and of the human moral state does not witness to determinism, but to free will. Free will, then, is the occasion for sin, and for God's uncompelled and gracious response in the incarnation of Christ. These are the very great matters that are clearly at stake in Scripture, giving man a choice to turn from sin and be forgiven by faith in Christ. Luther aptly wrote, "God our Father has made all things depend on faith so that whoever has faith will have everything, and whoever does not have faith will have nothing."[542] Yet if everything is determined by double predestination how can everything depend on faith? The deterministic system propounded by Luther in *The Bondage of the Will*, in which everything is decided by foreknowledge and predestination, would appear to diminish the incisive and conclusive character of Jesus' death on the cross, with its sacrifice, tears, pain, forsakenness, and love, and the glorious victory and triumph of His resurrection. It is Christ, not decrees, the gospel calls men to receive *by faith*.

Of particular import in this way is Jesus' prayer in the garden of Gethsemane. An overemphasis on eternal decrees, and on making God's foreknowledge into a sort of fate as Calvinism tends to do,[543] makes Jesus' prayer in

---

connection or in a rigorous order of physical causation. Thought is transcendence as regards the phenomena of space, Will is transcendence as regards the events of time; the double transcendence involves the complete supernatural character of man." Andrew Martin Fairbairn, *The Philosophy of the Christian Religion* (New York: Macmillan, 1902), 77–78.

542 Luther, *The Freedom of a Christian*, ed. Lull, 601.

543 C. Norman Kraus writes concerning Calvinism, foreknowledge, and free will: "In Protestant theology there has been a continuing debate about the relation of human free will and God's foreknowledge; that is, omniscience related to future events. The Calvinist tradition has held that God's knowledge must of necessity be equated with his decree, because God can know as certain only what he himself has destined to happen and will certainly accomplish. That is, he knows an event is certain to happen because he has decreed it to happen. If this is true, human freedom is limited by God's knowledge. In the Calvinist view, to say God foreknows means the same as that God foreordains. . . . this kind of rationalistic argument goes beyond the limits of the human analogy to describe God with definitive certainty. In any case, the Bible in no way uses the concept of God's knowledge to depreciate human freedom and responsibility. God has given us freedom to respond, and he knows us as free creatures. His purposes

submitting His will to the Father ostensibly meaningless if all things concerning the salvation of man are already predestined. M. William Ury writes, "A proper interpretation of the prayer in Gethsemane disallows predetermination without the consent of the Savior (Luke 22:42). Jesus prays, 'Father, if you are willing (*boulē*) . . . yet not my will (*thelēma*), but yours be done.'"[544] Ury continues, in analyzing the significance of Jesus' Prayer: "The critical issues pertaining to human will are revealed here. Divine will is primarily revealed to humans as the desire to offer salvation. Humanity is invited to respond to that will and provision."[545] Christ's obedience to the Father, exemplified in the submitting of His will to God at Gethsemane, plays a particularly significant role in salvation in that His obedience, in the grip of overwhelming grief and dread, made possible His sacrifice. And His sinlessness fulfilled the law, since he was fully man and likewise mankind's best representative before God as the only begotten Son of the Father, so that his life, freely given on the cross, could be the vicarious offering to God for the forgiveness of the sins of man.

As for the grace of election, could it be that Christ and his work *comprise* predestination for the very reason that those found in him by faith are found in one who helped create the world and existed before time? Should predestination be seen as emphasizing God's grace in Christ, the pre-existent one, instead of his eternal decree of judgment for the reprobate? Should election perhaps be seen as carrying a primary meaning for Christians which denotes the purpose of being holy agents of blessing, instead of simply the privileged chosen few who are heaven-bound only because of a mysterious and seemingly arbitrary decree? Leonard Verduin expounds on these possibilities:

> Too commonly the theological concept of election has been equated with selection, a device whereby the one is pulled in and the other is pushed out. Although the biblical idea of election may at times contain the idea of selection, it is far richer than that. The complement of elec-

---

for humanity and his plan for their accomplishment are designed according to that knowledge." C. Norman Kraus, *God Our Savior: Theology in a Christological Mode* (Scottdale: Herald Press, 1991), 83–84.

544 M. William Ury, "Will," in *Evangelical Dictionary of Biblical Theology*.
545 Ibid.

tion is frequently not reprobation (or preterition) but rather "the rest." . . . Such was Israel's election—witness the "in thee and in thy seed shall all the families of men be blest." Such was the election of Paul the Apostle, a "chosen vessel, to carry my name to the Gentiles." Needless to say, election in this sense is related to the here and now. . . . The whole concept of election needs further study, especially the idea (found in the writings of St. Paul primarily) of election in pre-time. There is some reason to believe that the configuration of eternity and time is a framework, chosen to point up the idea of *grace*. In any event, the theological concept of election, or of predestination, must not be allowed to cancel out man's peculiar endowment as a creature geared to option.[546]

Within a free will theology, a view could be taken which sees *Christ alone* as the center and source of predestination and the grace of election rather than eternal decrees. As Paul wrote in his letter to the Ephesians: "Blessed be the God and Father of our Lord Jesus Christ, who has blessed us in Christ with *every* spiritual blessing in the heavenly places, even as he *chose us **in him** before the foundation of the world*, that we should be holy and blameless before him."[547]

A. W. Tozer describes this correlation between Christ and God's grace: "Grace takes its rise far back in the heart of God, in the awful and incomprehensible abyss of His holy being; but the channel through which it flows out to men is Jesus Christ, crucified and risen. The apostle Paul, who beyond all others is the exponent of grace in redemption, never disassociates God's grace from God's crucified Son. Always in his teaching the two are found together, organically one and inseparable."[548] This Christocentric view of predestination and election would appear to correspond with the personal and relational message and tenor of Scripture better than a narrowly syllogistic system of eternal decrees for double predestination.

Faith and grace and free will are all compatible if seen in a simple way and not viewed through the lens of any kind of constraining deterministic system. In other words, to be biblical these three can be seen as key elements

---

546 Verduin, *Somewhat less than God*, 98–99.
547 Emphasis added. Ephesians 1:3-4, (ESV).
548 Tozer, *The Knowledge of the Holy*, 93–94.

in the relationship between God and man, not as instruments in a vast preordained mechanism ordered by a fixed system of decrees. Faith is man's reception of God's grace, and free will must be actual in order for man to yield in faith to God's offer of Himself in Christ. Submission is not a work which can be credited to man's account and make him righteous, if so then the language begins to make no sense and words have no meaning. A person being saved by a lifeguard must submit himself and quit flailing away so that the rescuer can help him and save him. He must trust the lifeguard and not his own efforts.[549] This is what it means to have faith. It is actually the opposite of works, yet a decision is still involved and it is crucial. As Estep writes, this is "a faith that must be free and voluntary or it is no faith at all."[550]

Thus, the choice to surrender to God and to his gifts, agreeing with God regarding personal helplessness, is at the heart of faith. One writer has declared, "Faith, then, is *submission* to this judgment of God, *renunciation* of boasting in human power and values."[551] Will I trust God or my own efforts for deliverance from sin? Clearly, if surrender takes place in faith, then free will must remain a key factor in the salvation equation. Baptist theologian Robert Culpepper summarizes the essential role the freedom of man plays in God's loving plan of salvation:

> In dealing with man's sin problem God acts in such a way as to respect man's freedom. If coercion had been God's method of saving

---

[549] This illustration is consistent with Hubmaier's theology because the drowning person still can choose to receive help or to reject it by panicking or for whatever other reason he may not trust his savior. Perhaps in Calvinistic theology the illustration would be changed in that the person being saved is already dead or at best unconscious and the savior pulls him up out of the water and revives him. No choice is made on the part of the already drowned person. This would be consistent with Calvinistic anthropology: total depravity, which gives the impression of complete spiritual death and complete dissolution of the *imago dei* in man. But why not save all who are in this desperate need? Free will is the simple answer to why some are left to drown. They refused their rescuer. Jesus says, "how I longed to gather you in" . . . "but you would not."

[550] Estep, "Church and State," 271.

[551] C. Norman Kraus, *Jesus Christ Our Lord: Christology from a Disciple's Perspective*, rev. ed. (Scottdale: Herald Press, 1990), 235.

man from sin, the cross would never have become a reality. Indeed, if coercion had been God's method there would have been no need for redemption, for God would not have permitted human sin. In such a case men would have been puppets, mere automatons, obeying their Master because they had no choice. But from such automatons God could have expected no response of love. A puppet can no more love than he can disobey. In the perfect liberty of the Creator God chose to create man as man, with the power of contrary choice. Following the principle of noncoercion, God chose to offer redemption to man in such a way as to attract but not to compel, to appeal but not to coerce. The cross of Christ is the biblical testimony that God acts in a way consistent with his own nature, demonstrating his love while respecting man's freedom. Reconciliation, not revenge, is God's objective. Self-sacrifice, not self-assertion, is his method.[552]

C. Norman Kraus, a Mennonite theologian, expounds further on the essential nature of faith as decision, as trusting surrender to Christ's salvation rendered on the cross. He writes: "In this faith-decision about one's own existence we find liberation from the domination of self and are given new life. This is the meaning of resurrection, for this decision to 'surrender to death all that is one's own' includes trust in God who gives life to the dead."[553]

The will of the man is surrendered to the revealed will of God in the transaction of choosing God in Christ by faith. This surrender continues in the ongoing life of faith for the Christian. Hubmaier affirmed this idea of sanctified surrender concerning the believer, who cannot attain perfection in this life and lives by grace, not human effort. As he was saved by grace, so he lives by grace, knowing his weakness, doing the works of love:

> He will surrender himself to the will of Christ, who wants that we also should do to our neighbor as he has done to us and give our body, life, honor, possessions, and blood for his sake. This is the will of Christ.

---

[552] Robert H. Culpepper, *Interpreting the Atonement* (Grand Rapids: Eerdmans, 1966), 133.

[553] Kraus, *Jesus Christ Our Lord*, 235.

But since this is impossible for us to do, we should call upon God diligently for grace and strength, so that he might give them to us and might not count our weakness and imperfection to eternal damnation, to make us able to fulfill his will as much as he gives us grace. For if he does not give us grace, we are already lost. We have been human, and we are human, and we will remain human until death.[554]

Similarly, Kraus describes faith as trusting and fixing upon, in other words, holding fast in surrender to its great object, Christ: "Christ's life and death are the great exemplar of decision for God and others, and we appropriate his revelation by accepting his understanding of life as our own. This we do when we respond in faith to the proclamation of the gospel and commit ourselves in baptism to his way of life."[555]

Thus, there is a dynamic *personal* quality in a theology that includes an affirmation of free will. Hubmaier never denied God's sovereignty. He simply asserted that man has free will. He did not believe that either facet of reality canceled out the other. He did not discount God's determining power out of hand (as Luther did human free will), but only sought to balance it with responsibility on man's part to submit to that power. Hence a personal relationship between God and man is possible, indeed foundational, in Hubmaier's theology. Ian Ramsey spoke to this essential personal element in the concept of free will: "'Free will' does not deny determinism any more than it necessarily implies indeterminism; rather it claims a characteristically 'personal' situation which the language of causal connectedness never exhausts."[556] The logic of a "personal" theology transcends and engulfs the rationality of mechanistically causal theologies like those of Luther and Calvin.[557] Any personal

---

554 Hubmaier, *On the Christian Baptism of Believers*, Pipkin and Yoder, 148.

555 Kraus, *Jesus Christ Our Lord*, 235.

556 Ian T. Ramsey, *Religious Language* (New York: Macmillan, 1963), 171.

557 Yandall Woodfin elaborates on the link between freedom (as central to theology and soteriology) and personal faith: "*God is personal and salvation is essentially surrender to and encounter with the personal being of God himself.* Christian salvation is not the result of an impersonal mechanical force, submission to fate, nor one's assent to this concept even though it is a Christian doctrine. Rather, salvation is quite simply trust in Christ. . . . When . . . the whole

tone, which is especially abundant in Luther, seemingly must be smuggled into the language of theology and practice despite the looming deterministic presence of God's eternal decrees.

This theology of personalism is a key component of Anabaptist identity, according to Jarold Knox Zeman. He claims that it is based upon a reading of Scripture. "The personalism of the evangelical Anabaptists was rooted in their biblicism and represented a revolutionary challenge to the sixteenth-century establishment of church and state, whether Catholic or Protestant."[558] Zeman argues that the discipleship emphasis of the Anabaptists grew out of this personalism. It is a value concentrated on individual persons rather than on institutions or ideologies. He describes the Anabaptist view: "What ultimately matters, in the eyes of God and therefore also for us, his creatures and children, is not the interests of ecclesiastical and political organizations but rather the development of human beings as persons."[559] Cornelius Dyck explains further this fundamental personalism in the symmetry between grace and free will in Hubmaier's theology. He writes that, for Hubmaier, "grace is understood on two levels—the natural knowledge or conscience, by which

---

of Christian faith and theology is interpreted according to this personalistic model, the high priority of human freedom necessitates the possibility that one can ultimately reject God's personal love. The New Testament makes it perfectly clear that God does not wish 'that any should perish, but that all should reach repentance' (II Peter 3:9). But it also teaches with equal force that 'God is not mocked' (Gal. 6:7). When God therefore, as Brunner says, takes 'Himself, His love, infinitely seriously,' this means that he must also take man and his freedom 'infinitely seriously.' Wherever man in his sin rejects divine love, the wrath of God is inevitable and morally justified. 'Because it is true that Jesus Christ alone is the Light and the Life it cannot be otherwise than that outside of Christ there is darkness, death, destruction.'" Woodfin, *With All Your Mind: A Christian Philosophy* (Nashville: Abingdon, 1980), 235–236.

558 Zeman, "Anabaptism: A Replay of Medieval Themes or a Prelude to the Modern Age?," 264.

559 Ibid., 266. Zeman distinguishes the personalism of the Anabaptists from that of the Spiritualists since the Anabaptists stressed church fellowship, making them less strictly individualistic than the Spiritualists. Zeman noted that the Anabaptists did not stress subjectivism, the inner mystical, spiritual life, as did the Spiritualists, as much as they stressed the church and its continuation and expansion.

people know right from wrong and regeneration. In no case is it sacramentally substantive, a 'thing,' but God coming to people in Spirit and in power."[560] Therefore, according to Dyck, for Hubmaier, grace "is never separated from the coming of Christ as Savior and Lord. The possibility of holiness is, consequently, not based simply on following the example of Jesus, but on the work of Christ who sets people free to respond to him."[561] This personal response (in biblical terms, repentance, faith, and discipleship) is what God is seeking, so that His human creatures may 'know Him just as we are fully known.'

In his time, Hubmaier made clear the crucial role of free will, *as corollary to God's grace*, for a proper biblical balance in his theology. So much so that grace and free will inhere as two aspects of the same gracious offer in Christ: the grace of God *is* the *free* offer of salvation through the Word which men are at liberty to take up by a decision of faith. Yet some choose to reject God, and the responsibility for that choice cannot be escaped. Because of the nature of the overwhelmingly gracious and merciful sacrifice of God's own Son inherent in the offer of salvation, to snub God's overture of love is to choose darkness and death and prefer the prideful, powerless shell of the self, which cannot prevent its own demise. Hubmaier declared:

> Nevertheless, it is certain and sure that the crucified Christ wants all people to be saved and come to the recognition of the truth, 1Tim. 2:4. . . .
>
> For that is the grace and favor of God which he bears to us and with which he embraces us: that power which he offers us through his preached Word, so that we—it lies now in our power—can become children of God, also desire and complete his fatherly will and please him, John 1:12; Rev. 3:20.
>
> Grace comes to us, not out of us, so that no one boasts in himself but in the merits of our Lord Jesus Christ, I Cor. 1:4. For our flesh and blood cannot reach such sonship out of their own power, John 1:12; Matt. 16:17; I Cor. 15:50.

---

560 Dyck, "The Anabaptist Understanding of the Good News," 29.
561 Ibid.

Conclusion

Since, however, this sonship is offered to all people equally, for the seed of the divine Word falls equally in four kinds of earth, it follows that we have the equal power to accept the seed and to bear fruit, John 1:12; Matt. 18:19; Mark 16:15; Matt. 13:3ff.; Mark 4:3ff. If we do not do that, then it is not God who is guilty, or his seed, but the evil of the earth, that is, we ourselves.[562]

---

[562] Hubmaier, *Freedom of the Will, II*, Pipkin and Yoder, 467-468.

Bibliography

Books

Allen, Diogenes. *Philosophy for Understanding Theology*. Atlanta: John Knox Press, 1985.

The Ante-Nicene Fathers. Edited by Alexander Roberts and James Donaldson. 1885-1887, 10 vols. Repr. Albany, OR: Ages Software, 1997.

Armour, Rollin S. *Anabaptist Baptism: A Representative Study*. Studies in Anabaptist and Mennonite History. Scottdale: Herald Press, 1966.

Arnold, Eberhard. *The Early Anabaptists*. Rifton, NY: Plough Pub. House, 1984.

Augustine. *The Enchiridion on Faith, Hope and Love*. Edited by Henry Paolucci. South Bend: Regnery/Gateway, 1961.

___. *On Free Will*. In *Augustine: Earlier Writings*, ed. J. H. S. Burleigh. Library of Christian Classics. Philadelphia: Westminster Press, 1953.

Bainton, Roland H. *Erasmus of Christendom*. New York: Crossroad, 1969.

___. *Here I Stand: A Life of Martin Luther*. Nashville: Abingdon, 1978.

___. *The Reformation of the Sixteenth Century*. Boston: Beacon Press, 1952.

___. *Studies on the Reformation*. London, 1964.

———. *The Travail of Religious Liberty*. Philadelphia: Westminster Press, 1950.

Balke, Willem. *Calvin and the Anabaptist Radicals*. Grand Rapids: Eerdmans, 1981.

Barnes, Irwin. *Truth Is Immortal: The Story of the Baptists in Europe*. London: Carey Kingsgate Press, 1955.

Bartsch, J. *Geschichte die Gemeinde Jesu Christi*. Elkhart: Mennonite Publishing Company, 1898.

Bax, Ernest Belfort. *Rise and Fall of the Anabaptists*. New York: A.M. Kelley, 1970.

Beachy, Alvin. J. *The Concept of Grace in the Radical Reformation*. Cambridge: Harvard University Press, 1960.

Beck, Joseph. *Die Geschictsbuecher die Wiedertaeufer in Oesterreich-Ungarn*. Nieuwkoop: B. de Graaf, 1967.

Bender, Harold S. *The Anabaptist Vision*. Goshen: Mennonite Historical Society, 1945.

———. *The Anabaptists and Religious Liberty in the Sixteenth Century*. Philadelphia: Fortress Press, 1970.

———. *Conrad Grebel c. 1498–1526, The Founder of the Swiss Brethren sometimes called Anabaptists*. Scottdale: Herald Press, 1950.

———. *Mennonites and the their Heritage*. Akron: MCC, 1945.

Bergsten, Torsten. *Balthasar Hubmaier: Seine Stellung zu Reformation and Taeufertum, 1521–1528*. Kassel: Oncken, 1961.

Bergsten, Torsten. *Balthasar Hubmaier : Anabaptist Theologian and Martyr*. Edited by W. R. Estep. Valley Forge: Judson Press, 1978.

Berkeley, Grace Lane. *Strange Chief, the Story of a Glorious Heritage*. Philadelphia: The Judson Press, 1929.

Berkhof, Hendrikus. *Christian Faith*. Grand Rapids: Eerdmans, 1979.

Bibliography

Blanke, Fritz. *Brothers in Christ: The history of the oldest Anabaptist congregation, Zollikon, near Zurich, Switzerland.* Translated by Joseph Nordenhaug. Scottdale: Herald Press, 1961.

Bornkamm, Heinrich. *Luther in Mid-Career 1521–1530.* Edited with foreword by Karin Bornkamm, Translate by E. Theodore Bach. Philadelphia: Fortress Press, 1983.

Boyd, Stephen B. *Pilgram Marpeck: His Life and Social Theology.* Durham: Duke University Press, 1992.

Bromiley, G. W., ed. *Zwingli and Bullinger.* The Library of Christian Classics. Philadelphia: Westminster Press, 1953.

Brown, Harold O. J. *Heresies: Heresy and Orthodoxy in the History of the Church.* Peabody, MA: Hendrickson, 1988.

Burnaby, John, ed., *Augustine: Later Works.* Library of Christian Classics. Philadelphia: Westminster Press, 1955.

Calvin, John. *Institutes of the Christian Religion, 1536 Edition.* Translated by Ford Lewis Battles. Grand Rapids: Eerdmans, 1986.

____. *Treatises against the Anabaptists and against the Libertines: Translation, Introduction and Notes.* Edited and Translated by Benjamin Wirt Farley. Grand Rapids, MI: Baker Book House, 1982.

Caner, Emir Fethi. "Truth is Unkillable: The Life and Writings of Balthasar Hubmaier, Theologian of Anabaptism." Ph.D. diss., University of Texas at Arlington, 1999.

Chadwick, Henry. *The Early Church.* Rev. ed. London: Penguin Books, 1993.

Chadwick, Henry and G. R. Evans, eds. *Atlas of the Christian Church.* New York: Facts On File, 1987.

Clasen, Claus-Peter. *Anabaptism: A Social History, 1525–1618.* Ithaca: Cornell University Press, 1972.

Clifton, Chas S. *Encyclopedia of Heresies and Heretics*. New York: Barnes & Noble, 1998.

Conner, Walter T. *The Gospel of Redemption*. Nashville: Broadman Press, 1945.

Culpepper, Robert H. *Interpreting the Atonement*. Grand Rapids: Eerdmans, 1966.

Davis, Kenneth Ronald. *Anabaptism and Asceticism: A Study in Intellectual Origins*. Studies in Anabaptist and Mennonite History. Scottdale: Herald Press, 1974. Reprint, Eugene, OR: Wipf and Stock, 1998.

Denck, Hans. *Selected Writings of Hans Denck*. Edited by Edward Furcha and Ford Lewis Battles. Pittsburgh: Pickwick Press, 1975.

Denning, Carl Elvin. "The Life and Teachings of Balthasar Hubmaier." B.D. thesis, Northern Baptist Theological Seminary, 1945.

Dickens, A. G. *Reformation and Society in Sixteenth-Century Europe*. London: Harcourt, Brace & World, 1966; reprint 1968.

Driver, John. *Radical Faith: An Alternative History of the Christian Church*. Edited by Carrie Snyder. Kitchener: Pandora Press, 1999.

Durnbaugh, Donald F. *The Believer's Church: The History and Character of Radical Protestantism*. Scottdale: Herald Press, 1968.

Dyck, Cornelius J. *An Introduction to Mennonite History: A Popular History of the Anabaptists and the Mennonites*, 3d ed. Scottdale: Herald Press, 1993.

____. *Spiritual Life in Anabaptism*. Scottdale: Herald Press, 1995.

Erickson, Millard. *Introducing Christian Doctrine*, 2nd ed. Grand Rapids: Baker, 2001.

Estep, William R. Jr. *The Anabaptist Story: An Introduction to Sixteenth-Century Anabaptism*, 3d ed. Grand Rapids: Eerdmans, 1975.

____. *Renaissance and Reformation*. Grand Rapids: Eerdmans, 1986.

———, ed. *Anabaptist Beginnings (1523–1533): a source book*. Nieuwkoop: B. De Graaf, 1976.

Faber, Johannes. *Doctoris Joannes Fabri, adversus Doctorem Balthasarum pacimontanum : Anabaptistarum nostri saeculi, primum authorem, orthodoxae fidei catholica defensio*. Lypsie: Melchiorem Lottherum, 1528.

———. *Ursach warumb der Widerteuffer Patron unnd erster Anfenger Doctor Balthasar Hübmayer zu Wienn auff den zehendten Tag Martij. Anno. M.D.xxviij verbrennet sey*. Landshut: Johann Weyssenburger, 1528.

Fairbairn, Andrew Martin. *The Philosophy of the Christian Religion*. New York: Macmillan, 1902.

Fast, Heinhold, ed. *Quellen zur Geschichte der Täufer in der Schweiz*. Zweiter Band (Ostschweiz). Zürich: Theologischer Verlag Zürich, 1973.

Friedmann, Robert. *The Theology of Anabaptism: an Interpretation*. Studies in Anabaptist and Mennonite History. Scottdale: Herald Press, 1973.

Friesen, Abraham. *Erasmus, the Anabaptists, and the Great Commission*. Grand Rapids: Eerdmans, 1998.

Friesen, Paul T. "Balthasar Hubmeier: An Examination of His Political Ethic." M.A thesis, University of Saskatchewan, 1982.

Garrett, James Leo. *The Nature of The Church According to The Radical Continental Reformation*. Fort Worth: 1957.

Geisler, Norman. *Chosen But Free*. Minneapolis: Bethany House, 1999.

George, Timothy. *Theology of The Reformers*. Nashville: Broadman Press, 1988.

Goertz, Hans-Jürgen. *The Anabaptists*. Translated by Trevor Johnson. London: Routledge, 1988.

González, Justo L. *A History of Christian Thought*, 2 Vols. Nashville: Abingdon, 1971.

Gray, Paul Wesley. "Balthasar Hübmaier." Th.M. thesis, Dallas Theological Seminary, 1975.

Green, Michael. *Evangelism in the Early Church*. Grand Rapids: Eerdmans, 1970.

Gritsch, Eric W. *Thomas Müntzer: A Tragedy of Errors*. Minneapolis: Fortress Press, 1989.

Haas, Martin, comp. *Quellen zur Geschichte der Taeufer in der Schweiz*. 4. Band: Drei Taeufergespraeche. Zuerich; Theologischer Verlag, 1974.

Harder, Leland, ed. *The Sources of Swiss Anabaptism: The Grebel Letters and Related Documents*. Scottdale: Herald Press, 1985.

Harvey, Andrew, ed. *Teachings of the Christian Mystics*. Boston: Shambhala, 1998.

Heath, Richard. *Anabaptism: From its Rise at Zwickau to its Fall at Münster, 1521–1536*. Baptist Manuals: Historical and Biographical. London: Alexander and Shepheard, 1895.

Hershberger, Guy Franklin, ed. *The Recovery of the Anabaptist Vision: A Sixtieth Anniversary Tribute to Harold S. Bender*. Scottdale, PA: Herald Press, 1957.

Hillerbrand, Hans Joachim. *A Bibliography of Anabaptism, 1520–1630*. Elkhart: Institute of Mennonite Studies, 1962.

Hoekema, Anthony. *Created in God's Image*. Grand Rapids: Eerdmans, 1986.

Horst, Irvin Buckwalter. *Erasmus, the Anabaptists and the Problem of Religious Unity*. Haarlem: H. D. Tjeimk, 1967.

____. *The Radical Brethren: Anabaptism and the English Reformation to 1558*. Nieuwkoop: B. de Graaf, 1972.

Hubmaier, Balthasar. *Balthasar Hubmaier, Theologian of Anabaptism*. Translated by Wayne Pipkin and John H. Yoder. Classics of the Radical Reformation. Scottdale: Herald Press, 1989.

___. *Schriften*. Quellen zur Geschichte der Täufer 9. Edited by Torsten Bergsten and Gunnar Westin. Guetersloh, 1962.

Hubmaier, Balthasar. *The Writings of Balthasar Hubmaier*. Edited by W. O Lewis and George Dagged Davidson, 1939.

Hutterian Brethren, ed. *The Chronicle of the Hutterian Brethren*. Rifton, NY: Plough Publishing, 1987.

Inge, William Ralph. *Christian Ethics and Modern Problems*. New York: G. P. Putnam's Sons, 1930.

Janz, Denis, ed. *Three Reformation Catechisms: Catholic, Anabaptist, Lutheran*. Texts and Studies in Religion. New York: Edwin Mellen Press, 1982.

Johnson, Paul. *A History of Christianity*. New York: Touchstone, 1995.

Kelly, J. N. D. *Early Christian Doctrines*. Rev. ed. New York: Harper Collins, 1978.

Klaassen, Walter. *Anabaptism in Outline: Selected Primary Sources*. Scottdale, PA: Herald Press, 1981.

___. *Anabaptism: Neither Catholic nor Protestant*. Waterloo, Ont.: Conrad, 1973.

___. *Living at the End of the Ages: Apocalyptic Expectation in the Radical Reformation*. New York: University Press, 1992.

___. *Sixteenth Century Anabaptism: Defences, and Confessions and Refutations*. Waterloo, Ont.: Conrad Grebel College, Inst. of Anabaptist & Mennonite Studies, 1981.

Klaassen, Walter, ed. *Anabaptism Revisited: Essays on Anabaptist/Mennonite studies in honor of C. J. Dyck*. Scottdale: Herald Press, 1992

Klassen, William. *Covenant and Community: The Life, Writings and Hermeneutics of Pilgram Marpeck*. Grand Rapids: Eerdmans, 1968.

Krahn, Cornelius. *Dutch Anabaptism (1450–1600)*. Hague Nijhoff, 1968.

Kraus, C. Norman. *God Our Savior: Theology in a Christological Mode.* Scottdale: Herald Press, 1991.

____. *Jesus Christ Our Lord: Christology from a Disciple's Perspective*, rev. ed. Scottdale: Herald Press, 1990.

Langenwalter, J. H. *Christ's Headship of the Church According to Anabaptist Leaders Whose Followers Became Mennonites.* Berne, IN: Mennonite Book Concern, 1917.

Latourette, Kenneth Scott. *A History of Christianity,* 2 Vols. Rev. ed. Peabody, MA.: Prince Press, 1975.

Lederach, *A Third Way: Conversations About Anabaptist / Mennonite Faith.* Foreword by Tom Sine. Scottdale: Herald Press, 1980.

Lewis, C. S. *English Literature in the Sixteenth Century.* New York: Oxford University Press, 1954.

Lienhard, Marc, ed. *The Origins and Characteristics of Anabaptism: Proceedings of the Colloquium Organized by the Faculty of Protestant Theology of Strasbourg, 20-22 Feb., 1975 - Les debuts et les caracteristiques de l'anabaptism.* The Hague: Nijhoff, 1977.

Liland, Peder M. I. "Anabaptist Separatism : A Historical and Theological Study of the Contribution of Balthasar Hubmaier (ca. 1485–1528)." Ph.D. diss., Boston College-Andover Newton Theological School, 1983.

Lindsay, Thomas M. *A History of The Reformation,* 2 Vols. Second ed. Edinburgh: T. & T. Clark, 1948.

Littell, Franklin H. *The Free Church.* Boston: Starr King, 1957.

____. *The Origins of Sectarian Protestantism: a study of the Anabaptist View of the Church.* New York: Macmillan, 1964.

Loewen, Harry. *Luther and the Radicals: Another Look at Some Aspects of the Struggle Between Luther and the Radical Reformers.* Waterloo, ON: Wilfred Laurier University, 1974.

Bibliography

Loserth, Johann. *Doctor Balthasar Hubmaier und die Anfänge der Wiedertaufe in Mähren*. Brünn: R. Rohrer, 1893.

_____. *Wiclif and Hus*. Trans. M. J. Evans. New York: AMS Press, 1980.

Lull, Timothy, ed., *Martin Luther's Basic Theological Writings* (Minneapolis: Fortress Press, 1989.

Luther, Martin. *The Bondage of the Will*. In *Martin Luther's Basic Theological Writings*. Edited by Timothy Lull. Foreword by Jaroslav Pelikan. Minneapolis: Fortress Press, 1989.

_____. _____. *Concerning Rebaptism*. In *Martin Luther's Basic Theological Writings*. Edited by Timothy Lull. Foreword by Jaroslav Pelikan. Minneapolis: Fortress Press, 1989.

_____. *The Freedom of a Christian*. In *Martin Luther's Basic Theological Writings*. Edited by Timothy Lull. Foreword by Jaroslav Pelikan. Minneapolis: Fortress Press, 1989.

_____. *The Large Catechism*. Translated by F. Bente and W. H. T. Dau. In *The Master Christian Library*, version 8. Rio, WI: Ages Software, 2000.

_____. *Preface to the Letter of St. Paul to the Romans*. In *The Master Christian Library*, version 8. Rio, WI: Ages Software, 2000.

_____. *Table Talk*. Translated by William Hazlitt. London: Fount, 1995.

_____. *A Treatise on Good Works*. In *The Master Christian Library*, version 8. Rio, WI: Ages Software, 2000.

Mabry, Eddie Louis. *Balthasar Hubmaier's Doctrine of the Church*. Lanham: University Press of America, 1994.

_____. *Balthasar Hubmaier's Understanding of Faith*. Lanham: University Press of America, 1998.

Macoskey, Robert Arthur. "The Life and Thought of Balthasar Hubmaier, 1485–1528." Thesis, University of Edinburgh, 1977.

Marpeck, Pilgram. *The Writings of Pilgram Marpeck*. Translated and edited by William Klassen and Walter Klaassen. Classics of the Radical Reformation. Scottdale: Herald Press, 1978.

Martin, C. Joseph. *A Comparative Study of the Teachings of Balthasar Hubmaier and Peter Riedemann Concerning Church Discipline*. Goshen College Biblical Seminary, 1960.

Martin, Steven P. *The Role of Women as Understood by John Calvin, Balthasar Hubmaier, Menno Simons, Martyr's Mirror*. Elkhart, IN: S.P. Martin, 1983.

Mau, Wilhelm. *Balthasar Hubmaier*. Berlin: Walther Rothschild, 1912.

McGiffert, A. C. *Protestant Thought Before Kant*. New York: Harper, 1962.

McGlothlin, W. J. *The Course of Christian History*. New York: Macmillan, 1926.

McGrath, Alister E. *Iustitia Dei: A History of the Christian Doctrine of Justification*. 2^d ed. Cambridge: Cambridge University Press, 1998.

McGrath, William R. *The Anabaptists: Neither Catholics nor Protestants*. Seymour Mo.: Historical Christian Publishers, 1964.

____. *Separation Throughout Church History: Containing Choice Quotes and Testimonies on Christian Separation from the World*. Seymour, MO: Historical Mennonite Faith Publications, 1966.

McSorley, Harry J., C. S. P. *Luther: Right or Wrong?: An Ecumenical-Theological Study of Luther's Major Work, The Bondage of the Will*. New York: Newman Press, 1969.

Mecenseffy, Grete. *Quellen zur Geschichte der Taeufer: Oesterreich*. II. Teil. Gerd John: Guetersloh, 1972.

Miller, Lynn A. *Trail of the Martyrs: A guide to the sites of Anabaptist martyrdom*. Elkhart, IN: Schwaermer Press, 1984.

Mullett, Michael. *Radical Religious Movements in Early Modern Europe*. London, 1980.

Murphree, Bobby Warren. "The Theology of Balthasar Hubmaier." Th.M. thesis, Golden Gate Baptist Theological Seminary, 1958.

Murray, John. *The Epistle to the Romans*. The New International Commentary on the New Testament. Grand Rapids: Eerdmans, 1990.

Newman, Albert Henry. *A Manual of Church History*, 2 vols. Philadelphia: American Baptist Publication Society, 1953.

Newport, John P. *Life's Ultimate Questions: A Contemporary Philosophy of Religion*. Dallas: Word Publishing, 1989.

Niebuhr, Reinhold. *The Nature and Destiny of Man: A Christian Interpretation*, 2 vols., Library of Theological Ethics. Louisville: Westminster John Knox Press, 1996.

Nienkirchen, Charles William. "In the World But Not Of It: The Development of Separatist Motifs in Early Anabaptist Ecclesiology (1523-1528)." Ph.D. diss., University of Waterloo, 1985.

Oberman, Heiko. *Luther: Man Between God and the Devil*. Translated by Eileen Walliser-Schwarzbart. New York: Doubleday, 1992.

Oden, Thomas C. *Systematic Theology*. Vol. 1, *The Living God*. Peabody: Prince Press, 1987.

Olin, John C. ed. *Christian Humanism and the Reformation: Selected Writings of Erasmus*. 3^d ed. New York: Fordham University Press, 1987.

Olson, Roger E. *The Story of Christian Theology: Twenty Centuries of Tradition and Reform*. Downers Grove: InterVarsity Press, 1999.

Oyer, John. *Lutheran Reformers Against Anabaptists*. The Hague: Nijoff, 1964.

Pauck, Wilhelm. *The Heritage of the Reformation*. Glencoe: Free Press, 1961.

Packull, Werner O. *Mysticism and the Early South German-Austrian Anabaptist Movement, 1525-1531*. Studies in Anabaptist and Mennonite History. Scottdale, PA: Herald Press, 1977.

Pater, Calvin Augustine. *Karlstadt as the Father of the Baptist Movements: The Emergence of Lay Protestantism.* Toronto: University of Toronto Press, 1984.

Payne, E. A. *The Anabaptists of the 16th Century and their Influence on the Modern World.* London: Carey Kingsgate, 1948.

Pearse, Meic. *The Great Restoration: The Religious Radicals of the 16th and 17th Centuries.* Carlisle: Paternoster Press, 1998.

Pelikan, Jaroslav. *The Christian Tradition: A History of the Development of Doctrine.* Vol. 4, *Reformation of Church and Dogma (1300-1700).* Chicago: University of Chicago Press, 1984.

Penner, Bruno A. "The Anabaptist view of the Scriptures." M.A. diss., Bethany Biblical Seminary, and Mennonite Biblical Seminary, Chicago, 1955.

Pike, Edward Carey. *The Story of the Anabaptists.* Eras of Nonconformity. London: Thomas Law, 1904

Pipkin, H. Wayne, ed. *Essays in Anabaptist Theology.* Elkhart, IN: Institute of Mennonite Studies, 1994.

Placher, William C. *A History of Christian Theology: An Introduction.* Philadelphia: Westminster Press, 1983.

Pries, Edmund. *The historical context of Anabaptist oath refusal in Zurich: 1525-1532.* Waterloo, Ontario: Edmund Pries, 1988.

Ramsey, Ian T. *Religious Language: An Empirical Placing of Theological Phrases.* New York: Macmillan, 1963.

Rempel, John D. *The Lord's Supper in Anabaptism: A Study in the Christology of Balthasar Hubmaier, Pilgram Marpeck, and Dirk Philips.* Studies in Anabaptist and Mennonite History 33. Scottdale: Herald Press, 1993.

Rideman, Peter. *Account of our Religion, Doctrine and Faith.* Rifton, NY: Plough Publishing Co., 1970.

Bibliography

Ross, James and Mary McLaughlin, eds. *The Portable Renaissance Reader* New York: Penguin Books, 1981.

Roth, Willard E., ed. *What About Church History?* Scottdale: Herald Press, 1964.

Rupp, Gordon. *Luther's Progress to the Diet of Worms, 1521.* Greenwich: Seabury Press, 1951.

Rupp, E. Gordon and Philip S. Watson, eds. *Luther and Erasmus: Free Will and Salvation.* Library of Christian Classics. Philadelphia: Westminster Press, 1969.

Ruth, John L. *The Believer's Church Story.* Elgin, IL: Brethren Press, 1982.

Sachsse, Carl. *D. Balthasar Hubmaier als Theologe.* Neue Studien zur Geschichte der Theologie und der Kirche, 20. Berlin: Trowitzsch, 1914.

Schreiber, Heinrich. *Balthasar Hubmaier, Stifter der Wiedertäufer auf dem Schwarzwalde.* Freiburg in Breisgau: Universitahäts-Buchhandlung von A. Emmerling, 1973.

Schulze, R. Wilhelm. *Neuere Forschungen über Balthasar Hubmaier von Waldshut.* Lahr/Schwarzwald: Moritz Schuenburg Verlag, 1957.

Shenk, Wilbert R., ed. *Anabaptism and Mission.* Scottdale, Herald Press, 1984.

Smithson, R. J. *The Anabaptists: Their Contribution to Our Protestant Heritage.* London: James Clarke & Co., 1935.

Snyder, C. Arnold. *Anabaptist History and Theology.* Rev. Student ed. Kitchener, Ontario: Pandora Press, 1997.

____. *The Life and Thought of Michael Sattler.* Foreword by Cornelius J. Dyck. Scottdale, PA; Kitchener, ON: Herald Press, 1984.

Snyder, C. Arnold and Linda A. Huebert Hecht, eds. *Profiles of Anabaptist Women: Sixteenth-Century Reforming Pioneers.* Studies in Women and Religion. Waterloo, Ont.: Wilfrid Laurier University Press, 1997.

Snyder, Howard A. *The Community of the King*. Downers Grove: Inter-Varsity Press, 1977.

Stayer, James M. *Anabaptists and the Sword*. Lawrence: Coronado Press, 1972.

Stayer, James M. and Werner O. Packull, eds. *The Anabaptists and Thomas Muentzer*. Dubuque: Kendall Hunt, 1980.

Swartley, Willard M. *Essays on Biblical Interpretation: Anabaptist-Mennonite Perspectives*: Text-Reader Series. Elkhart, IN: Institute of Mennonite Studies, 1984.

Thomas, Owen C. *Introduction to Theology*, Rev. ed. Harrisburg, PA: Morehouse Publishing, 1983.

Torbet, Robert G. *A History of the Baptists*, 3d ed. Valley Forge: Judson Press, 1963.

Tozer, A. W. *The Knowledge of the Holy*. San Francisco: Harper and Row, 1961.

Van Braght, Thielemann, ed. *The Bloody Theatre or Martyr's Mirror of the Defenseless Christians Who Baptized Only Upon Confession of Faith, and Who Suffered and Died for the Testimony of Jesus, Their Saviour, From the Time of Christ to the Year A. D. 1660*. 2d English ed. Translated by Joseph F. Sohm. Scottdale: Herald Press, 1999.

Vedder, Henry C. *Balthasar Hübmaier the Leader of the Anabaptists*. New York: Putnam, 1905; reprint, New York: AMS Press, 1971.

Verduin, Leonard. *The Reformers and their Stepchildren*. With a foreword by Franklin H. Littell. Grand Rapids: Eerdmans, 1964.

_____. *Somewhat less than God: The Biblical View of Man*. Grand Rapids: Eerdmans, 1970.

Vos, Karle. *Balthasar Hubmaier*. Haarlem: Vereeniging voor de Verstrooiden, 1916.

Wagner, Murray L. *Petr Chelcicky: A Radical Separatist in Hussite Bohemia*. Studies in Anabaptist and Mennonite History. Foreword by Jarold K. Zeman. Scottdale, PA; Kitchener, ON: Herald Press, 1983.

Bibliography

Walker, Williston. *A History of the Christian Church*. New York: Scribners, 1959.

Weaver, J. Denny. *Becoming Anabaptist: The Origin and Significance of Sixteenth-Century Anabaptism*. Foreword by Leonard Gross. Scottdale: Herald Press, 1987.

Wenger, John Christian. *Even unto Death: The Heroic Witness of the Sixteenth-Century Anabaptists*. Richmond: Knox, 1961.

Westin, Gunnar. *The Free Church Through the Ages*. Translated by Virgil A. Olson. Nashville: Broadman, 1958.

Williams, George Huntston. *The Radical Reformation*, 3d ed. Kirksville: Sixteenth Century Journal Publishers, 1962.

Williams, George H. and Angel M. Mergal, eds. *Spiritual and Anabaptist Writers*. Library of Christian Classics. Philadelphia: Westminister Press, 1957.

Windhorst, Christof. *Täuferisches Taufverständnis : Balthasar Hubmaiers Lehre zwischen traditioneller und reformatorischer Theologie*. Studies in Medieval and Reformation Thought. Leiden: Brill, 1976.

Winter, Ernst F., ed. *Erasmus - Luther: Discourse on Free Will*. New York: Continuum Publishing, 1989.

Wiswedel, W. *Balthasar Hubmaier : der Vorkämpfer für Glaubens- und Gewissensfreiheit*. Kassel: J. G. Oncken Nachf., 1939.

Woodfin, Yandall. *With All Your Mind: A Christian Philosophy*. Nashville: Abingdon, 1980.

Wray, Frank. "History in the Eyes of the Sixteenth Century Anabaptists." Ph.D. diss., Yale University, 1954

Yoder, John H. *The Schleitheim Confession*. Introduction by Leonard Gross. Scottdale, PA: Herald Press, 1977.

Zachman, Randall C. *The Assurance of Faith: Conscience in the Theology of Martin Luther and John Calvin*. Minneapolis: Fortress Press, 1993.

Zeman, Jarold K. *The Anabaptists and the Czech Brethren in Moravia, 1526–1628; A Study of Origins and Contacts.* The Hague: Mouton, 1969.

Zuck, Lowell H., ed. *Christianity and Revolution: Radical Christian Testimonies 1520–1650.* Philadelphia: Temple University Press, 1976.

Zwingli, Ulrich. *Early Writings.* Edited by Samuel Macauley Jackson. Durham, NC: The Labyrinth Press, 1987.

Articles and Essays

Bainton, Roland H. "The Great Commission." *Mennonite Life* 7 (1953): 183–89.

Beachy, Alvin J. "The Grace of God in Christ as Understood by Five Major Anabaptist Writers." *Mennonite Quarterly Review* 37 (January 1963): 5–33, 52.

Bender, Harold S. "These are My People: The Nature of the Church and its Disciple- ship according to the New Testament." *Mennonite Quarterly Review* 37 (January 1963): 53–56.

Blough, Neal. "Pilgram Marpeck, Martin Luther and the Humanity of Christ." *Mennonite Quarterly Review* 61 (April 1987): 203–212.

Boyd, Stephen Blake. "Pilgram Marpeck and the Justice of Christ." *Mennonite Quarterly Review* 60 (April 1986): 202–203.

Burson, Scott R. and Jerry L. Walls. "God's Sovereignty and Human Significance: Predestination, Divine Election and the Power to Choose Freely." In *C. S. Lewis and Francis Schaeffer: Lessons for a New Century from the Most Influential Apologists of Our Time,* 64–80. Downers Grove: InterVarsity Press, 1998.

Corley, Bruce. "Interpreting Paul's Conversion—Then and Now." In *The Road from Damascus: The Impact of Paul's Conversion on His Life, Thought, and Ministry.* Edited by Richard N. Longenecker. Grand Rapids: Eerdmans, 1997.

Davis, Kenneth R. "Erasmus as a Progenitor of Anabaptist Theology and Piety." *Mennonite Quarterly Review* 47 (1973): 163–178.

___. "Menno Simons and the Radical Reformation." In *Great Leaders of the Christian Church*, John D. Woodbridge, ed., 242–246. Chicago: Moody Press, 1988.

Dyck, Cornelius J. "The Anabaptist Understanding of the Good News." In *Anabaptism and Mission*, Wilbert R. Shenk, ed., 24–39. Scottdale: Herald Press, 1984.

Estep, William R. "The Anabaptist View of Salvation." *Southwestern Journal of Theology* 20, no.2 (1978):32–49.

___. "Balthasar Hubmaier: Martyr without Honor." *Baptist History and Heritage* 13, no.2 (April, 1978): 5–10, 27.

___. "Church and State." In *The People of God: Essays on the Believers' Church*, ed. Paul A. Basden and David S. Dockery, 267–276. Nashville: Broadman & Holman, 1991.

___. Review of *Balthasar Hubmaier: Theologian of Anabaptism*, edited and translated by H. Wayne Pipkin and John Howard Yoder. *Journal of Church & State* 32 (Spring 1990): 420.

Estep, William R. Review of *The Lord's Supper in Anabaptism: A Study in the Christology of Balthasar Hubmaier, Pilgram Marpeck, and Dirk Philips*, by John D. Rempel. *Southwestern Journal of Theology* 37 (Spring 1995): 50–51.

Fast, Heinhold. "The Dependence of the First Anabaptists on Luther, Erasmus and Zwingli." *Mennonite Quarterly Review* 30 (April 1956): 104–19.

Fast, Heinhold and John H. Yoder. "How to Deal with Anabaptists; An Unpublished Letter of Heinrich Bullinger." *Mennonite Quarterly Review* (April 1959) :83–95.

Friedmann, Robert. "Concerning the True Soldier of Christ." *Mennonite Quarterly Review* 5 (April 1931): 87–99.

___. "The Doctrine of Original Sin as Held by the Anabaptists of he Sixteenth Century." *Mennonite Quarterly Review* 35 (July 1969): 206–214.

Frost, S. E. "Fate Versus Free Will." In *Basic Teachings of the Great Philosophers* , 127–152. Rev. ed. Garden City: Doubleday, 1962.

González, Justo L. "Anabaptism and the Radical Reformation." In *A History of Christian Thought*. Rev. ed. Vol. 3, *From the Protestant Reformation to the Twentieth Century*. Nashville: Abingdon Press, 1975.

Hall, Thor. "Possibilities of Erasmian Influence on Denck and Hubmaier in Their Views on the Freedom of the Will." *Mennonite Quarterly Review* 35 (April 1961):149–170.

Heimann, Franz, "The Hutterite Doctrines of Church and Common Life: A Study of Peter Riedemann's Confession of Faith of 1540." *Mennonite Quarterly Review* 26 (January 1952): 22–47; 26 (April 1952): 142–160.

Hillerbrand, Hans J. "The Origin of Sixteenth-Century Anabaptism: Another Look." *Archiv für Reformationsgeschichte* 53 (1962): 152–180

Hošek, Frant. Xaver. "Life of Balthazar Hubmeyer, the Founder of 'New Christianity' in Moravia," Translated by W. W. Everts, *Texas Baptist Historical and Biographical Magazine*, 1981.

Hubmaier, Balthasar. "Schriften." Edited by Gunnar Westin and Torsten Bergsten. *Mennonite Quarterly Review* 38 (January 1964): 64–65.

Kiwiet, John J. "Anabaptist Views of the Church." In *The People of God: Essays on the Believers' Church*, ed. Paul A. Basden and David S. Dockery, 225–234. Nashville: Broadman & Holman, 1991.

Klaassen, Walter. "A Fire That Spread: Anabaptist Beginnings." *Christian History* 4 (1985): 7–9.

____. "Anabaptism: Neither Catholic Nor Protestant." *Christian History* 4 (1985): 10–12, 34–35.

____. "Some Anabaptist views on the doctrine of the Holy Spirit." *Mennonite Quarterly Review* 35 (April 1961): 130–139.

____. "Speaking in Simplicity: Balthasar Hubmaier." *Mennonite Quarterly Review* 40 (April 1966): 139–147.

____. "Spiritualization in the Reformation." *Mennonite Quarterly Review* 37:67–77.

Klassen, Herbert. "The Life and Teachings of Hans Hut." *Mennonite Quarterly Review* 33 (1959): 171–205; 267–304.

Kraybill, Donald B. "Yieldedness and Accountability in Traditional Anabaptist Communities." In *Anabaptist Currents: History in Conversation with the Present*, ed. Carl F. Bowman and Stephen L. Longenecker, 269–280. Bridgewater, VA: Forum for Religious Studies, Penobscot Press, 1995.

Kreider, R. S. "Anabaptism and Humanism: An Inquiry into the Relationship of Humanism to the Evangelical Anabaptists." *Mennonite Quarterly Review* 26 (1952): 123–141.

Leth, Carl M. "Balthasar Hubmaier's 'Catholic' Exegesis: Matthew 16:18–19 and the Power of the Keys." In *Biblical Interpretation in the Era of the Reformation: Essays Presented to David C. Steinmetz in Honor of His Sixtieth Birthday*, ed. John Thompson and Richard A. Muller, 103–117. Grand Rapids: Eerdmans, 1996.

Leth, Carl M. "Recent Research in the History of the Tyrol-Moravian Anabaptists." *Mennonite Quarterly Review* 2 (January 1928): 5–15.

Macoskey, R. A. "The Contemporary Relevance of Balthasar Hubmaier's Concept of the Church." *Foundations* 6 (April 1963): 99–122.

McClendon, James Wm., Jr. "Balthasar Hubmaier, Catholic Anabaptist." In *Essays in Anabaptist Theology*, ed. H. Wayne Pipkin, 71–81. Elkhart: Institute of Mennonite Studies, 1994.

Moore, John Allen. "Balthasar Hubmaier: Truth Is Immortal." In *Anabaptist Portraits*, 165–242. Foreword by Leonard Gross. Scottdale, PA: Herald Press, 1984.

Moore, Walter L. Jr. "Catholic Teacher and Anabaptist Pupil: The Relationship between John Eck and Balthasar Hubmaier." *Archive for Reformation History* 72 (1981): 68–97.

Neuwmann, Gerhard J. "Anabaptist Position on Baptism and the Lord's Supper." *Mennonite Quarterly Review* 35 (1961): 140–48.

Oosterbaan J. A. "The Reformation of the Reformation: Fundamentals of Anabaptist Theology," *Mennonite Quarterly Review* 51 (July 1977): 171-196.

Packull, Werner O. "Balthasar Hubmaier's Gift to John Eck, July 18, 1516." *Mennonite Quarterly Review* 63 (October 1989): 428-432.

____. "Denck's Alleged Baptism by Hubmaier: Its Significance for the Origin of South German-Austrian Anabaptism." *Mennonite Quarterly Review* 47 (October 1973): 327-338.

Peachey, Paul. "The Radical Reformation." In *The Origins and Characteristics of Anabaptism / Les debuts et les caracteristiques de l'anabaptisme*, ed. Marc Lienhard, 10-26. The Hague, Netherlands: Martinus Nijhoff, 1977.

Pipkin, H. Wayne. *Zwingli and Hubmaier*. Paper presented at The Sixteenth Century Studies Conference, October 18, 1991, in the session on Zwingli and the radicals. Elkhart, IN: H. W. Pipkin, 1991.

____. Review of *Balthasar Hubmaier's Understanding of Faith*, by Eddie Mabry. *Mennonite Quarterly Review* 74 (October 2000): 629-630.

____. "The Baptismal Theology of Balthasar Hubmaier." *Mennonite Quarterly Review* 65 (January 1991): 34-53.

Poettcker, Henry. "Menno Simons' View of the Bible as Authority." In *The Heritage of Menno Simons: A Legacy of Faith (A Sixtieth Anniversary Tribute to Cornelius Krahn)*, ed. Cornelius J. Dyck, 31-54. Newton, KA: Mennonite Publication Office, 1962.

Price, Theron D. "The Anabaptist View of the Church." *Review and Expositor* 51 (1954): 187-203.

Rupp. E. Gordon. "Thomas Muentzer, Hans Hut and the Gospel of All Creatures." Reprint from *Bulletin of the John Rylands Library*, XLIII, 1961.

Snyder, Arnold. "Beyond Polygenesis: Recovering the Unity and Diversity of Anabaptist Theology." In *Essays in Anabaptist Theology*, ed. H. Wayne Pipkin, 1-33. Elkhart, Ind.:Institute of Mennonite Studies, 1994.

Stayer, James M. "The Radical Reformation." In *Handbook of European History, 1400-1600: Late Middle Ages, Renaissance, and Reformation.* Vol. 2, *Visions, Programs, and Outcomes,* ed. Thomas Brady Jr., Heiko Oberman, and James Tracy, 249-282. Grand Rapids: Eerdmans, 1995.

———. "The Swiss Brethren: An Exercise in Historical Definition." *Church History* 47 (June 1978): 174-95.

Stayer, James M. and W. O. Packull and K. Deppermann. "From Monogenesis to Polygenesis: The Historical Discussion of Anabaptist Origins." *Mennonite Quarterly Review* 49 (April 1975): 83-121.

Stealey, Sydnor L. "Balthasar Hubmaier and Some Perennial Religious Problems." *The Review and Expositor* 40 (October 1943), 403-422.

Steinmetz, David Curtis. "Balthasar Hubmaier (1485?-1528): Free Will and Covenant." In *Reformers in the Wings.* Philadelphia: Fortress, 1971.

———. "The Baptism of John and the Baptism of Jesus in Huldrych Zwingli, Balthasar Hubmaier and late Medieval Theology." In *Continuity and Discontinuity in Church History: Essays Presented to George Huntston Williams on the Occasion of His 65th Birthday,* ed. Forrester Church and Timothy George, 169-181. Leiden: E. J. Brill, 1979.

———. "Luther and Hubmaier on the Freedom of the Human Will." In *Luther in Context.* Grand Rapids: Baker Books, 1962.

———. "Luther und Hubmaier im Streit um die Freiheit des menschlichen Willens." *Evangelische Theologie* 6 (1983): 512-526.

Steinmetz, David Curtis. "Scholasticism and Radical Reform: Nominalist Motifs in the Theology of Balthasar Hubmaier." *Mennonite Quarterly Review* 45 (April 1971) :123-144.

Weaver, J. Denny. "Discipleship Redefined: Four Sixteenth Century Anabaptists." *Mennonite Quarterly Review* 54 (October 1980): 255-279.

Williams, George H. "Sanctification in the Testimony of Several So-Called Schwärmer." *Mennonite Quarterly Review* 42 (January 1968): 5-25.

Windhorst, Christof. "Balthasar Hubmaier: Professor, Preacher, Politician." In *Profiles of Radical Reformers: Biographical Sketches from Thomas Müntzer to Paracelsus*, ed. Hans-Jürgen Goertz, 144–157. Kitchener: Herald Press, 1982.

Wiswedel, Wilhelm. "The Inner and Outer Word: A Study in the Anabaptist Doctrine of Scripture." In *Essays in Anabaptist Theology*, ed. H. Wayne Pipkin. Elkhart: Institute of Mennonite Studies, 1994.

Yoder, John Howard. "Balthasar Hubmaier and the beginnings of Swiss Anabaptism." *Mennonite Quarterly Review* 33 (January 1959): 5–17.

___. "The Believers' Church Conferences in Historical perspective." *Mennonite Quarterly Review* 65 (January 1991): 5–19.

___. "The Hermeneutics of the Anabaptists." *Mennonite Quarterly Review* 41 (1967): 291–308.

Zeman, Jarold Knox. "Anabaptism: A Replay of Medieval Themes or a Prelude to the Modern Age?" *Mennonite Quarterly Review* 70 (1976): 259–71.

www.ingramcontent.com/pod-product-compliance
Lightning Source LLC
Chambersburg PA
CBHW050253010526
44107CB00003B/302